Towards the Virtual Organization

FOR FURTHER INFORMATION

If you would like to discuss the subject of the book further either out of personal interest or with respect to your organization then the authors would be pleased to hear from you. They can be contacted in the following way:

Dr Peter Whitlam & Mr Richard Hale
Partners
The Asset Partnership
Broom Hill
21 Cliff Drive
Cromer
Norfolk NR27 0AW
United Kingdom

Telephone and Fax: (44) 1263 515150

e-mail: whitlam@asset.co.uk
                      rhale@asset.co.uk

ACKNOWLEDGEMENTS

We would like to thank the many people and organizations which have helped contribute to this book, either by way of formal contributions or through informal discussion. Thanks are also due to our clients who have clearly provided us with a rich source of material in looking at the changing shape of organizations.

Special thanks are due to the following people who have helped with our research and case studies:

Dr Arthur Rothwell — De Montfort University, Leicester
Stephen Shearon — ACNielsen
Gilceia Amaral E Silva — Oxford Brookes University

and the following organizations:

ACNielsen
AlliedSignal
Andersen Consulting
BP Oil
Cellnet
Coca-Cola
Compaq
Emslie Phelps Consultancy
Esselte
Nationwide Building Society
The Perrier Group
Railtrack
Scottish Hydro-Electric
Motorola
Saratoga
Xilinx

Introduction and background

*We are well into the new millennium,
indeed most organizations are currently
employing people and engaged in
practices that will still be in place well
beyond the year 2000*

In this introductory chapter we:

■ Commence by briefly describing the changing business context against which this book is set
■ Describe our background rationale for writing this book and provide understanding of our unique research which provides the theoretical underpinning
■ Define our model and use of the term *the virtual organization* and briefly contrast this with more traditional operating business environments
■ Discuss ways in which readers can use the Change Assessment Orientation Survey (Ch.A.O.S.) to assess the position of their organization in relation to best practice, prior to managing organizational change
■ Briefly explore the structure and content of the book to help the reader navigate through the chapters in the most appropriate way

The changing business environment

In today's business environment, organizations face accelerating change resulting in increasing levels of uncertainty, instability, turbulence and insecurity. For many, this is an attractive concoction of opportunity, spiced with excitement and challenge and, as is so often the case with such heady emotions, part of the thrill is rooted in a fear of the unknown.

Ironically, in recent years many organizations will have experienced the less savoury aspects of change; this may have meant having to face up to the reality of a profound reorganization of their business or the prospect of no business at all. For those within the organization, whether operating as leaders or followers, this has created a melting pot of human emotions. To this end, we have seen and maybe experienced fear and excitement, delight and anger, stress and anxiety, passion and endless confusion.

For those who are charged with leading organizations into the future it is no longer sufficient to simply restructure, offer a change seminar for the survivors and counsel the bereaved. True leaders will not only shape the future by creating a powerful vision behind which others can unite, they will also be capable of mobilizing people to challenge attitudes, develop new abilities, form new teams and ultimately create new organizations.

Grand as this may sound, the facts are that it is already happening and through our consultancy practice and ongoing organizational research, we have worked and are currently working with some of the most successful businesses to identify what it is that distinguishes them from their less successful neighbours.

Using the rigour of academic research methodologies combined with the practicality of leading edge organizational development we have identified the characteristics of best practice in such organizations. What we have found is that the real change masters of the future will not only create an organizational vision and put in place strategies to achieve this, but more importantly they will always start by fully and comprehensively understanding their current position.

To the uninformed this may seem self evident, yet we would suggest that such organizational position analysis is generally a highly subjective process which tends to be introspective and frequently results in developing strategies that are focused more on organizational survival than success. Consequently, this often results in organizations repeating mistakes from their past, rather than seeking to adopt new ways of looking at things. Indeed, our studies clearly show that for an organization to become a *virtual organization* it is a fundamental part of this process is for them to unlearn or forget the ways of the past, or as one chief executive put it: 'Its Okay to look back at the past but we mustn't stare, to do so is to condemn ourselves to repeating the same mistakes'.

Rationale for the book

As part of the fundamental requirement for effective organizational position analysis we would contend that an organization needs to consider its performance not only against itself, not even against others, but against 'the best of the others'.

In effect this is the rationale for writing this book; using our research we are now able to provide the reader with actual data   for benchmarking and assessing his or her organizational readiness for not simply managing change as a one-off event, but institutionalizing continuous change. Furthermore, by benchmarking organizational performance against current best practice it is possible to adopt an outward looking and open-minded stance to the future.

In this book we look at real business examples, as well as provide the theoretical framework and practical tools for assessing your organization's readiness to meet the future. It is through this pragmatic approach, underpinned by sound academic research, that the reader is likely to increase the chances of success in moving the organization towards the virtual organization model.

Throughout our research it will be seen that we have engaged in direct studies of organizations and in some of these organizations we have worked with them in helping manage the change process. Additionally, we have spent some time studying the work of others and consulting both academic and industrial authorities regarding our work on the virtual organization.

The concept of the virtual organization

It seems that one of the major new buzzwords of the late 1990s is 'virtual'; we have heard of virtual book shops, virtual universities, virtual shopping malls, virtual offices and, of course, virtual reality. So is the virtual world simply a passing fad or is it something which is truly changing the way we live our lives and the way we work and communicate?

Despite the proliferation of virtuality it is difficult to find a common definition of 'virtual' which is applicable in all of its uses. We do believe, however, that the concept has real value when addressing the subject of organizational development; and as a concept it is not so much about managing in the sense of planning, controlling, directing and organizing, but more concerned with the notion of continuous or institutionalized change. This implies not management but a process which is both self regulatory and self perpetuating. For this reason we propose the following definition of the virtual organization:

'The virtual organization is the name given to any organization which is continually evolving, redefining and reinventing itself for practical business purposes.'

The critical characteristics of such organizations include the following qualities. Virtual organizations:

- Institutionalize organizational change, and
- Demonstrate focused strategic direction and purpose, thus
- Enabling individuals to optimize their potential to contribute, by
- Creating new forms or shapes,
- Developing dynamic communication, and
- Creating cultures which support continual organizational adaptation.

In the basic sense virtual organizations engage proactively in the following activities:

- Gathering data (both from inside and outside the organization)
- Information analysis
- Formulating strategies for success rather than survival
- Exploiting technology
- Powerful goal setting
- Measurement in all areas
- Entrepreneurial skills
- Influencing effectively (rather than over-use of power)
- Empowering people throughout the organization
- Helping others to take risks
- Managing ambiguity.

There are, of course, a number of potential down sides to the virtual organization. For instance, people often work at a distance and are expected to use initiative which can lead to freedom and release; however, by contrast, there are inherent risks of disenfranchisement, isolation and confusion.

The title *Towards the virtual organization* was agreed because our research showed that many successful organizations appear to have been moving towards a genuinely different approach to doing business. Mostly this appears to have been achieved more by accident than design, but like many other accidental discoveries it seems to be working for these organizations.

In terms of the above definition these organizations have created businesses which are evidently a force to be reckoned with; but in their most advanced form are actually difficult to see, touch or define. In the virtual sense, it was not necessarily clear where the organization ended and another one began; in fact some overtly sought to become 'boundaryless'. They were often so fluid in the way they operated that in some cases they could not even explain too easily how they were structured or what were the secrets of success; it was clear, though, that they were absolutely focused on building a dynamic business for the future.

We have developed, and will explore throughout this book, a model brought about a radical culture change by improving communications both in terms of systems and behaviours, but which failed to address the subject of its positioning in the marketplace. Or the high-technology consultancy in start-up mode which spent the first year defining a corporate culture before generating a viable business; by the time it was ready to operate the marketplace had changed so significantly that it had missed the opportunity.

Virtual organizations will address all four of the factors described above and will do so simultaneously in order to exploit the environmental demands for change.

In the next section we provide a brief overview of the style of the book as well as the subjects covered in each of the chapters. This should serve as a guide to help the reader decide which parts of the book to focus on, depending on the particular interests or needs of the organization.

Getting the best from this book

Working with a number of international organizations from a range of different sectors, and having assessed their organizational health in respect of their change orientation, we have identified that they appear to take the necessary steps in respect of direction, structure, systems communication and culture and are not simply orientated towards the acceptance of change as a singular event but see change as the norm in a process of continuous adaptation.

Throughout the book we share case study material from over 1000 international organizations which took part in the original research, as well as from other writers and researchers. These real examples have helped us in the formulation of the model which underpins the Change Assessment Orientation Survey (Ch.A.O.S.).

The Change Assessment Orientation Survey (Ch.A.O.S.)

This is the instrument which will enable you to compare your organization with others, either in your sector or more generally. It enables you to assess your organization's change orientation against the four key variables. A modified copy of this instrument is contained in Appendix I.

The Ch.A.O.S. instrument has been developed over a period of many years and has been independently tested for its reliability and validity; furthermore, through our ongoing consultancy we have been able to collate valuable benchmark data by business and industry sector. This means that apart from being able to see how an organization stands in relative terms across the four factors, you will be able to make comparisons with other organizations and with established norms. A generic summary of this data is provided in Appendix II.

The result is that you can see how well your organization measures up as a virtual organization and how prepared it is to embark on the journey of organizational change. Initially you may simply wish to complete the Ch.A.O.S. instrument individually; subsequently, you may wish to ask others to complete it. Equally, you may wish to use the survey as a way of assessing the relative strengths and weaknesses of different parts of your business against the model.

You are encouraged to use this instrument as widely as possible across functions and at different levels within the organization. This will enable valuable internal comparisons and can assist in evaluating the impact which recent change initiatives may have had. Additionally, it is strongly recommended that the survey is used on a regular basis, so that comparative data can be produced over time in order to identify trends and areas for particular attention, as well as pinpointing pockets of best practice which can be shared elsewhere.

Alternatively, you may choose to take a problem-focused approach and use this instrument to carry out a diagnosis on a particular part of the business where you understand there to be a problem but where you feel that more in depth analysis is required. Indeed, we have used the survey in all of the ways discussed above with a number of organizations and we will be sharing our findings throughout the book.

Additionally, if you would like to receive further, and more accurate, benchmarking data regarding how your organization compares to others, you might wish to contact the authors for more detailed analysis and feedback (see the contacts page at the front of the book for details).

Throughout the book, in addition to sharing the findings from the organizations participating in the original research, we also draw heavily on our experience with a number of client organizations which are currently wrestling with the subject of their organizational development in a rapidly changing environment.

In particular, we will cite positive examples from organizations such as Motorola, 3M, Dunn and Bradstreet (ACNielsen), Coca-Cola and AlliedSignal. The obvious appeal here is that such organizations or their products are widely known. Increasingly, we are finding ourselves advising such large organizations as to how they might operate more like the smaller, more virtual organizations with which they need to collaborate or compete.

There is also much to be gained from looking at some of the smallest of businesses compared to the international giants. As we have said, being small does improve the likelihood of being able to successfully make the journey towards virtual organization status. It is particularly interesting to explore the very high levels of profitability that can be achieved in such small virtual organizations.

It is also felt that there is some benefit to be gained from looking at the less positive examples; these are drawn from actual organizations, though as a point of principle we will always present these organizations anonymously, at most referring to the sector or type of business.

Throughout the book you will also find a number of *Pause for thought* sections. These ask you to reflect on key points drawn from the subject being discussed. The objective here is to ensure that the book is used in a practical way and that it provokes constructive thinking which helps you to move your organization successfully through the change process. Indeed, if using this book in a team context, these issues can be considered individually, then discussed collectively.

Summary of chapters

Chapter 2—The world in transition

There is an argument which says that in order to understand the way organizations are changing, there is first a need to try to make sense of broader societal trends. It is suggested that organizations might be seen as microcosms of the wider societies within which they operate. Indeed, there is much evidence to support this notion.

In this chapter we explore examples of societal changes drawn from a broad range of political, economic, social and technological issues that have in the past, and are continuing to drive and influence change within organizations. The issue of the rate of change is explored and we explain the concept of the change curve as a way of recognizing the impact of accelerating change in your own business environment. You are asked to reflect on the accelerating change curve in your own industry.

Some historical perspective is provided regarding the linkage between organizational change and changes in history. This enables a link to be made between the trends which have been emerging through the 1990s, with extrapolation and speculation regarding the shape of organizations in the 21st century. We take a look at some of the work of the futurists who have attempted to look forward to the future of organizations and society.

We then look at some of the general trends which we identified in the successful organizations with whom we are either currently working, or whom we have researched, namely:

■ The importance of actively demonstrating concern for staff rather than paying lip service to the notion.

- The requirement for increasing employee participation at all levels of the organization.
- The need to be continually innovative, seeking step changes rather than incremental business improvements.
- The importance of entrepreneurial skills and the need to manage the excesses of organizational control.
- Continuing customer (and supplier) orientation, both within and outside the organization.
- The increasing importance of relationship building and influencing others.

These trends signify some of the key characteristics which we believe successful organizations will need to possess in the future. Those organizations which sit more towards the virtual end of the continuum tended to display these characteristics significantly more strongly and consistently than more traditional organizations.

Chapter 3—Beyond the learning organization

There is clearly a need for organizations to look at learning as an ongoing and continuous process and to look beyond simply the training course or training intervention. There is a need to create a climate where people accept the need to continually learn and develop; in other words, to develop learning behaviours as well as processes and systems.

This chapter focuses in particular on the debate surrounding the concept of the learning organization. This is a subject which has attracted a great deal of debate in recent years and is of particular relevance to the development of our concept of the virtual organization.

There are many different definitions of the learning organization and undoubtedly the work in this area has raised the awareness of the importance of creating a culture of learning throughout the organization. In many ways the research in this area is inconclusive and it has been suggested that the learning organization is little more than an aspirational concept. However, because of the evident relationship between the process of adaptation and that of learning, and the importance of change which is discussed earlier, we believe it is helpful at this stage to review some of the key literature in this field. In some ways this leads to an academic debate, but we do move on to look at the practical steps which organizations might take in order to effectively institutionalize change and learning. We also discuss some examples of how organizations we have worked with are approaching organizational adaptation.

In terms of our own contribution to the learning organization debate, we suggest that there is a need for organizations to recognize the need for unlearning rather than simply imposing new thinking on the old fabric. Here we draw on a model which was originally developed from our studies of successful individuals in organizations and which we have increasingly come to recognize can be applied equally powerfully on an organizational level. This model shows how organizations engage in what we describe as internal dialogue (talking within the business), which may be influenced by a number of external sources. Among these external sources are people and organizations which might be perceived as experts. The combination of the organization's internal dialogue and the influence of the perceived experts will lead to the development of an organizational climate or comfort zone. In effect, the organization develops its own internal belief systems which can then become self perpetuating. Organizations may go to great lengths to ensure they operate within their own climate or comfort zone and in many cases this can become a significant change-inhibiting force.

We conclude this chapter by looking at practical ways in which the organization might manage such barriers and hence improve the process of change.

Chapter 4—The virtual organization: A journey not a destination

In this chapter we expand on the explanation of our model of the four organizational factors which the virtual organization excels in and identify that in order to manage continuous change successfully, a business needs to focus on these issues:

■ Direction
■ Form
■ Communication
■ Adaptation.

The evolution of the model is covered with some detailed explanation of the research methodology, including our case study work with a number of different organizations ranging from the more traditional to those which appear to operate more like virtual organizations.

Furthermore, we have expanded on the Ch.A.O.S. instrument; a practical tool which can help readers to see how their organization currently measures up to what has been identified as 'best practice'. At this stage the Ch.A.O.S. instrument is explored in detail. Advice is provided regarding how the tool can be used in a practical sense and generic data from other organizations which have completed the survey is provided for benchmarking purposes.

The book then moves on to explore the four key factors of the model in more detail and we use the analogy of a journey, rather than a destination, to depict the sense of perpetual change which the organization is likely to embark upon.

Chapter 5— Preparing for the journey

Different approaches to strategic planning are considered in this chapter and an argument is presented to suggest that traditional approaches to strategic thinking are no longer sufficient if an organization wishes to survive the turbulence of the business environment in the future.

Special reference is made to the importance of vision and the way in which vision can align individuals behind a specific course of intended action. Practical steps for articulating the organizational vision are provided and various examples are drawn from a range of organizations and teams. In the virtual organization it is likely that individuals will work in small teams consequently, the principles of developing a dynamic vision apply equally to functional, multi-disciplinary and specialist teams.

Many organizations have attempted to develop mission statements, possibly viewing them as the quick route to uniting people who might otherwise have differing objectives. Effective organizations, however, recognize that the process of building a vision must involve employees at all levels. This is normally an uncomfortable process and more than a semantic discussion; different perspectives are brought to the table and worked through and the real *raison d'être* is agreed.

Some organizations go on to clarify their values; these are the key beliefs which underpin everything they do and aspire to. We have found that all organizations have such values, though only some consciously explore them and overtly declare them internally and externally. In more traditional organizations we found a more closed approach, often due to a fear that employees or customers might hold the company to their stated values, particularly where there are differences of opinion. The increasing tendency for organizations to clarify their values seems to be linked to the accelerating rate of change which companies are experiencing. Being specific in terms of strategies and plans is difficult in times of rapid and ongoing change; the plan for next month, or next quarter could be blown away due to events which are impossible to anticipate but which emerge next week. Values, however, are more enduring; they establish certain rules and behaviours by which members are to operate consistently over long periods of time.

By stating their values and actively working to them, and being seen by others to do so, organizations also achieve a secondary objective which many organizations seek to achieve, that of building integrity.

Where an individual member of the organization has personal values and beliefs which are out of kilter with those of the organization, the impact of such dissonance can be most destructive. We present a practical approach to defining values and beliefs, and questioning both where these actually come from and the implications of holding onto them in the future.

Chapter 6—Selecting the vehicle

In this chapter we move on to consider the second of the four key factors in the model, the *form* or shape of the organization. Form is the word used to suggest a new way for businesses to organize themselves. The word 'structure' is deliberately avoided as it appears to suggest too rigid a way of organizing work aimed at achieving the corporate vision. Furthermore, structure suggests a focus mainly on organizational structure in terms of reporting relationship and the hierarchy. In the virtual organization, reporting relationships are likely to be messy and often unexplained, and hierarchical relationships are not particularly important. What appears to be required is a far greater level of flexibility.

In the past it was possible to gain a reasonable understanding of how a business operated by asking for a copy of the organization chart; this would tell you about reporting structures, relationships, where the power was held and how decisions were made with a reasonable level of reliability. This is less and less the case and it is certainly untrue of the virtual organization. First, it is unlikely that there will be a classic organization chart or family tree in the virtual organization. If there is, then it will probably be out of date almost as soon as it is written because of the rapid rate of change.

Second, it is unlikely to provide information regarding decision making and power bases because power is related to factors other than status and so decision making is often devolved to operational levels and to those at the customer or client interface. Status is less of a currency; more important is being able to contribute to the development of the business—it is unique contribution which is valued.

Approaches to managing human resources in the virtual organization do not fit with the traditional approach. While real opportunities for development are likely to exist, only a certain type of person will really succeed in this environment; he or she will need to be personally driven by a sense of personal destiny and will demonstrate certain behavioural skills and attitudes.

Remuneration tends to fluctuate depending on the fortunes of the business and overall the principles of a meritocracy are well accepted; if you make a contribution you will be rewarded. There are unlikely to be any passengers. All will share in the rewards, as will bear the cost of the pain.

Because of the need for flexibility and the changing content of jobs the critical factor is not so much what you do but how you do it. Competencies focused around critical behaviours which are transferable from one task to another are the means by which jobs are defined and performance is measured. So performance is measured by looking at the extent to which certain behaviours are displayed. The profile of each job may well be unique and is bound to change; strict demarcation of jobs is unhelpful in that it restricts flexibility and for many individuals this demands a significant mind shift in terms of how one approaches one's job.

Individuals will not be rewarded for what they say, nor will they gain prestige for what they know; the only thing that really matters is what they actually do. In the virtual organization performance is all.

Structurally, there is a move towards a blurring of job, departmental and functional boundaries and the distinction between the organization and the outside world is becoming less clear, too. Suppliers work on the client site, organizations work alongside their customers. Members of the organization may simultaneously be part of several teams and possibly more than one organization. This throws the traditional employment contract into question.

In the more radical cases the virtual organization makes use of the virtual office. There is no place for the prestigious city office; the office will move with the person, who will move to the location of the work. Flexibility and responsiveness provide competitive edge and the ability to be able to respond to the clients' or customers' needs and to work where they want you when they want you is important. Titles, where they exist, are primarily used for interaction with more traditional organizations.

Some managers in making the transition from more traditional approaches find it difficult to abolish the status symbols such as the offices, cars, titles, and the team of subordinates carrying out menial and sometimes meaningless tasks.

To summarize, of all the four factors in our model it is probably the factor of form that presents both individuals and organizations with the greatest challenge. To be successful, it will require a paradigm shift in the way we think about employment. Some individuals will readily grasp the opportunity of working in a redefined organizational form with both hands; most will come over to these new ways of working slowly over time and several will actively resist. Some, of course, will be unable to make the transition.

Chapter 7—The fuel for the journey

The process of *communication* is explored as the third key factor in the model. Successful change orientated organizations appear to communicate simultaneously in all directions, with special systems designed to enable communications both upwards and sideways. In a similar way, such organizations also continuously communicate with others outside the organization. This also would include effective communications with their suppliers and customers and may even extend to include their competitors.

Formal systems for communication would be minimal and in many ways the style of communicating might appear to be somewhat chaotic and unorganized. We look at how successful organizations are exploiting the technology of communications and how this can provide a competitive edge in terms of the ability to process, manage and manipulate data speedily and accurately. This contrasts with the experience of organizations where communication is over structured and formalized to the extent that it inhibits progress. In these organizations the rules regarding communication serve to reinforce the hierarchy. Often a channel of communication is used simply in order to comply with the rules, even though it may be a slower and less effective route. In such organizations there tends to be more internal communication than communication with the outside world; these companies see themselves almost as operating in a self contained world. Ironically, often there is a plethora of data and not enough communication.

By contrast, those aspiring to the virtual organization approach will tend to recognize the need to communicate quickly and directly, using the most appropriate method. Where the numbers of members are small then communication is verbal and regular, arguably constant. Ideas are bounced around, feedback is openly given and opinions are encouraged rather than suppressed.

It is acknowledged that the issue of corporate culture is one of the mechanisms by which a business communicates, consequently special reference is made to this aspect of communication. Key areas of consideration are issues such as the level of honesty in communication, the value of initiative, the challenging of senior management, risk taking, innovation and the role of fun.

Employees are truly empowered to take decisions and to take risks, but this is not an excuse for senior people to abdicate responsibility and to withdraw support. Empowering organizations take care of the empowered, as well as developing the leaders with the necessary skills and confidence. People are treated with a degree of dignity and respect whatever their role or contribution, and there are either explicit or implicit codes of conduct with regard to communication, whether between individuals or within or between teams.

Establishing trust and integrity in this environment is a challenge. Integrity is a difficult concept to get to grips with; how do you define it, what does it look like in practice and, an even more testing question, how do you develop it? It is no coincidence that in a climate of radical change, where organizations are working in sometimes loose networks and forming alliances, often with their current or potential competitors, that the issue of integrity has emerged as a major organizational issue. We have found that the need to build integrity is a recurring core value among those organizations which measured up effectively against the virtual organization model.

Furthermore, it appears that in successful organizations in the future the team will be the normal unit of performance and there is a real need to address the issue of successful team building. We look at the characteristics of successful teams in the future and consider some of the most recent research in this area which dispels some of the long held myths about team working. We also look at the characteristics of what we describe as dysfunctional teams which so often threaten to paralyse the organization.

Chapter 8—Test driving the future

This last of the four key factors, organizational *adaptation* provides focus for exploring the ways in which the virtual organization will actually adapt and institutionalize change. This will be driven by external factors. In a sense, the organization will be continually re-inventing itself and will be able to blend in with and stand out from its environment almost at will; it and the people within it will possess 'chameleon-like' qualities.

At an individual level, adaptation means maintaining an open mind and being prepared to continually acquire the new skills required to perform. Learning is seen as a continual rather than a one-off experience. The body of knowledge in many respects is changing and growing on a daily basis; the accepted wisdom now may be dated tomorrow and this means individuals need to be constantly scanning the environment to keep up to date, because this is what will give them competitive edge.

Organizational adaptation is examined in two ways. First, we look at the existence of formal mechanisms, most of which would tend to be concerned with systems approaches to managing change or learning. This includes the design, development and delivery of training using a wide range of leading edge techniques. This includes self managed learning, experiential learning and the use of mentoring.

Second, we examine the actual behaviours that are exhibited by the individuals within the virtual organization. These behaviours are inextricably linked to the process of adaptation and include special emphasis on the use of, for instance, initiative, creativity, decisiveness and risk taking. Leaders will need to develop an adaptive approach among organizational members. Critical skills are focused on enabling or facilitating change, and building the confidence of others to cope effectively with change.

In this chapter we look at some of the approaches to adaptation taken by a range of organizations, some which might be considered to be creative in any case and others which are attempting to bring about major cultural change.

Chapter 9—Reviewing the journey

Here we pull together by way of summary the key messages from the book. The model of organizational development is reviewed once more. Additionally, a case study is presented which is based on a fictional organization set in the future. This is designed to leave the reader with some thought provoking images of how we might be working in the future.

The world in transition

*Change is the law of life. And those who
look only to the past or present are
certain to miss the future*

JOHN F KENNEDY

In this chapter we:

■ Argue that in order to understand some of the changes required within organizations there is a need to look outside the organization and consider some of the changes taking place in society at large
■ Discuss some of the views proposed by those who have tried to anticipate the shape of society and organizations in the future
■ Explain the concept of the accelerating change curve and the impact this has on different business sectors and ask the reader to consider the rate of change in his or her sector and organization
■ Look at how the reducing 'body of knowledge' is influencing which behaviours will be important in the organization of the future
■ Describe the key organizational trends which we have identified and contrast the approaches taken by organizations which are more traditional to those which are more like virtual organizations

Looking beyond the organization

In order to contextualize the subject of organizational change, it is revealing to track some of the changes which are taking place outside the organization on a broader level. The last few years have seen major changes taking place and significant trends in the political, economic, social and technological fields. Many futurists have attempted to look at these trends and extrapolate in order to create a vision of the future. While this is far from a precise science there are some findings which are likely to have a major impact on the shape of organizations in the future.

Several of these trends have a particular relevance for the amount and the type of changes that can be expected to occur within any given organization. Naturally, such changes bring with them the requirement to acquire new knowledge and skills. An issue which also needs to be considered and which we explore in more depth throughout the book is the subject of 'unlearning'; there is considerable evidence to suggest that managing the change process is not just about learning new ways of operating but about simultaneously questioning some of our existing beliefs and attitudes.

In his book, *Megatrends,* John Naisbitt (1984) used content analysis to study research and writings covering a period of almost 20 years to identify what was happening in the wider world. In particular, he highlighted what he believed to be the most significant trends within Western society. Although the study was undertaken in the US, most of the trends identified would appear to be transferable and provide insights into understanding our environment on a global basis. Included here were the following major environmental trends:

■ We no longer have the luxury of operating within an isolated self-sufficient economic system; we must surely recognize that we are now subject to increased uncertainty due to our membership of the wider global economy. Likewise, there is evidence to suggest that we need to let go of the idea that we are an industrial society and must address the task of exploiting our new role as an information society. This has major implications for organizational structures and individual and team behaviours and is throwing the whole balance of power in the organization into turmoil.

■ We are giving up our dependence on hierarchical structures in favour of informal networks and more flexible structures. Decentralization is enabling us to perform in a way that is critical if we are to be responsive to the needs of our customers. Again, this is impacting on the way individuals and teams are operating and calls for a new approach to building and maintaining relationships.

■ The rate of technological change is so rapid that it is no longer sufficient to plan on learning new skills which will be used for the foreseeable future. More realistically there is a need to continuously acquire new skills in order to exploit the potential of technology; this calls for a new individual and organizational mind-set. Furthermore, if we fail to do this and our competitors do, then rather than standing still we are likely to be falling behind as fast as the technology is progressing.

■ In many aspects of life there is a move towards the individual taking responsibility for his or her own destiny. This questions a previous reliance on the organization, the state or the institution to take care of the individual. Increasingly, the individual has to shoulder responsibility for matters such as learning, economic survival and future direction. At the same time, the choices and options required by individuals are increasing. In particular, this appears to be one of the trends influencing the expectations that employees have of their careers.

These trends only represent a few of the total suggested by Naisbitt.

However, it is in understanding the backcloth of this external environment and the implications for organizations, that we become increasingly aware of the need for greater organizational ability in the way in which we adapt, develop, continually evolve and grow. It is interesting to consider how such trends which were identified over a decade ago have continued to develop and how many of the predicted changes have materialized.

In our own study, Whitlam (1990) was able to isolate the fact that organizations which appeared to be managing change more successfully than others seemed to be demonstrating certain characteristics and responding to the external factors which clearly impacted upon them; we discuss these later in this chapter.

Undoubtedly we have seen a major shift in society and the realization of a number of the predictions suggested by Naisbitt, such as the move from a national to a global economy. It is interesting to observe, though, that against many of the trends there is, in fact, the backlash of an almost contradictory or paradoxical counter-movement. With changing and reducing trade barriers organizations are moving into new regions of the world, seeking out production facilities and trying to create the markets for their products. If we look more closely at how organizations are managing the move from a national to a global society, we hear major corporations such as AlliedSignal talk about the need to operate on a 'glocal' basis; that is, working very much on an international basis but also recognizing the social responsibility and sensitivities which are expected more locally. In a similar way, Toyota declares that its guiding principles are to 'be a company of the world' and 'to pursue continuing growth through efficient, global management' while 'serving the greater good of people everywhere by devoting careful attention to safety and the environment' and 'becoming a contributing member of the community in every nation'.

Rifkin (1995) paints an alarming picture for the future of the world of work in the light of the current technological revolution. In the past when a technological revolution threatened the labour market we might have considered the emergence of new markets as the saviour in terms of creating new job opportunities. So, in the early part of the 20th century, agricultural labourers were drawn into the mechanical sectors and vocations. From the middle of the century onwards, the service sector has emerged as a real force and one which has absorbed much of the blue collar labour of the past:

Today, however, as all these sectors fall victim to rapid restructuring and automation, no 'significant' new sector has developed to absorb the millions who are being displaced. The only new sector on the horizon is the knowledge sector, an elite group of industries and professional disciplines responsible for ushering in the new high-tech automated economy of the future.

More recently, Naisbitt (1994) has suggested that:

- Big organizations are deconstructing and reconstructing as networks of autonomous units
- Networking and entrepreneurial skills are coming to the fore
- Strategic alliances are replacing mergers and take-overs
- Competition is required even with your strongest competitors
- Everyone will need to become a politician.

Such generalizations seem to be borne out by the specific examples; it has been recognized, for instance, in the automotive industry that historical strategies of vertical integration where organizations such as Ford owned the mines, the rubber plantation, as well as the motor factory, are no longer workable. As there are no limits on who can or will develop expertise, there is a need for organizations to be able to move quickly, to be able to form alliances and to demonstrate flexibility. Again, let us look at one of the other guiding principles of Toyota: 'to build lasting relationships with business partners around the world'.

Clearly such good intentions are more than simply good public relations or the makings of idealistic vision; they are happening. But the challenges for individuals within the corporation cannot be understated. To operate successfully in this political and social environment calls for particular skills. Recently, an Australian general manager of a Swedish multinational spoke of the challenges of selling into China:

Yes, cultural differences are significant but it is not possible to generalize about the Chinese culture—selling in the South is very different to selling in the North of China. At the same time I am working from an Australian background which is quite different from that of my senior managers who come from our Northern European headquarters.

(Anon)

There is a need identified here to be sensitive to cultural differences and to be able to adapt according to rapidly changing circumstances. At the same time employees often find themselves working as part of a team which is spread across the globe.

Some would say that this should be more easy than ever because of the speed and effectiveness of communications technology, but in reality one's ability to communicate at such a distance is limited. Here, we are learning to operate in new ways, where the technology is driving the changes in behaviour; and here, too, there are often entrenched behaviours and expectations which have to be 'unlearned' before one can expect to really embrace the new technology. Interestingly, one of the major factors holding major corporations back from really committing to the information superhighway, through the Internet, for instance, is fear; fear of a security risk, fear of losing control, fear of not knowing with whom employees will be communicating and fear of the loss of carefully guarded commercial intelligence.

As the corporate giants tread carefully into the future, the relative small fry are seizing opportunities and recognizing that their size is no longer their Achilles heel but provides them with the opportunity to move at pace, to take decisions speedily, to take risks and to carve their path through the chaos.

The accelerating change curve

Much has been written in recent years of the changing shape of organizations and of the move away from the traditional hierarchical structures towards flatter and more flexible forms of organization. Organizational change initiatives have often carried the labels 'delayering', 'decentralizing' and 'down-sizing'. For some time, writers, such as Burns and Stalker (1961), have suggested that there is a relationship between changing external environmental factors and the changing shape of organizations; stable environments appear to prompt a more mechanistic, bureaucratic and top down structure and unstable environments lead to more flexible approaches.

While it seems there has been an implicit suggestion that all organizations are moving in this direction, the evidence suggests that at the current time we can see evidence of a continuum of organizational structures and styles ranging from the more traditional to what we will describe as the virtual. Charles Handy has proposed the model of the 'clover leaf' organization with the small core of workers managing bought in labour and specialists and, indeed, we have seen evidence of this model in action. It should be emphasised, though, that this is not yet the norm; there is considerable evidence in fact to suggest the traditional bureaucracy is still alive and well (Guest and Mackenzie Davey, 1996).

If it is accepted that we are experiencing a dramatic rate of environmental change due to the forces of technology, social expectations and shifting economic boundaries, and that organizations need to move away from the traditional model in order to survive, then what is the future for such traditional bureaucracies? In order to address this question it is essential to consider a critical variable here, that of the 'accelerating change curve' for any given industry. The concept of the accelerating change curve suggests that at any given time any industry, and their respective organizations, are experiencing change and that for different industries the rate of change will vary at different times. This concept is shown visually in Fig. 2.1.

Irrespective of whatever industry we are considering, the pattern appears the same; slow incremental change over many decades,   then

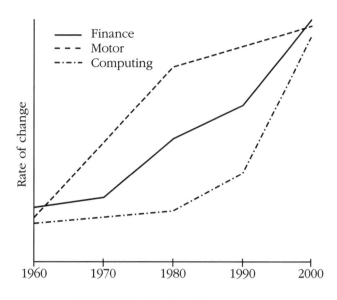

Fig. 2.1   Accelerating change curve

suddenly a dramatic steep increase, often driven by technological developments. For some industries these accelerated changes occurred in the 1960s, whereas for others it is happening right now and for others it has yet to take place. Take place it will, however, and when it does that industry will never be the same again. It is also particularly interesting to note the impact that an industry's accelerated change curve can have on other organizations, not only from within its own sector but outside of it, too.

Looking closer at the accelerated change curve we suggest, for example, that for the motor industry, the 1960s and 1970s saw a massive level of change with the advent of the Japanese into the market in competition with the US. This in turn proved a key factor behind the quality revolution. Interestingly, the developments in terms of the technology of the product may have been less revolutionary than those of, say, the computing industry but the approach to production and improving standards has led to a new mind-set with respect to manufacturing, marketing, quality and meeting customer needs.

In the computing industry we show that the rate of change has continued to climb throughout the last 20 years or so and shows little sign of abating. The first programmable digital computers were invented in the early 1940s and were up to 50 foot long. By the early 1950s, there were less than six computers in the world and IBM predicted there would be a market in the future for no more than 25 computers, only to change tack within a couple of years and venture into commercial production. By the early 1970s, microchip technology had emerged and the 1980s and 1990s have seen the development of a number of specialist computer related markets, not least of all that of the software industry. In 1991, companies spent more money on computing and communications equipment than the combined amount spent on industrial, mining, farm and construction equipment (Pritchett, 1996).

Increasingly the industry pioneers attempt to anticipate the shape of computing in the future and also to actually shape the future by creating new technologies and markets. Images which may have inhabited the world of science fiction are becoming science-fact; computers which can out-think the world chess master, holographic images of human beings able to interact with real people, virtual reality meetings—the list goes on and barely a day passes without profound computing related developments being revealed.

Despite the reality of such emerging capabilities our ability to predict the future with any degree of reliability is doubtful. To what extent will there be computers in every home and how will they be used? Will technologies become truly integrated? Will social behaviour change as a result of technological capabilities? Just how will the information super-highway evolve? There are more questions than answers and any players in this market have to be nimble enough to adjust if the technology takes a twist or a turn or even becomes obsolete.

The finance industry, which for some time has enjoyed a fair degree of stability, now faces a rapid rate of change. Here the timing of the acceleration of the change curve is different, but nonetheless significant. Affected by factors such as globalization, changing national economic and political boundaries, deregulation, increased consumer choice and the information revolution, this market is requiring a whole new approach from its players. This in turn is demanding not just new skills and knowledge but a new perception of the customer. As one branch manager from a major financial services organization said to us:

My technical knowledge is now a secondary factor—the products and interest rates change almost weekly anyway, so I am always having to learn new things—what is more important is the need for me to apply certain approaches—skills really. For instance I must always be looking for opportunities to develop the business, to forge new relationships and to be flexible in meeting the needs of my customers.

(Anon)

Customers have become more demanding, they can obtain more information and have more choice. At the same time as experiencing these changes in the customer relationship, the finance sector is now feeling the real impact of technological change. Not only does this affect the range and choice of financial products which can be made available, but it throws into question the role of the thousands of clerical and administrative personnel who have formed the backbone of the industry in the past. In 1996, the introduction of electronic share-trading on the London stock exchange meant that a computer now takes care of all transactions which had previously been carried out with 'real' paper certificates; yes, you can have a hard copy of the certificate if you wish, but that is more to comfort the traditionalist than for any functional purpose. The vision of the paperless office which many foresaw in the early 1980s has been some time coming but now seems to be emerging as a real proposition; it has been predicted that up to 40 per cent of jobs in commercial banking will be lost over a period of just seven years.

There are two important considerations when considering the accelerated change curve. First, real change is seldom seen as a straight upwards line; more appropriately, it might be seen as a combination of incremental and step changes. However, it is only when it is considered against the rate of past changes that the extent and implications of the change can be calculated.

Second, where the rate of change is slow, evolutionary and incremental, then individuals and organizations are close to the 'body of knowledge'. The body of knowledge in this context refers to the knowledge which is known and more importantly, recorded in writing and made available for others to find and utilize.   Where the body of knowledge is great, then it is not too difficult finding answers to particular problems. In effect, organizations search to understand how others may have addressed similar issues in the past and they then use this information to help themselves in solving their own problems.

In contrast, where the change curve is particularly steep, then the body of knowledge tends to be considerably diminished. As a result it is not so easy for an organization to find answers to what might appear to be complex problems. It is less feasible to go to the local university, business school or library and find material as to how others have tackled this problem. The problem is likely to be unique without anybody having faced, let alone resolved, it in the past. Even if others have encountered similar problems then, with a reduced body of knowledge, they are not likely to have actually recorded their actions. In such difficult circumstances what is required is a new set of managerial behaviours. Arguably, for leaders this calls for personal skills in developing and asking questions rather than seeing the leadership role as one where it is necessary to have all the answers.

Reflecting on the accelerating change curve in your industry or organization may prompt thoughts regarding the implications for both individuals within the organization and for the organization itself. For the individual there is a requirement to cope with an increasing rate of change and this imposes real psychological demands which some seem better equipped to contend with than others. For some individuals the change will be viewed as a loss of something valuable or important, whereas for others it will be the anxiety of the unknown that causes the greatest problems. Irrespective of the response we can anticipate that individuals will need to be managed through specific stages in the process.

If one accepts that change is in many ways synonymous with learning, in other words it is difficult to effect change without some learning taking place, then it might be proposed that a critical skill in the future will be the ability to learn. While the importance of individual responsibility for learning cannot be underestimated, there has been a significant growth in the popularity of the concept of the 'learning organization' in recent years. This has led to the proposition that the organization as an entity can continuously learn and transform itself. We examine this argument in more detail in the next chapter, but suffice to say at this stage that organizational as well as individual learning is vital if the environment is subject to rapid and accelerating change.

It has been previously proposed in theoretical approaches to systems analysis that organizations have to contend with uncertainty at various levels, ranging from interpersonal uncertainty, technological uncertainty and uncertainty to do with the environment on a broader scale. Thompson (1967), has suggested that this means managers need to take a co-ordinating, participative and empowering approach and that organizations need to address the subject of their environment in a proactive way in order to scan and anticipate changes which are taking place as well as attempting to influence wider change.

As previously discussed, one of the major challenges presented by the accelerating change curve is that there is less opportunity to fall back on recognized knowledge or ways of doing things. By contrast, in more stable and unchanging environments there is a recognized body of knowledge to refer to. In the rapidly changing environment there is often a need to actually define the way of operating for the first time.

So far we have emphasized the importance of the accelerating change curve for different sectors of industry and commerce. Generally, though, it is likely that the accelerating change curve will hit all areas of working life and all sectors, even if the timing is different in individual cases. Many have spoken of the information revolution and suggested that we are now experiencing a revolution which is on a par with the industrial revolution of the past. The only problem with this analogy is that classically a period of revolution is followed by stability, albeit in a changed state. There is no evidence to suggest, however, that with the revolution we are currently experiencing there will be a period of stability to follow.

In an attempt, however, to identify a picture of what successful organizations are likely to look like in the future we researched over 1000 different European organizations, to examine what they felt to be the key changes taking place in terms of how organizations are operating (Whitlam, 1990). Culpin (1989), has undertaken a similar study but in this case using content analysis and there is clearly some commonality in the findings of both research projects. We have found that there are specific issues which we believe successful organizations will need to address in the future in order to succeed and we describe these below as significant organizational trends.

Significant organizational trends

The research that we undertook involved us in using over 1000 questionnaires distributed across Europe which looked at the subject of change and patterns within organizations. Overall, from analysing the responses we were able to identify the following seven significant trends.

Importance of demonstrating concern for people

We found that organizations will, in the future, be particularly challenged by the requirement to show a real concern for their people. At first glance it might appear that many organizations do this; but on closer examination there is often a major difference between what it is believed happens and what actually happens in practice. As we previously described, we found a number of traditional organizations which seemed on the face of it to show concern for their 'staff' (they tended to use the word 'staff' more than 'members' or 'people') and would make a number of tangible offerings by way of social and financial support and fringe benefits. Such support in the traditional sense tended to focus around, for instance, pensions, staff restaurants, staff associations, discounts on products, social clubs, paid holiday entitlement and welfare facilities. There was no doubting that such benefits were indeed real and had a perceived value for the recipients.

What was interesting in these cases, though, was that the organizations which readily quoted such factors as evidence of their concern for staff tended to show such concern with a sense of paternalistic pride. Talking to the staff themselves also revealed a reciprocal sense of dependence on the 'father figure', that is, father in the form of the organization. In such cases it was often felt by the staff that the concern which was shown tended to be applied in a generalized rather than individualistic way; initiatives, schemes and benefits would apply to the whole group who were viewed as a cohort, rather than recognizing individual needs and preferences. Not that such concern for staff should be undervalued, more it was a concern which manifested itself differently when compared with organizations which appeared to be leading their field in a climate of accelerating change.

There was, however, a significant downside to the concern for staff as described above. In the traditional organization such a paternalistic culture worked well for so long as things remained stable. Where, however, we saw such organizations being forced into change without being ready for it, often the entire foundation upon which the paternalistic culture was based would be swept away. Staff who had assumed that there was an organizational loyalty towards them which they clearly returned were found to be unwanted, unskilled for new activity and unable to cope outside of the old institution. The psychological damage in some cases was irreparable: such people had not only learned to be dependent on the organization, they had developed a sense of learned helplessness.

This contrasted dramatically with more forward thinking organizations which were able to manage the messiness of change while at the same time showing concern for their people. The word 'people' is chosen advisedly here, because in these organizations there was evidence that people were recognized for their own personal ability to contribute to the business in their own unique way. In addition to this, in those organizations which tended to align more closely with our concept of virtual organizations it was not always absolutely clear cut who the members were, or at least there were categories of member other than just 'staff'. So there would be players with a significant role to play in ensuring the success of the organization, but rather than necessarily being employed on a traditional full-time basis they might fit a number of other categories, such as:

■ Consultants and/or external advisors
■ Secondees from other organizations, such as customers or suppliers
■ Sub-contracted specialists
■ Family members.

Rather than assuming that such external parties should be treated as outsiders, virtual organizations are more likely to welcome such people into the organization and make them feel part of the team. There is a recognition here of the need to show a concern for such people in order to keep them motivated and focused and to be able to draw on their particular contribution.

But this is easier said than done. How realistically can an organization show concern for people who may have other interests and loyalties. There is potentially an inherent dichotomy here between the individual's needs, motivators and values and those of the organization. Take, for instance, the position of the sub-contracted expert; let's look at it from the individual's perspective. He or she may be contracted into the organization for a fixed term or may be balancing a commitment to a number of different organizations at the same time. The main personal motive is to continue to remain an expert and a marketable commodity. This means updating skills, continuing to balance a variety of tasks and clients and not becoming overly dependent on one organization. Does this mean that this person should be treated as any less a member of the organization than, say, a core employee? Successful organizations are redefining the whole scope of who constitutes a member and are working to include rather than exclude such members; they are included on training programmes, remuneration packages, given access to employee benefits and development opportunities and are openly recognized for their contribution to the business.

This issue was highlighted in the media industry in the UK at the end of the 1980s, with the publication of a major study by The Institute of Manpower Studies (1989) into employment trends and skills requirements. It was suggested that the key to success of the industry in the future was likely to be the development of freelancers and it was found that their needs were being miserably neglected in comparison to those of core employees. It was reported that:

Skilled manpower in the freelance and independent sectors needs access to training which is of sufficient quantity, of good quality, appropriate in content and level, at times and in modes appropriate to working patterns, in relevant locations, capable of rapid introduction and/or modification to meet constantly changing needs and affordable at point of delivery. These needs are not currently being met.

Organizations which effectively manage non-core workers and show genuine concern for them, may or may not have in place tightly defined contractual arrangements; more important is a sense of trust and integrity on the side of both parties. Yes, it may be easier for both parties to walk away from one another but there is a mutual interest in building a lasting relationship. For traditional organizations the ability to manage with such contractual vagueness causes some considerable discomfort.

As well as managing peripheral workers effectively, successful organizations in the future will tend to recognize individual differences and indeed encourage celebration of such differences. Such recognition of individual differences will tend to pervade all aspects of people management. There will be individual choice over remuneration packages, such as that seen with the 'cafeteria benefits' approach, recognition of different development needs, and the provision of choice. Some organizations have overtly declared that recognizing individualism is a core value; Motorola, for instance, talks of the 'individual dignity entitlement' and works to integrate this philosophy with many aspects of its management of people. In such cases, status in the hierarchical sense is a less dominant theme than in the traditional organization; the special contribution of individuals is more important than their title or, to use a military term, how many stripes they have on their arms.

Of course, such a focus on the individual presents particular difficulties when it comes to administration. Instead of being able to design the system and then allowing it to run itself, there is a need for more flexibility. Rules and regulations take second place to concern for people. This does not mean that anything less than effective performance is accepted; on the contrary, in such organizations there is a strong emphasis on being able to define effective performance and measure individuals against such criteria. Furthermore, there is a readiness to confront poor performance and to tackle differences of opinion in a mature way. By contrast, in some of the traditional organizations there is a tendency to avoid such confrontation, with poor performers often promoted to their level of incompetence or moved sideways into what are misguidedly referred to as specialist roles.

Continual employee involvement

The second major organizational trend which we identified was that increasingly organizations will be required to actively involve their people at all levels. Involvement in this context means both ensuring effective communication regarding the developments in the business as well as involvement in decision making. Out of choice we would tend to avoid the perennial buzzword 'empowerment' because this again seems to be a widely used and often misused word, which some organizations have adopted more because it is fashionable than because they wish to adopt truly empowering approaches.

Involving organizations genuinely recognize the benefit to be gained from drawing on the talents of members. This means demonstrating trust in employees and confidence in their abilities and creating a climate where mistakes are tolerated, used and processed as learning opportunities.

In contrast, many traditional organizations and their senior managers are restricted by real fears that by involving their staff more there will be a loss of personal power and a threat to the *status quo*. With such a mind-set we often detected an arrogance which suggested, usually erroneously, that those at a lower level in the hierarchy had little to contribute by way of ideas, initiative or motivation. There was real evidence of McGregor's 'Theory X' type managers holding out in a fast changing world. Their mind-set might be described as follows:

■ People dislike work and will avoid it if they can
■ People must be forced or bribed to put out the right level of effort
■ People would rather be directed than accept responsibility, which they avoid
■ People are motivated mainly by money
■ Most people have little creativity.

The following quotation from a manager, cited by Peters and Waterman in *In search of excellence* (1982), seems to sum up this mentality:

Our control systems are designed under the apparent assumption that 90 per cent of the people are ne'er do wells, just waiting to lie, cheat, steal or otherwise screw us. We demoralize 95 per cent of the work force who do act as adults by designing systems to cover our tails against the 5 per cent who really are bad actors.

However, when we probed into such organizations there was often evidence to suggest that the reverse was actually true; this can be seen by the example of the case study organization below.

CASE
STUDY
2.1

The need for involvement

A major national transport organization had called in consultants to advise regarding organizational development with the goal of improving morale, motivation and the performance of the staff, particularly those at the more junior levels.

This was an organization where high length of service was the norm but career progression tended to be slow and for many of those at the more operational end of the business they did not really view themselves as having a career so much as a job.

In taking the brief from senior management, the consultants were told that in particular there was a need to investigate the junior operational staff because they seemed to be poorly motivated and simply plodding from one day to the next without any desire to really contribute to the business, which was undergoing significant culture change. The task of the consultants was to identify whether these people should be kept on in the new shape organization and to identify the root cause of the problem and make recommendations accordingly.

The consultants conducted a campaign of structured interviews with some fascinating findings. Overall, their report back to the senior management team came as something of a shock: they reported that this junior level of personnel were among the most highly motivated people they had encountered. Interviews revealed that all of those seen felt there was little opportunity for development at work and that they were resigned to 'just doing a job' and some admitted they were cruising through to retirement. They felt they were stereotyped as operational staff and not afforded respect by their seniors. However, there was real evidence of high motivation, drive and ability which was being channelled into activities outside of work. Included in the group interviewed were the following individuals:

■ A marathon runner who was running at national level.
■ A mother of five who had set up a parent support group which involved her in liaising with professional people, convening and chairing meetings, publishing a newsletter and organizing a telephone help line.
■ A writer who had written dozens of children's books which had been published internationally.
■ A lecturer who was giving evening school tuition at a local college.
■ A computer expert who had become an authority on the information superhighway.
■ A charity worker who had raised thousands of pounds for a children's cancer charity.

Each of these people identified above, and there were more, had demonstrated extreme levels of human motivation in order to overcome serious time and financial constraints and achieve real successes in their chosen area. The only pity was that none of these people were able to say that their supervisors or managers at work actually knew of their achievements. Furthermore, when the consultants challenged these individuals to consider how they might transfer or make use of their skills in the workplace or in their future career they were unable to see a connection. They simply believed that 'work was work' and these were external interests. In effect, what the consultants found was that as individuals these employees were so over-controlled ('Theory X' thinking) that they felt that their work was something that they had little or no control over or ability to improve.

So, the findings of the consultants in reporting back to senior managers were that there was real evidence that they had some of the most motivated people at the operational end of the business, but that they did not even know it. There was a need to find out about the people and their interests and skills, rather than stereotype them as one group. Additionally, there was an opportunity to involve these individuals in getting them to look at their own roles and making real suggestions as to how these could be improved.

From an organizational perspective the business needed to unlearn or forget the emphasis that had been placed on control, then to set these individuals free to realize their potential in the corporate environment.

We found that there were many Western organizations, fitting the traditional model, which had attempted to implement learning from the model Japanese organizations under the banner of Total Quality Management, Continuous Improvement, Business Process Re-Engineering, *Kaizen* or Empowerment. Often they accepted the argument on an intellectual level, that there was much to be gained from involving employees more in decision making, but there was often a resistance to making such approaches work on an emotional level.

Traditional managers saw their power base being eroded and failed to see that their role should evolve to one of facilitating and developing processes rather than instructing and controlling. We even saw some managers allowing such initiatives to fail by passively resisting such change while appearing to be supportive. So, for instance, in one case a manager was overtly encouraging devolved decision making while deliberately withholding the provision of relevant training to equip employees with the skills and confidence required to present their ideas upwards in a convincing manner.

We contrast this with organizations which have truly embraced the concept of involvement: Hitachi has estimated that it receives 4.15 million suggestions from 80 000 personnel per week and Toyota has estimated that 2 million suggestions were received in 1987 from 84 000 staff, 97 per cent of which were implemented (Eccles, 1993).

There is, of course, a danger in looking to the Japanese for all the answers; there is no doubt that there are difficulties which the Japanese experience with the application of their approach. For instance, in some cases *kaisen,* or continuous improvement techniques, are taken to extreme. The production environment is placed under extreme pressure to work more quickly and stress is deliberately created so that mistakes and difficulties can be identified; having found the weak points pressure is then exerted to improve or correct methods. This places considerable pressure upon employees to keep up, resulting in extreme levels of human stress, to the extent that the Japanese now have a word to describe production related illnesses, *karochi.*

The Japanese approach to involvement in decision making, though, is an interesting one. Clearly there are implications for involving more people in decision making, not least of all the fact that this approach takes more time. It has been recognized for some time, though, that true consensus, while difficult to achieve, results in better quality decisions than voting or autocratic approaches. The real significance of involving others in decision making, however, should be seen against a future time perspective.

As can be seen in Fig. 2.2, key variables in decision making might be considered to be the speed at which the decision is taken, the quality of the decision and the level of subsequent support from employees. In a traditional and autocratic culture, decisions will typically be taken by the more senior person who imposes such decisions upon those below, who are then expected to implement such decisions and co-operate. The advantage here is the speed of decision making, the disadvantage is the level of buy-in; the implementers may implement with little belief in or acceptance of such decisions or may even passively resist implementation.

We have seen some alarming examples of this in organizations. One

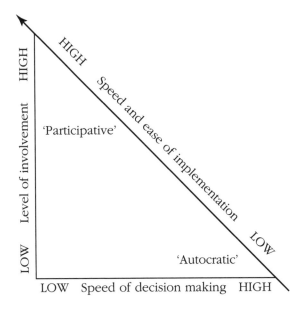

Fig. 2.2 Decision making and implementation

senior manager, for instance, described a situation where the sales team in a local national office deliberately overpriced a product so that it would not sell. The rationale for this was that they did not really believe in the product because it was imposed on them by the corporation at headquarters level. The real issue, of course, was to do with lack of involvement and hence lack of buy-in to the decision.

This non-participative approach to involvement in decision making is still prevalent in many traditional organizations. Even where the traditional organization has established some formal means of encouraging participation, for example through quality circles, suggestion schemes or works councils, the level of involvement in decisions which really are fundamental to the business can often be seriously questioned.

When the level of involvement in the decision making process is high, then it may actually take longer to arrive at a consensus. The real benefit is seen, though, when implementing the decision. Because the decision has been arrived at through a consultative and participative process, then the level of support for the decision is likely to be higher. Implementation therefore becomes easier due to both the level of psychological support and the fact that potential difficulties will have been anticipated through increased involvement and the discussion of different perspectives.

So effective organizations will in the future, we believe, both show concern for their members and will involve them in the business, recognizing the potential which people at all levels have to offer. This brings us to the third of the seven characteristics which we identified— the development of entrepreneurial skills.

Encouraging entrepreneurial skills

Organizations which seemed to be thriving, as opposed to just surviving, in the rapidly changing environment tended to encourage members at all levels to constantly seek ways of developing the business. Clearly it is unrealistic to expect members at all levels and in all functions to be able to contribute by way of developing the actual product or service because one's ability to do this is determined in part by specialist knowledge and skills. Often entrepreneurial skill really meant intrepreneurial skill, in that members would identify ways of improving the business from within; included here were examples of employees taking the initiative by improving existing processes or replacing them with better ones. This meant providing such members with discretion to make decisions and to act.

Motorola, for instance, overtly declares that effective managers should behave as follows:

■ Use mistakes as opportunities to learn/teach not punish
■ Creatively ask questions
■ Involve others in brainstorming and decision making
■ Reward/recognize openly those who go beyond the minimum.

In a similar vein the individual employee is actively encouraged to behave as follows:

■ Take initiative and tackle a problem without having it assigned to them
■ Be willing to challenge/change policies (challenge the status quo) to improve organizational effectiveness
■ Look for ways to exceed expectations and go beyond what is expected
■ Treat goals and objectives as a minimum as opposed to a limit.

This is an interesting approach because what Motorola is seeking to do is to define a model of successful performance. This, they believe, increases the chances of all employees achieving success.

There were other interesting approaches taken to encourage and reinforce appropriate entrepreneurial behaviours. One organization has a prize parking place outside the company's main offices reserved for the 'employee of the month'; contrast this with many organizations which only reserve such prestigious places for the most senior executives, thus reinforcing the importance of the hierarchy and the status quo. Another organization actually seeks to reward individual employees who take some sort of risk which doesn't quite come off. This approach is used to reinforce the importance of risk taking rather than stifle such opportunities.

More traditional organizations tended to operate in a control focused way. In the traditional hierarchical and functional structure there was a tendency for employees to be limited to working and making decisions relevant only to their own work area or specialism. There were clearly defined boundaries within which one had to operate and anyone who stepped over these boundaries would be dealt with in no uncertain terms. This culture tended to restrict any initiative and often we found people at the middle and junior levels of the organization who had little or no real knowledge or understanding as to what was going on in the business outside of their own area. In organizations more able to cope with change there was a conscious effort to break down such boundaries and in many cases this was overtly declared in a stated objective to become boundaryless.

Frequently in the more traditional organizations we found examples of rules and regulations which managers found difficult to justify. Often these rules were intended to enforce uniformity and by definition had the effect of reducing and inhibiting individuality. Sometimes the rules were based more on tradition and folklore than on any particular rationale; in these cases behaviours were often seen to be stylized and ritualistic. There were many examples:

- The company where everyone was issued with company neck-ties and told that if they were seen not wearing them they would be disciplined.
- Rules surrounding the etiquette of running meetings, often forcing people to attend meetings where they had little to offer or gain, but where they attended because of their formal position.
- Many examples of rules and regulations surrounding meal times and the way to behave in the company dining room. This included men having to keep their jackets on while dining and young graduates having to receive etiquette training in aspects of how to eat correctly.
- A personnel manual that included over three pages describing when, and under what conditions, employees could use the toilets.
- A five-page policy, 'The inclement weather policy', detailing how managers should deal with staff attendance in situations of adverse weather conditions.

Clearly these examples may at first seem ridiculous in the extreme. Nevertheless, it is important to recognize how such organizational behaviour develops. It is often driven by a burning desire to control and thus be able to predict, and consequently manage, the future. Indeed, this is early evidence of man's insecurity or fear of the unknown.

Often such rules and regulations had the effect of reducing individuality and thus entrepreneurial spirit. There was also evidence in many cases of a self fulfilling prophecy in action, whereby employees would be treated more like delinquent children and, as a result of being treated in this way, this is how they behaved.

Focus on innovation

In some ways, this fourth characteristic which we identified in successfully adapting organizations was linked to the above factor, 'entrepreneurial skills'. Here, though, the emphasis is placed more on encouraging steps rather than incremental innovation as well as innovative behaviours.

The need for innovation is driven by three factors: first, it is the organizational response to operating in the midst of the accelerated change curve where there are no obvious solutions; second, the constant search for competitive advantage is also fuelling the need for the continuing emphasis on innovation; third, technology is providing numerous insights into the way in which services and products may possibly develop.

In order to be truly innovative there is a requirement to actually make a time and financial commitment to innovation. Often organizations like 3M are held up as examples to us all. In reality, it is only in parts of 3M, for instance, where employees are allowed up to 15 per cent of their paid employment time to work on innovative projects of their own choosing. These projects need not be directly related to their current work and the company believes that by allowing employees to do this, while the number of commercially successful innovations may be relatively low compared to the number of projects pursued, those that do make it are often truly innovative in that they break new ground and create new markets or product ranges.

While size of organizations in many cases tended to inhibit innovation, 3M has proven that large multinationals can truly innovate if they make a significant commitment to do so. 3M are active in 57 countries and employ around 85 000 people world-wide, re-investing around seven per cent of their turnover in research and development and producing over 60 000 different products in over 100 distinct technologies. Each year, 30 per cent of sales comes from products that did not actually exist four years earlier. The figures speak for themselves.

Increasingly, large companies are recognizing the benefits of working together with smaller companies and vice versa, in order to encourage innovation. In the UK, the M4 innovation network has recently been established with government backing to enable collaboration and cross learning between big and small companies and educational and research institutions; it includes such major organizations as 3M, National Power and Black and Decker.

In order for any company to embrace such an approach there is a need to break down some of the inhibiting barriers which might exist in the traditional context, where sharing information is often seen as threatening. Innovative companies recognize that there is a need to collaborate, to form alliances and to share. They also realize that they do not have all the answers; they are open minded.

In less innovative organizations there tends to be a fear associated with risk taking. Often it is recognized that those who stepped outside of the boundaries in the past were considered eccentric, did not fit and did not survive. It was in this area that we found that the 'right first time' philosophy, often associated with Total Quality Management initiatives and with quality standards, could potentially mitigate against innovation and creativity by reinforcing non-innovative behaviours such as compliance, analysis and attention to detail.

Focus on customer orientation

It might be considered that since the 1980s we have seen a quality revolution, which in turn has focused on customer orientation working its way through most industries in the service sector. At the same time, there has been a recognition that the same principles which hold good for customer care with regard to the external customer or client, the purchaser of the organization's goods or services, actually can be applied with equally good effect within the organization. Despite the message from the past, as espoused by the likes of Peters and Waterman in the 1980s, it seems that only some organizations have really taken the 'close to the customer' message to heart. Too often we see examples of organizations focusing on giving customers what they think they want, rather than treating them as real stakeholders and making sure their needs are really identified and then met.

It is ironic that often the best case studies can be drawn from negative examples:

A group of customers using a large hotel wanting to arrange to have breakfast at 7.15 a.m. and being told by a manager that breakfast starts at 7.30 a.m. but that they were 'welcome to sit and wait for 15 minutes'. There is an interesting footnote to this story. When the predicament was being discussed by the customers, the conversation was overheard by a part-time waitress who spoke directly to the chef who immediately agreed to the 7.15

a.m. breakfast. This raises some interesting questions concerning who has the real power and influence in the organization.

Another hotel that goes to great lengths to point the way to the customer car park, which is approximately 100 metres from the entrance, while displaying many signs that management only are able to park outside the front door of the hotel. Inside the hotel are signs saying 'The Customer's Needs are Paramount'.

Then there was the airline which claimed to have revolutionized its approach to customer care through a major culture change programme, which was supported by training for all of its employees. On a long haul flight one customer, holding a small baby, was queuing to use the toilet when suddenly an air stewardess jumped the queue and pushed in front without a word of explanation.

The case of the high street bank which launched a major advertising campaign claiming to have refocused its efforts around listening to the customers' needs, also provided some evidence of how the good intentions often failed to be translated into action. One customer who was requesting an extension of an overdraft facility in the run up to her wedding was asked by her bank manager if she would consider postponing the wedding. Needless to say she promptly tranferred her account elsewhere and was married as planned. Furthermore, a competitor bank was delighted to then take on this new customer and her husband.

Emphasis on measurement

We found that there was a tendency in successful organizations to focus on measurement and to attempt to measure even in areas where measurement is not so easy. This was not just about financial measures or quality measures and standards. Measurement in this context frequently entailed the measurement of behaviours and skills and in some cases the factors which have previously been described as 'soft'. We found evidence of organizations attempting to take a more scientific approach to measuring some of these supposedly softer issues.

The early 1990s saw major emphasis being placed in many organizations on measurement; however, the emphasis was often skewed much more towards 'hard' than 'soft' measures. So managers were set specific financial objectives, sales executives were set tough financial targets and manufacturing managers worked to demanding production schedules. The emphasis was placed on achieving one's targets, in some cases at any price. It was assumed that this was the way to beat the competition and to continuously raise standards. In effect, such organizations were focusing almost entirely on outputs. The downside to such an output focused approach was that often process related issues were ignored. So a salesperson could be set a demanding sales target, with a real and tangible reward for being the best which is defined as selling more than their colleagues. They would be rewarded handsomely, regardless of how they achieved their result. This could, in the worse cases, mean engaging in destructive, internally competitive behaviour and causing more actual carnage than benefit in the long term.

Some organizations have now come to realize the dangers of prioritizing just hard targets and are achieving more balance by carefully thinking through and defining the critical behaviours or competencies which should be displayed in a job role. The focus on behaviours is an input focused approach and has become more relevant, and at the same time the actual task related skills have decreased in importance. As the knowledge and skill required for successful performance in jobs is changing on an almost daily basis, the key is to be able to facilitate effective learning and to address the enduringly important behaviours.

The other major growth area where we have seen successful organizations instigate clear measures of performance is in benchmarking. Successful organizations are aware of how they measure up against best practice and this normally means some formal approach to drawing internal comparisons as well as comparisons with other organizations or professionals. Some companies will use recognized national standards to measure themselves against. Where these are used, for instance the use of the Investors in People standard in the UK, comparisons are made with a view to achieving continuous improvement above and beyond the standard. In Chapter 8 we look in more detail at how organizations are approaching the use of benchmarking data in order to continually improve and adapt.

Additionally, and linked to the subject of measurement and goal setting, we found organizations with the ability to create strong pictures of how the future could be. Where we saw examples of powerful leadership, one of the characteristics of the leader was the ability to translate such pictures into a vision which could be shared at all levels of the organization. This is a subject we explore later in Chapter 4, where we discuss the qualities of effective leaders and approaches to vision building.

Influence not authority

The final significant finding was that within successful organizations there was a significant increase in the emphasis being placed on influencing skills, rather than gaining authority from more traditional sources such as position power or coercion. It is becoming more difficult for managers and leaders to rely on traditional sources of position power in order to make things happen and this might be seen to be due to the following factors. As more specialisms are developing and as technological advances are creating pockets of expertise, those with position power may not actually possess expert power. Conversely, the experts need not be the most senior people in the hierarchy. Furthermore, it seems that people are becoming more demanding of their leaders in terms of expecting to be consulted and persuaded rather than ordered or punished.

The other key factor leading to the need for influencing skills is the fact that with the increasing level of collaboration across organizations and, for instance, the trend towards outsourcing there is a need to genuinely persuade others over whom one may have no formal authority. In other publications we look in detail at the subject of personal influencing skills and share some of our research into the specific skills of influencing (Hale and Whitlam, 1995). This has identified that successful influencing means managing impressions, building rapport, communicating well, recognizing non-verbal communication and being able to confront. Additionally, we have found that managers and leaders who are effective in influencing others tend to engage in certain goal orientated thinking or cognitive approaches.

So far we have identified a number of key factors which we believe organizations will need to address in order to operate successfully when faced with an increasing rate of change. Those organizations we would describe as being close to the model of the virtual organization would tend to address these themes in a proactive way. You might at this stage like to think about the way in which your organization measures up against these seven factors.

PAUSE FOR THOUGHT

Consider the seven organizational trends identified above and rate your own organization against these factors:

	Low	High
Concern for people	0———————	—10
Employee involvement	0———————	—10
Entrepreneurial skills	0———————	—10
Innovation	0———————	—10
Customer orientation	0———————	—10
Importance of measurement	0———————	—10
Influence not authority	0———————	—10

Justify your rating with examples of where the characteristics are strongly or weakly demonstrated. It can also be instructive to consider the historical context of the current rating by identifying whether the trend is upwards or downwards.

You may wish to ask members of your organization at different levels to carry out the same exercise in order to see whether similar or different perceptions are held throughout the organization.

What might account for any differences in perception?

In this chapter we have looked at the world in transition from two perspectives. We have considered some of the key trends and changes taking place outside of the organization in the world at large. Then, on the basis that starting to understand some of these macro level developments will help us to understand some of the changes taking place in the corporate environment, we have moved our focus of attention to looking at key organizational trends.

In the next chapter we continue to explore the subject of organizational change and development and will review some of the emergent themes in recent years, in particular the notion of the 'learning organization'. This is helpful as a means of aiding us to understand how organizations might well cope with the accelerating change curve. Additionally, we add to the debate regarding how organizations might manage change effectively by exploring the notion of organizational values, beliefs and the concept of an organizational 'self-concept'.

References

Burns, T. and Stalker, G.M., *The Management of Innovation*, Tavistock, 1961.

Culpin, R., Leadership Style and Human Resource Management, *Management Decisions*, 7(1) (1989).

Eccles, T., The Deceptive Allure of Empowerment, *Long Range Planning*, 26(6) (1993).

Guest, D. and Mackenzie Davey, K., *People Management*, 22 (1996).

Hale, R. and Whitlam, P.J., *The Power of Personal Influence*, McGraw-Hill, Maidenhead, 1995.

Institute of Manpower Studies, *Skill Search: Television, Film and Video Industry Employment Patterns and Training Needs*, Report No. 186, Brighton, 1989.

Naisbitt, J., *Megatrends*, Futura, 1984.

Naisbitt, J., *Global Paradox*, Nicholas Brealey, London, 1994.

Peters, T., and Waterman, R., *In Search of Excellence*, Harper & Row, 1982.

Pritchett, *New Work Habits for a Radically Changing World*, Pritchett & Associates, Tyne & Wear, 1996.

Rifkin, J., *End of Work*, Tarcher/Putnam, New York, 1995.

Thompson, J.D., *Organizations In Action*, McGraw-Hill, New York, 1967.

Whitlam P.J., *Assessing Organizational Learning Effectiveness*, M.Phil Dissertation, International Management Centres, 1990.

Beyond the learning organization

*'To improve is to change, to be perfect is
to change often'*

WINSTON CHURCHILL

In this chapter we:

■ Review the debate surrounding the concept of the 'learning organization' which has arisen with the increasing rate of change in recent years
■ Recognize the impact of an organization's attitudes, values and beliefs on its current performance and future potential
■ Explain the notion of learned helplessness
■ Explore the process by which an organization develops its self-image which then either contributes to success or inhibits future growth
■ Consider the role of those outside the organization in contributing to the development of organizational beliefs
■ Explore three ways in which organizations can manage the barriers and develop the appropriate attitudes, values and beliefs which include flooding, organizational desensitization and the use of involved vision building.

Learning organization—aspiration or reality?

Much has been written in recent years of the concept of the learning organization, to the extent that this expression has entered the common vocabulary in the world of organizational development. Undoubtedly this interest in the learning organization has been influenced by the increasing rate of change or accelerating change curve which we discussed in the previous chapter. From as far back as the early 1980s, and building on the work of other theorists, Revans (1982) proposed that:

'learning must equal or be greater than environmental change or the organization will not survive'.

Faced with unprecedented rates of change, in terms of technology, social and economic factors, there is a need to ensure that the organization and the people within it are able to keep pace with and meet the changing expectations and demands of customers, stakeholders, suppliers, competitors and employees.

The fact that the learning or knowledge of the organization's members has a real value is increasingly being recognized. This may currently be clearly seen in the more technical industries, where new technical knowledge which is gained by members while in the organization's employ must be retained; in fact, to lose the individuals and their knowledge presents a real threat. This has clearly contributed to the growth in the area of patents, copyright and legislation and contractual obligations regarding intellectual property.

There has also been a recognition that simply acquiring new knowledge or skills is insufficient; the knowledge and skill needed for success tomorrow may be irrelevant next week or next month. There is more to be gained by learning to learn and so some organizations have attempted to create a learning culture which does more than simply provide a suite of courses to meet specific and static needs. Indeed in our own research, Whitlam (1990) quite clearly showed that organizations that are successful in the new millennium will find that there is a decreasing emphasis on training systems such as programmes and performance appraisal systems, and a much greater emphasis on developing learning behaviours such as initiative or risk taking and learning processes like knowing how to access resources.

This raises some interesting questions like 'Is it actually possible to develop behaviours like initiative or risk taking?' and 'How exactly do we empower or enable individuals to exploit learning processes such as how to access resources?'. These issues are related to the organization's attitudes and beliefs and are inextricably linked to the prevailing culture or climate. Some proponents of the learning organization concept suggest that one can address learning from both the perspective of the individual members and the organization itself; organizations as well as individuals can learn.

Despite the high level of interest and the liberal way in which the term is bandied about, some differences of opinion exist as to a consensus of either a model, theory or definition of organizational learning. Here we review some of the research in this area and suggest that as an aspirational concept the learning organization is useful. However, there is little evidence, even when looking at best practice, to suggest that the perfect learning organization really exists. In most cases it is accepted that this is really a concept which corporations might work towards, rather than being a fixed point that is reached, then sustained. In this sense the research in this area has proved useful for some organizations and for change agents; it provides guiding principles to work to and models to work with. Here we provide a brief overview and critique of the literature in this area.

Critique of the literature

Definitions of the learning organization abound; we feel no need to add to the list, but it is helpful to summarize some of the most well known definitions and thoughts from leading thinkers in this area. Both academics and practitioners have contributed here, and there are many examples of collaborative exercises where the two have come together to try to find some sort of answer as to how the learning organization should be developed in the future. For instance, MIT in America has established the Center For Organizational Learning and lists among its members Ford, Harley Davidson, Electronic Data Systems, Federal Express, AT&T, Philips and Intel—all organizations which are seeking a breakthrough in the search for best practice through the sharing of ideas among corporations and academics.

Historically, debate surrounding organizational development and design has focused on structural, strategic and, more recently, cultural issues. In a sense the learning organization debate has emerged out of a recognition that there is a need to address processes and behaviours and to manage change and uncertainty. Hofman and Senge (1993), call for a whole new way of thinking about organizations: a need to create a vision of the organization which people want to work for and which thrives in an environment of increasing interdependency and change. They talk of learning organizations which:

... are both more generative and more adaptive than traditional organizations. Because of their commitment, openness, the ability to deal with complexity, people find security not in stability but in the dynamic equilibrium between holding on and letting go—holding on and letting go of beliefs, assumptions, and certainties.

It is this notion of individual and organizational beliefs which we pick up on and explore later in this chapter. It is also suggested that we tend to be limited by our perception of the leader of the organization who tends to fit the traditional stereotype of the hero-leader, leading from the front as an inspirational individual. Arguably, in the learning organization we need to think more of leaders at all levels and even of the concept of collective leadership. These views are interesting in that they question some previously held basic assumptions regarding the way in which organizations are managed and led. They are also consistent with our picture of the changing nature of leadership.

John Burgoyne (1995), suggests an almost spiritual connotation when he talks about society moving to a stage where people actually look to organizations for meaning in their lives, particularly as their belief in the state weakens. He suggests different levels of organization:

- *Habit driven organizations*—This is the lowest level in the model and is where habits are learnt and become entrenched. It is suggested that this actually inhibits the learning of relevant new skills and knowledge.
- *Adaptive organizations*—At the next level are organizations which have learnt how to change habits and which adapt to changes which might be taking place in their environment.
- *Stable organizations*—At the next level are organizations which are able to actually influence their environment and stabilize their position in order to secure their longevity. Burgoyne admits these may be rare, but he quotes organizations such as Coca-Cola, McDonald's and IBM as examples.

This is a useful model to help us consider the stage of learning within the organization. Interestingly, the three 'stable' organizations quoted are all large corporations; it is worth considering whether it is possible for the relatively small organizations to operate at this level. It may be the case that we are seeing a major change here and in the future it is possible that smaller, dynamic organizations which might be described as virtual organizations will be able to exert more of an influence, either collectively or individually, on their external environment and on larger corporations, than has hitherto been the case.

Pedler et al. (1991), define the learning company as '... an organization that facilitates the learning of all its members and continually transforms itself'. Here we see one of the most significant aspects of the learning organization concept, namely that of the organization itself learning as opposed to simply its members. This is about a process of continuous change rather than seeing change and learning as a one-off or sporadic event.

When debating the learning organization there is often a confusion between the issues of individual versus organizational learning. For the sake of clarity, individual learning can be taken to include the formal and informal processes by which the individual learns within the organizational context. As such, it embraces training, development and educational processes, as well as more informal activities related to the process of individual learning.

By contrast, organizational learning is taken to mean the process by, and through, which the organization itself actually learns. Essentially, it is concerned with the acquisition of corporate knowledge, skills and attitudes, as well as broader systems issues. However, within such a framework individual learning within the organization will undoubtedly be a constituent part.

If we define learning itself as: 'a lasting change of behaviour based on experience', then clearly such a definition can be seen as applicable to either individual learning or organizational learning. The important part of this definition is the word *lasting*. Our research indicates that many organizations appear to achieve a temporary change of behaviour, often as a result of some major change programme, but when this change is studied over time, the results are often disappointing. In terms of individual learning, Whitlam (1993) found that where individuals have undertaken behavioural skills programmes, and where their performance has been monitored over time, the transference of achieving *a lasting change of behaviour* is as follows:

On immediate completion of the initial change process	99%
3 months after the initial process	63%
6 months after the initial process	49%
9 months after the initial process	17%
1 year after the initial process	6%

Although these figures are of themselves valuable, it is more interesting to consider the underlying reasons for such an apparently poor transference of newly acquired knowledge and skills. In the vast majority of cases, the most significant issue appears to be related to cognitive processes, in particular the impact of an individual's attitudes and beliefs on actual performance. Ironically in change programmes, such cognitive processes seldom appear to be explored explicitly, often because of the underlying assumption that these things will somehow take care of themselves. Clearly, this is not the case.

Many writers, researchers and academics have wrestled with the issue of organizational learning in an attempt to try to establish whether organizations themselves can learn, and if so, how. There are almost as many angles on this as writers, with some approaching the subject as learning specialists, some as psychologists and others as organizational development consultants. A leading thinker in this field is Argyris (1977), who suggested the notion of 'double loop learning'. He says:

Organizational learning is the process of detecting and correcting error. Error is for our purpose any feature of knowledge or knowing that inhibits learning. When the process enables the organization to carry on its present policies or achieve its objectives the process may be called single loop learning. If the organization was capable not only of detecting error but of questioning the underlying policies and goals as well as its own programme ... it might be called double loop learning.

In their publication, Barham *et al.* (1988) state:

> The learning organization can be described as one in which learning is not restricted to discrete chunks of training activity, either fragmented or systematic, but is one where it has become a continuous process, and where on the job learning has become a way of life.

We could go on summarizing the views and findings in this field, however at this stage it is worth trying to synthesize some of the consistent messages which are emerging about the learning organization. Organizational learning might be seen as:

- An organizational not just an individual process, however it works through individuals
- Closely linked to the processes that the organization adopts
- Involving fundamental change
- Occurring at several levels of the organization
- Institutionalized in systems.

Trying to draw together the various strands of thinking about the learning organization is not easy; the concept it seems is just that — a concept. And even those organizations which are often held up as models of the learning organization, often fail to live up to the hype. It is not unusual to find that members of the organization are actually unaware of their learning organization status. Dolan (1995), bemoaned the fact that he could find little by way of practical guidance from the thinking of the ideas of key learning organization writers; spurred on to contact 12 of the most quoted companies he found that key people in two-thirds of these organizations actually knew nothing of their apparent status.

So, are there any practical applications and recommendations which emerge from the massive amount of deliberation on the learning organization? How exactly is a learning organization developed or, if it is accepted that this is really an aspirational concept, then how is it possible to move towards the aspiration?

Practical steps

Garratt (1995), admits the idea of learning and change in organizations is nothing new. However, he suggests that there are four key essentials:

- People need regular and rigorous help
- Learning needs robust organizational systems and a positive organizational climate to move the learning to where it is needed
- Learning should be seen as valued by the organization for achieving its objectives

■ The organization should be designed so as to be able to continuously transform itself.

Certainly our experience has suggested that in effective organizations there will need to be robust systems which contribute to the learning culture. However, we found that as the organization moved more towards the learning organization model the reliance on systems became less important and the significance of effective learning behaviours and processes increased.

The link which Garratt identifies between learning and the organization achieving its objectives is important. We have come across several examples of organizations where the actual systems for training and development may be strong, and rigorously implemented, but where training has either evolved into a separate business within the organization, or where it is perceived as little more than an unnecessary hindrance to the real business.

In more successful organizations which are closer to the learning organization model, learning is closely integrated with the business, the function and the individual job; line personnel would see themselves as continuously learning and continuously developing others. Training functions provide specialist support and expertise and facilitate learning, rather than deliver repeat courses. Their role is to identify best practice, either from within the organization or from without, and to find ways of spreading such knowledge and skill to the areas of real need.

Interestingly, in the virtual organization we believe the approach to learning is taken even further: learning is totally integrated with everyday activities on the part of all organizational members. There is less need for formal systems and procedures because individuals will tend to demonstrate a strong learning orientation anyway.

In recent years we have seen a movement towards encouraging individuals to take responsibility for their own learning and personal development. While this may have been implicit in the relationship between the organization and the professional or most senior people, this has not always been the case with those working at the more operational levels in the business. There is still evidence in some traditional organizations of a learned helplessness, whereby the individual assumes that he or she will be cared for and that if there is a need for development the organization will make, even has a duty to make, relevant provision. In many organizations it is now recognized that the leaders have a key role in creating the environment for others to learn and to want to learn. This is different from a role of deciding on the training need and making the solution available. The trend, as Naisbitt (1982) has suggested, is away from institutional support and towards self-help.

In order to encourage this sort of self-help approach to learning and personal development many organizations are making training and development available to their members, based on their personal preferences more than organizational relevance. Ford popularized this approach with its Employee Development and Assistance Programme which was launched in 1987. The company and the trade unions representing the company's 44,000 hourly paid and salaried employees run the scheme, which offers financial assistance to employees for a wide range of courses and opportunities for personal development, education and training. Employees can apply for assistance in almost any field. Overall, the emphasis is placed on the acquisition of new skills rather than on training for the current role. There are examples of hourly paid clerks enrolling on six-year social science degrees and drivers learning German to help them in communications on cross border trips.

Many in the automobile industry, doing as some proponents of the learning organization suggest, followed suit in copying this practice. It is now commonplace to find open learning centres in organizations such as British Aerospace, GEC, Coca-Cola & Schweppes Beverages. In the case of the latter the learning centre contains learning materials not directly related to individual jobs but of broader educational interest. This was based on the assumption that any learning was a good thing and was to be encouraged and that the objective was really to encourage a habit of learning. Also individuals would often come in to pick up a video tape on a personal subject such as sailing, and on impulse would take a distance learning package on a work related subject such as time management.

Some organizations talk of 'virtual learning spaces', referring to places where people come together to learn without having to move right out of the working environment. Again, this reflects the trend of moving training back to the workplace and seeking opportunities for continuous learning.

One might ask how an organization should be designed so as to be able to continuously transform itself. It may appear that there is an inherent conflict here between the need to establish some structure or design and to be organizationally and structurally flexible. This is not an easy matter to address and throws into question many of our long held beliefs about the need for structure, accountability, job descriptions and control. In order to be able to transform itself, the organization needs to contend with messiness, disorder, lack of structure, moving goal posts and change. There is little place for empire building and status symbols; expertise and power bases are changing and developing continuously, often at the lower levels of the hierarchy, if there is one. We found that in the virtual organization this issue is addressed by establishing a mind-set among members which supported a fluid structure; we use the word 'form' as we feel this more accurately captures the spirit of change and continuous adaptation and this is explored in more detail in Chapter 6.

Burgoyne (1995), also makes some practical recommendations about becoming a learning organization. He emphasizes, among other things:

- A learning approach to strategy and a participative approach to policy making
- 'Informating', which is really about the effective use of technology to communicate
- Internal cross functional communication
- Rewards to incentivize learning and the development of a learning culture
- Boundary workers as information scanners
- Inter-company learning through, for instance, benchmarking and imitation
- Self development processes.

There is much to be said for all of these headings and many of the recommendations are consistent with our observations of the virtual organization. Indeed, it might be considered that the virtual organization does incorporate many of the concepts of the learning organization but it also goes on beyond this to address issues encompassing strategy, form, communications and adaptation in a particularly dynamic way as explored in Chapters 5 to 8.

In the virtual organization, strategy formulation and policy making are very much dynamic processes which tend to involve all members of the organization. In some traditional organizations there is a belief that such processes are participative but on closer examination the level of participation involves little more than the facility to seek clarification and understanding rather than truly influence policy and strategy. Virtual organizations recognize that due to the actual level of expertise held at all levels in the organization, and in order to capture the creativity of its people, there is a real need to allow people at all levels to influence the direction and nature of the business.

As in the Burgoyne summary, we found that the issue of communication was critical to success and certainly virtual organizations tend to combine both formal and informal communication processes and if anything would err on the side of over communication. As suggested by Burgoyne, there is a willingness to embrace the technology which allows for more rapid and effective communication. This contrasts with examples of more traditional organizations, which have a tendency to under communicate, to view communication more as a one-way, usually top-down process, while sometimes paying lip service to upward communication through, for example, team briefing and other similar initiatives.

The importance of boundary workers as scanners of the environment is increasingly important and this can again clearly be seen to relate to the increasing need to identify and understand developments which may be taking place in the organization's business, technical, social or economic environment. Additionally, the fact that we now suffer more from information overload than underload also suggests the need to process and manage such information, much of which originates from beyond the organization itself. The need to scan such developments is accentuated due to the increasing rate of change. Furthermore, in scanning from the boundaries one may just catch sight of scanners from other organizations. Increasingly there is a need to form relationships with such people and to view them as potential collaborators rather than as a threat. This calls for particular skills and, for many, a new mind set. The importance of collaboration is effectively illustrated by Morgan (1985), who says:

Competitive collaboration can either enhance or destroy a firm's independence ... the firm most capable of learning from its partners will be the firm that, ultimately, most enhances both its strategic options and its strategic freedom.

Collaboration allows access to competence deeply woven into a partner's organizational fabric; skills that are more tacit than explicit, bundles of technology rather than stand-alone technologies, knowledge and skills that are the results of organizational learning, rather than sheer inventiveness.

The same author (Morgan, 1988) describes the managerial behaviours needed by companies in the future:

- Managing complexity
- Reading the environment
- Leadership and vision
- Promoting creativity, learning and innovation
- Human resource management
- Developing contextual competencies
- Skills of remote management
- Using information technology as a transformative force
- Proactive management.

Many of these characteristics reinforce the factors listed by Burgoyne and identified through our own research.

So, it would appear that there are some guiding factors which organizations might do well to be aware of if aspiring toward learning organization status. You might at this stage wish to consider how you believe your own organization measures up by reflecting on the following questions.

PAUSE FOR THOUGHT

Are you led by one 'hero' leader or is leadership collectively shared and is it seen at all levels of the organization?

How entrenched are habits and how does this inhibit learning?

Does your organization mainly react to its environment or is it in a position to influence its environment?

To what extent does your organization question its underlying policies and goals?

How well linked is learning to the organization's purpose and business?

How does your business continually adapt?

To what extent are learning behaviours encouraged such as risk taking, initiative or challenging senior management?

What attitudes exist in your organization which may inhibit the process of change?

How are people encouraged to take responsibility for their own learning?

Is learning accessible to everyone in the organization?

What use is made of technology to manage information and learn new things?

How are individuals rewarded for their learning?

How does your organization scan the external environment, both formally and informally?

Realizing organizational change

We would question whether there is a place for the moral high ground when exploring the development of the learning organization. Ultimately, the organization and its members will be working towards their collective and individual objectives, respectively; these will vary considerably from one organization to the next and from person to person.

It has been suggested that organizations should work towards securing their own longevity and stability in a turbulent world, or even that their ultimate goal should be to achieve 'a good death'. It may be that such ideals are adopted by some organizations, but it is questionable whether we can define generally applicable, fundamental goals for all organizations to work towards. To do so would be arrogant; there is an increasing level of diversity in terms of organizational purpose.

It is often claimed that the prime motive of the organization is to satisfy its shareholders; for many organizational members in the corporate world the shareholders are simply a changing, faceless and disparate group of anonymous people and institutions. While satisfying shareholders may well be vital to future survival, one has to question whether this is really a fundamental goal behind which those beneath the very senior levels can really unite.

A new picture is emerging where organizations may be working towards their own unique goals. These could, for example, include the following:

- To provide a satisfying and enjoyable environment for members
- To evolve to a stage where the business can be sold to others or bought by its members
- To survive for the working life-time of its leader
- To contribute to human or environmental well being
- To make its mark in corporate history
- To push back the boundaries of human endeavour.

While we do not claim to be able to define generically applicable goals for organizations of the future, there are certain key factors which successful organizations are likely to need to address; not least that of the ability to adapt and manage the process of change itself.

All too often there is an assumption that if the organization wishes to change and to develop new skills, even beliefs, then this is possible by overlaying new skills and beliefs over the old ones. If the learning experience is intense enough, then this should overcome any difficulty of entrenched views and opinions. This argument is basically flawed and accounts for the failure of many change initiatives which have addressed change at only a superficial level; new techniques, processes and ideas are introduced but they are simply overlaid on the existing belief structure. In order to bring about radical change in the business, it is likely that fundamental beliefs and values will need to be questioned. If the organization has a long history, then existing beliefs and values are more likely to be entrenched and difficult to challenge.

To make matters worse, it is often the case that organizations are unaware of their own values and beliefs—at least until they are challenged. Sometimes organizations, particularly where there is a

Fig. 3.1   A model of organizational behaviour

tradition of time-serving employment or where the culture is especially strong, will develop a self concept which is actually distorted. Let's look at how this comes about. In order to explore the subject of the organization's beliefs and values we will draw on a model which we have developed through our work with individuals in organizations, and which we have increasingly come to recognize can be applied in a team or organizational context, too.

A model of organizational behaviour is shown in Fig. 3.1, which suggests that organizations do things; in other words, they behave. As a result of their behaviour they will engage in some form of internal dialogue between the members of that organization regarding their actions. This sort of organizational dialogue can take many forms. They will sometimes be negative and sometimes positive, although people appear to have a tendency to be more critical than positive. As a result we hear people throughout the business say things like:

'That's just like us—typical—always getting the communication wrong.'

'We are great designers but our marketing always lets us down.'

'There we go again, five minutes behind the competition.'

Of course, these are all examples of negative conversations, but often there are positive examples as well. So we hear comments such as:

'We employ the best graduates in the country.'

'Our engineers are world leaders.'

'Our greatest strength is our cost control.'

Such reflections are a part of everyday organizational life and will be the result of individuals reviewing organizational activities, successful or otherwise. In this sense they will relate to operational and everyday occurrences; however, the nature of such conversations will tend to be fairly consistent as they are closely related to the organization's self-image.

In addition to such internal conversations which contribute to the organization's self-image, there is the influence of those who might be described as perceived experts. These are either organizations or people whom the business allow to influence its thinking about itself. Whether these 'experts' are truly expert is irrelevant; the significant issue is that they affect the thinking of the organization, either positively or negatively. They may come from a number of sources, for instance, the City, newspapers, customers, competitors, non-executive directors, consultants, senior managers or previous leaders.

The combination of two factors, what people within the organization say to one another and the views expressed by others outside the organization, results in the creation of an organizational self-concept. This is the predominant picture which the organization holds onto and as such it tends to be enduring. It includes such things as perceived strengths, weaknesses, potential and more. It is the sum total of all the beliefs and attitudes which are held by those within the organization. The cycle closes as the organization continues to act in accordance with its self-concept or beliefs. Consequently, if we believe we are 'poor at marketing' we continue to act in a way that is consistent with such a belief. Furthermore, it is likely that we will demonstrate in our behaviour the nature of our thinking about ourselves and this will be seen by others. We see this as a self perpetuating model which helps to explain some of the phenomenal upturns or downturns that we see in many different organizations' fortunes.

Of course, the greater the history of the organization the more likely it is that there will emerge a powerful mythology surrounding people who have succeeded as a result of working within the self-image or who have failed as a result of working outside of it. So, for example, we hear comments such as:

'He is a real XYZ man—cost conscious, great in controlling overheads, but no leader.

'He got to the top by pushing and shoving and sheer force of character —that's how anyone gets on around here.'

'She knows how to deal with clients—that's what counts.'

'He just did not fit in—too much of an individual.'

So the organization develops a self-image the power of which should not be underestimated; to be required to reappraise the organizational self-concept is extremely stressful. However, in order to bring about major change and indeed to respond to or even anticipate environmental change, there is often a need to question the underlying assumptions of the business—its values and beliefs.

The self-image might also be viewed as the organization's comfort zone, as suggested in Fig. 3.2. This is the zone within which the organization prefers to operate, and, if threatened with having to operate outside of it, is likely to feel extreme discomfort. This comfort zone comprises everything to do with the organization's history, beliefs, values, knowledge and skills. To be expected to operate outside of this zone, for example to behave in different ways, to acquire new knowledge, to change strategies, to question the status quo, is likely to meet with resistance. This is particularly the case where the organization has a well established self-concept as a result of a long history or because the culture is particularly strong. Interestingly, even where there is evidence of a positive self-concept and the culture is consistent, there are pitfalls with regard to effecting real change. In these cases, there is often resistance to change due to a pride in the organization's uniqueness.

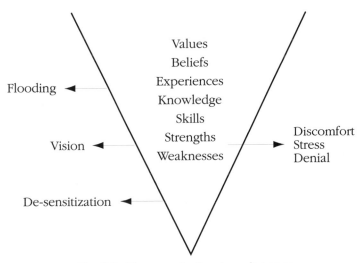

Fig. 3.2 The organizational comfort zone

How, then, can an organization overcome the barriers which resist change and which seek to keep the organization working within its own comfort zone? Is it possible for the organization to develop a new or different self-image? We believe it is, but there is a need to decide on which approach to take. Here we look at three approaches to expanding the organizational comfort zone: flooding, desensitization and the use of powerful vision.

Expanding the organizational comfort zone

Flooding is a technique which has been used in the field of individual psychology for some time. This is where in order to confront a personal need for a change in thinking, for instance in order to overcome a major phobia, the individual is flooded with the difficult experience in the hope that he or she will emerge suitably cured. While flooding can be a very powerful experience for those who survive it, it can be very damaging for those who do not. One might say that those who do not survive the experience drown and do not live to tell the tale. On an organizational level we also see examples of flooding experiences, where the organization is exposed to radically different approaches over an intense time period. Such a flooding experience might be seen with the appointment of a new chief executive or in times of take-over or merger. The new regime and style of management and leadership is imposed with little consultation, under the assumption that there are winners and losers and that it would simply be inappropriate and too time consuming to use a more participative approach to bring about change. As an approach, this can be effective for the organization in the long term, though as with personal flooding, there will inevitably be casualties, those who are unable or unwilling to make such a radical personal change.

The second approach to moving the organization outside of its comfort zone, and in so doing to move towards the achievement of its potential, we describe as desensitization. Here, the approach is a much more gradual one: changes are brought about in a step by step, incremental way. So, certain leaders or visionaries are likely to see how things could be and they attempt to encourage the members of the organization to make the required changes in a gradual way. There is likely to be more consultation with members of the organization at different levels and there is more sensitivity to the needs of individuals. Over time, people are desensitized to the fear of change or the new picture of how things could and should be. As an approach, clearly desensitization is more time consuming than flooding, but generally it is safer. The danger is that while you are bringing about incremental change, others are making step changes.

Finally, we have seen the use of vision as a means of moving organizations out of their comfort zone and towards a picture of how things could be. Used in a practical and involving way, vision can prove to be a particularly powerful means of effecting organizational change. This calls for a leader and a number of other organizational members to have the vision or imagination to be able to picture the future. Such people are recognizable by their willingness and ability to talk in a confident and enthusiastic way about how things could be. They then create and convey images to others in the organization in order to mobilize them in the direction of the new vision. Effectively, the visionaries focus on changing the thinking of the organization. With a change in thinking there follows a change in the behaviour of those in the organization. Unfortunately, there has been much misuse of the term vision in some organizations and a misunderstanding as to how effective vision building can work.

The power of vision

Buxton Mineral Water Company (part of The Perrier Group) in the early 1990s were faced with the challenge of gaining BS5750/ISO 9000 quickly. Strategically this was seen as particularly important given the benzene scare within the Perrier product.

Up to the point the plant had been acquired by Perrier, it had been operated along the lines of a very traditional manufacturing environment with strong control and an established hierarchy. Indeed, it was hardly the epitome of a progressive organization; many of its human resource practices were woefully inadequate.

The organization implemented a major organizational change programme that was designed to drive home the importance of total quality management in the plant. This was treated with a high level of scepticism and suspicion.

The senior management team were the first to undertake the change programme and as part of this process they developed a powerful organizational vision in respect of taking the business forward. All the senior team were involved in developing this vision statement; but more than this, they subsequently presented this to the organization and genuinely invited feedback from all employees. The statement was widely published and proudly displayed all over the plant. Ultimately, this vision statement became a living testament to where the business was going and how it would achieve its goal.

The programme was then cascaded down the organization and every employee was involved in some way or another. Each had to understand the vision and be able to identify their own unique contribution to its achievement. The results were dramatic—not only did the performance of the overall plant improve significantly, but the plant achieved the quality standard at its first attempt, which in itself was a creditable achievement given the history of the plant.

In many ways the use of a vision statement in itself is not that important; what does appear to matter is the way in which the vision is developed, communicated and owned by everyone. We look in more detail at the process of building a vision in Chapter 5.

At this stage you may wish to consider the following questions regarding the self-image of your organization and how change is currently managed.

PAUSE FOR THOUGHT

What are the positive things that your people are likely to say about your business?

What things would they say you are not good at?

Where did they learn these things?

How can these negative beliefs be challenged?

Who have been, and who are the perceived experts or outsiders who influence your organizations self-image?

To what extent are these positive or negative 'experts'?

Do you use flooding to drive change in your business?

How successful has this been?

Have you experienced the use of organizational desensitization?

If you have a vision, how was it developed and how much use is made of it?

So far in the book we have reviewed some of the major changes taking place on a macro level, which clearly are making a major impact on the need for organizations to change. We have seen that the actual rate of change in many sectors is increasing and we have considered the implications of this for organizations in terms of how they manage issues such as innovation and adaptation. In this chapter in particular, we have suggested that change is synonymous with learning and that the debate surrounding the concept of the learning organization has been brought about due to the increasing need for effective adaptation in what is increasingly seen as a knowledge based organizational environment.

The learning organization debate, we suggest, has contributed significantly to the subject of organizational development. However, there are many different angles on the subject and the idea of a learning organization does tend to be something for companies to aspire to. Significant aspects of the work conducted on the learning organization relate to the idea of the organization itself learning, as opposed to just the individuals within it and the idea of organizations continually transforming themselves. Frequently, though, the reality of supposed learning organizations fails to keep pace with the well intended models.

It does seem, however, when we look at organizations that have attempted to establish themselves as learning organizations, that there is an over emphasis on training systems and processes, often at the expense of considering how learning can be integrated, even institutionalized, within the corporate culture.

Many of the qualities described by the learning organization enthusiasts are, of course, undeniably appropriate and relevant in the virtual organization. We believe, though, that in the virtual organization there *is* evidence of learning being institutionalized as part of the very fabric of the organization. It is seen that members of the organization, at all levels and in all functions, learn continuously in a variety of ways. Interestingly, in the virtual organization formal learning systems and processes may be reduced, but actual learning is increased. We look at this in more detail later in the book particularly in Chapter 8 where we discuss organizational adaptation.

At this stage, though, we will move on to explain the nature of our own research, which has enabled us to formulate a model of organizational development against which any organization can be measured and which will demonstrate the extent to which an organization might be described as prepared for and capable of making the changes required in order to excel in the four factors which characterize the virtual organization.

Naturally, not all organizations will want to become virtual organizations. However as we believe that the virtual organization is more than simply a concept—there are examples of organizations displaying virtual organization activity and characteristics—it is worth even the most traditional organizations in the (currently) most stable environment considering whether and when they will have to either interact with or even move towards becoming virtual organizations.

References

Argyris, C., Double Loop Learning in Organizations, *Harvard Business Review*, September/October, 1977.

Barham, K., Frazer, J. and Health, L., *Management for the Future*, F.M.E./Ashridge, 1988.

Burgoyne, J., Feeding Minds to Grow The Business, *People Management*, September, 1995.

Dolan, S., A Different Use of Natural Resources, *People Management*, October, 1995.

Garratt, R., An Old Idea That Has Come of Age, *People Management*, September, 1995.

Hofman, F. and Senge, P.M., Communities of Commitment: The Heart of Learning Organizations', *Organizational Dynamics*, 2(2), Autumn, 1993.

Morgan, G,. *When Competitors Compete*, Jossey Bass, 1985.

Morgan, G., *Riding the Waves of Change*, Jossey Bass, 1988.

Naisbitt, J., *Megatrends*, Futura, 1982.

Pedler, M., Burgoyne, J. and Boydell, T., *The Learning Company*, McGraw-Hill, Maidenhead, 1991.

Revans, R, *The Origins and Growth of Action Learning*, Chartwell-Bratt, Bromley & Lund, 1982.

Whitlam, P., Assessing Organizational Learning Effectiveness, M.Phil dissertation, International Management Centres, 1990.

Whitlam, P.J., Imagery in Goal Achievement, D.Phil dissertation, International Management Centres, 1993.

The virtual organization— a journey not a destination

We have tried to restore the dying art of going out and capturing what is perceived as the possible

JAMES IONSON
(Team Leader, Strategic
Defence Initiative)

In this chapter we:

- Discuss the background to our research which has enhanced our understanding of the process of effective organizational change and contributed to the development of our understanding of the virtual organization
- Describe a model of successful organizational performance as identified in our research
- Describe typical differences between traditional and virtual organizations using the model as the basis for objective comparison
- Explain some ways that the Change Assessment Orientation Survey (Ch.A.O.S.) has been used by a number of organizations
- Illustrate how to use Ch.A.O.S. and consider how the results can be best used to focus attention on performance improvement

The learning and the virtual organization

In the previous chapter we looked at some of the work of other writers and researchers who have sought to understand the concept of the learning organization. We began to present our view that our concept of the virtual organization goes beyond that already discussed in the learning organization debate. While there are a number of rather different approaches to the subject of organizational learning (or change effectiveness), it seems that there is a common recognition of the need to look at the means by which the organization can actually maximize the benefits of the learning of its members. Similarly, it is recognized that learning will help organizations to manage the process of change or transformation. Our fundamental premise is that:

$$\boxed{\begin{array}{c} \text{Change} = \text{Learning} \\ \text{and} \\ \text{Learning} = \text{Change} \end{array}}$$

We believe that learning is actually synonymous with change. In order to change we have to learn, and by learning we precipitate change. This we believe is true for both the individual and the organization. Therefore, when we learn new skills or approaches we provide the vehicle for both personal and organizational change.

In our research we have studied the subject of organizational change in an effort to try to understand the shape of organizations in the future. This work has led us towards a clearer picture of what is often referred to as 'the learning organization'. It seems that much of the work in the learning organization arena tends to focus primarily on training systems and processes, rather than on looking at how organizations can successfully create a genuine learning culture. A key outcome from our own research has been to suggest that in the future, organizations will, with respect to learning, actually achieve organizational learning by transcending training systems and processes and by creating a real culture of learning. Furthermore, we suggest that when such organizations also address critical issues related to their direction and purpose, their organizational structure and form, and their approach to communication, they might be described as virtual organizations. In formulating a model which defines four critical factors—direction, form, communication and adaptation—we have then been able to look at how any organization deals with these four factors and, therefore, the extent to which the organization might be described as a virtual organization.

While we have heard reference to the virtual organization by some managers and writers on the subject, this seems to be a relatively unexplored area compared to the mass of debate surrounding the concept of the learning organization.

Despite the recency of the virtual organization entering our vocabulary, however, we have seen evidence that these organizations do already exist. Virtual organizations in the truest sense may be relatively few and far between, but there is evidence that many organizations are progressing fast in their journey towards becoming virtual organizations. Furthermore, the evolution of such organizations may well be eroding the power base and influence of traditional organizations. The most alarming aspect of this is that by definition the virtual organization is difficult to really understand and may be deceptively powerful, particularly if looking out through traditional corporate eyes. Because of this many are unaware of the potential threat which exists to the traditional organization. The threat comes not just in terms of virtual organizations potentially stealing market share, but is seen in the sense that traditional organizations are increasingly having to deal with organizations that are closer to the virtual organization model — and this is causing some considerable discomfort.

Additionally, it appears that many organizations which might be described as virtual organizations against our model do not actually carry high profile brand names which are instantly recognizable; they may be small in size, they may actually use different names for different activities and in many ways they actually blend into their environment rather than stand out from it. Only on closer examination does one start to realize the power of such organizations—their ability to adapt, to respond quickly to changing circumstances and their specialist expertise. In addition to the smaller hidden army of virtual organizations there is much evidence of certain larger high profile organizations attempting to move toward the virtual organization model. If they are finding it difficult or consider it inappropriate at this time to move the whole organization in this direction, then they are experimenting with virtual organization concepts in key parts of their business.

Summary of research

Our studies have involved a combination of primary and secondary research methods. We have studied the literature, discussed the subject with organizations and leading authorities and carried out detailed case studies with specific international organizations. This has led to a new categorization of organizational types ranging from what we describe as the traditional organization, organizations which embrace the learning organization concept, through to the virtual organization.

One of our objectives in conducting this research was to be able to produce a tangible and practical output which would help organizations to assess their current status and help them identify their readiness for change. The Change Assessment Orientation Survey (Ch.A.O.S.) has been developed from the model which emerged out of the research. This has already been used by a number of international organizations in order to identify specific organizational development issues which need to be addressed. Similarly, it has been used as a measure of culture and to identify within a business the areas of good practice and areas for particular focus.

A generic version of this instrument is provided in Appendix I and can be used by the owner of this book in order to provide an initial assessment of his or her organizational status against our model. Equally this version of the instrument can be copied and used within the organization in order to provide a range of perspectives from different personnel or functions. If used at regular intervals over an extended period of time it will provide a picture of progression and organizational development. Furthermore, if having profiled your own organization against this model you feel there are particular aspects of the business which need to be addressed as a matter of priority in order to prepare for and manage change, then you will be able to pay particular attention to the relevant chapters which follow.

Aims of the research

The primary aims of our research were threefold. First, we aimed to examine the notion of the learning organization and organizational change, and within this context explore the rationale behind the current level of interest. Second, through action research, we wanted to identify a framework for understanding the concept of the learning organization (and what emerged as the virtual organization). Third, there was an intention to produce a diagnostic instrument, so that organizations could easily assess their current capability, against the findings of this research.

Against this background, and the apparent complexity of exploring this issue, it was considered useful to apply a structured approach to the study. Therefore the approach shown in Appendix III, the research path, was taken. Effectively, the research progressed through the following stages.

Stage 1—Analysis

As a result of our initial studies which included looking at the existing body of knowledge, it became clear that no widely acceptable definitions or models of the learning organization or change management existed. This confirmed our belief that, as a project, this study must in the first instance focus on providing a model for understanding the subject, and then provide a method which would enable organizations to be assessed against this model.

Stage 2—Decision making

Questions were considered to be centred around the following issues:

■ What does effective learning and change in organizations look like?
■ What skills are necessary to bring about effective continual or institutionalized change?

- What do successful organizations currently do, deliberately or accidentally to ensure transformation?
- What else could an organization do to promote organizational change, as well as to help individuals learn more effectively?

Having evaluated the full range of research options, it was decided to use the following approach:

- Structured interviews
- Questionnaires
- Extended case study.

It was recognized that secondary research would be available through the use of a literature review, speaking to other researchers and using some smaller case studies. This secondary research was to provide the initial framework for developing the structured interviews and the questionnaires.

Summary of secondary research case studies

Part of the secondary research consisted of identifying and examining historical data in relationship to businesses which had apparently achieved a remarkable transformation from being a business in trouble, to achieving significant success.

Emphasis was placed on finding case studies where comparisons could be made with industries of a similar structure, complexity and organization as that involved in the extended case study. Numerous organizations were examined, however it was finally decided to focus on the following organizations which were seen to have achieved considerable transformation:

- The Post Office
- Sheffield Forgemasters Ltd

The first of these case studies focuses primarily on individual learning, whereas with the second, the emphasis is on broader organizational change.

Redefining learning at the Post Office

CASE STUDY 4.1

The early 1980s were turbulent times for many British industries. This was typified by the type of situation which faced The Post Office.

Firstly, the organization had repositioned itself to become a more commercially orientated business, while at the same time optimizing the opportunities presented by the use of new technologies.

Second, as a result of this repositioning of the strategic objectives, dramatic organizational restructuring was taking place. Within the Letter Division the structure was rationalized from 10 regions into four business territories.

Finally, an extensive programme of mechanization was being introduced to assist in the growing volume of business, and to help in combating the impact of competitive activity. The mechanization programme was aimed at creating 80 mechanized letter offices (MLOs) which were disseminated throughout the key postal districts.

To support this latter initiative, considerable investment had been made particularly in providing formal training for supervisors. It was the apparent lack of success with this specific issue that forms the focus of this study. Naturally, it was anticipated that the output of the above changes would considerably impact on productivity. In general it was recognized that in order to ensure success, many of the ramifications of these changes would need to be effectively managed by both supervisors and first-line managers. This raised several questions regarding the competencies of this population and their ability to cope with the proposed changes, which were more akin to production style methods than the more traditional ways of processing mail. In particular this would require these employees to develop both effective control skills combined with a more assertive style of management. Hence the investment in training.

Within a short period of time it became self-evident that despite the level of off-job training that had been provided, a high percentage of supervisors were experiencing difficulty in adapting to the new role requirements. An initial task force was set up to investigate this problem. Their brief was to investigate and define the extent of the problem, as well as to pilot different small schemes aimed at ensuring that supervisors could be assisted in acquiring the necessary new skills for the new order organization.

Various research investigations were undertaken, which included an attitude survey which only served to confirm the opinion that morale in this population was low. More significant than this, though, the group found that there was no correlation between those staff displaying effective performance, and the formal training that had been received. Indeed, in some cases the most effective performers had received no training, but had somehow learnt in the time honoured tradition of on-job problem solving, often through seeking help from others or by asking numerous questions.

This finding seemed to raise three important questions:

- Why had some supervisors learnt successfully on the job, as opposed to through formal training courses?
- What in particular had these individuals done?
- Could such lessons be transferable to others?

It appeared that there was some evidence to support the notion that learning in itself might be considered a skill. For some of these employees the skill of learning seemed to have been forgotten. For years, these supervisors with their previous well-learnt skills, seemed to have become habitual performers demonstrating what might best be described as robotic behaviour, as described by Cunningham (1987). While this was a positive advantage when automatic reactions were called for, it could easily reduce the motivation to explore and challenge situations, thus producing an over-dependence on 'experts' to resolve issues not covered in the automatic process.

At a time when the contribution of training was beginning to be recognized more and more as an important weapon in the battle to gain competitive advantage, this actually might have been seen more as an issue of learning than training. Consequently, the task of The Post Office appeared to be to rekindle the learning process in employees who had forgotten how to learn effectively. As an issue, this had been previously explored by Knowles (1973):

'It is a tragic fact that most of us know how to be taught; but few of us know how to learn.'

The task force turned to the Study of Human Learning at Brunel University. Professor Laurie Thomas explained:

'While new techniques make teaching more effective, the disadvantage is that the learner learns what the trainer or teacher thinks they should know.'

He continued :

'Another disadvantage is that efficient instruction often removes the need for personal skill and judgement, particularly in relationship to learning through every day activities.'

Naturally, this was the exact opposite of what was required within the new roles; there was a need for employees who could learn effectively while actually doing the job. While the effectiveness of training techniques had improved, training was still largely viewed as inefficient; therefore some individuals needed help in order to take control of their own learning process.

The project team then set about creating the right conditions for learning. They recognized that:

1. The skill of learning, or re-learning, must be actively managed. This should be included as a common component in all training programmes.
2. The learner must see personal value in the learning opportunity. Organizational benefit alone would not be sufficient.
3. Previous effective performers may need considerable encouragement to accept the fact that they have on-going learning needs and opportunities.
4. Being sent on a course can imply criticism, this in itself may cause resistance to learning.
5. Individual learning is unique; mass production training techniques do not recognize this; therefore the focus should be on the issue of individualism.
6. Responsibility for learning must rest with the learner; however, the organization should have an obligation to assist the individual in discharging this responsibility.

7. Most learners learn better with support, the nature of such support is critical.
8. More knowledge can be acquired by emphasizing learning rather than training.

Having specified the above conditions, The Post Office, together with Brunel University, decided to set up a pilot scheme for self-managed learning. A central issue appeared to be the need to recognize individualism in the learning process and so the use of coaching was considered.

A framework of selection criteria was set up in order to identify and measure the most suitable employees to undertake the coaching role. The characteristics that were sought were broad ranging and included: recognized competence, self-organization, respect and high face validity among colleagues.

The role of the coach was to be clearly defined. Essentially it was a supporting role, however some basic training was to be made available. In particular skills would be provided in the sphere of problem solving, decision making and planning.

The programme was not without its sceptics; like many organizations employees had over the years seen other initiatives arrive and all too often fail, mostly due to lack of follow-through. Interestingly, to combat this problem the initiative received some visible support from senior management. This support, however, was mostly of a low profile nature.

Within a short period of time the initial and limited pilot started to show some successful results and soon the programme was extended nationally.

To evaluate a project of this kind presents numerous difficulties. The way the process evolved in one office does not necessarily mean that the same process would occur in another. Consequently the process can be seen primarily as organic rather than mechanistic. Many of the benefits can be seen as nebulas, particularly issues related to attitude and some behavioural changes. Subsequently much of the evidence was anecdotal.

However, on a more tangible note, it was found that during the period of the early pilot programme, a significant performance improvement was recorded against recognized standards for handling first class mail, as well as for second class mail. Over the same period, unit costs per standard hour had fallen by 14 per cent. Nevertheless, at the time of the pilot several other variables could have had an impact on some of these performance indicators.

The overall durability of the programme had yet to be proved; however, there seems little doubt that self-managed learning, in this case through a learner coach, is capable of bringing about performance improvement and influencing the bottom line. Indeed, for some individuals the experience of learning how to learn seems to have had a dramatic life changing impact.

Maintaining a self-learning environment does not appear to have been that difficult. Success appears to have been caused by The Post Office providing basic resources, including the need for continuing coaching selection and development.

In examining the conditions that were created to encourage the process of learning, it was seen that they could be classified under the following major headings:

- Systems—Training programmes, organizational roles and responsibility and performance appraisal;

- Culture—Learning values, encouragement and positive attitudes;

- Strategy—Learning versus training, linked to business needs.

These findings tended to suggest that these three variables might ultimately form part of any model of effective individual learning in organizations.

We now move on to consider another case of transformation where the emphasis appeared to be placed on organizational rather than individual learning; nevertheless, the results were equally remarkable.

Organizational learning at Sheffield Forgemasters Ltd

CASE STUDY 4.2

Sheffield Forgemasters Ltd had been formed in 1982, ostensibly as the white hope of the high technology end of the UK steel industry. The company was formed by the merging of two British businesses of specialist steel makers and forgers. Each partner of the merger was the inheritor of a great tradition of innovation in steel making. Both had recently received considerable investment in plant, but when both organizations merged neither of them was particularly profitable and consequently they faced a serious challenge.

By the mid-1980s, the organization lost in excess of £55 million; this included the loss of merger pump priming cash of £40 million and debts of £120 million plus.

In May of 1985, the business was operating at a loss of £2 million per month and the financial institutions gave notice of foreclosure. As a last ditch attempt to remedy the situation, a new chairman was appointed and given a limited time to turn things around.

Within the organization, the following features were evident:

- Inter trade union rivalry
- Morale was extremely low with considerable evidence of fear, mistrust and suspicion
- Quality was poor; waste was accounting for over 10 per cent of costs.
- The organization was highly centralized with almost 30 per cent of the staff of 3990 located in a monolithic head office
- The organizational structure was complex, with the business being hierarchical resulting in awkward and unclear systems of direct and indirect reporting
- Communications at best were inefficient, while at worst they were non-existent
- Management style was autocratic. There was evidence of a class system throughout the industry and this was particularly evident in this organization.

Initially action was taken to simplify the organizational structure. This involved the business being decentralized into three operating businesses. A managing director was appointed to the operating companies and each was required to restructure their own business and place special emphasis on improving communications and the ability of people to work in teams.

As a result of this restructuring, the head office was reduced from over 500 staff to less than ten. Effectively, all the responsibility and accountability was devolved downwards into the line.

As a method of gaining some quick and visible success, efforts were directed at salvaging blatant waste. This resulted in dramatic savings of £5 million within the first three months and consequently, was to lead to the introduction of a quality initiative throughout the entire production facility.

In the sphere of resourcing, deliberate plans and actions were taken to introduce individuals who did not have a traditional background in the steel business. It was observed that such individuals often brought with them a 'freshness or innocence' capable of being a catalyst for change.

Considerable resources were allocated to the process of training. Special attention was given to the following areas:

■ Team building
■ Communications
■ Improving quality
■ Performance review
■ Effective problem solving.

All training was positioned in such a way as to ensure it was learner centred. This contrasted enormously with what had previously been provided, where training was mostly extremely didactic and in response to a particular crisis or problem.

Having defined the organizational mission, strategic intent and value systems, considerable time and effort was invested in ensuring everybody knew and understood the same thing. Likewise, when performance results were published by the chairperson, they personally corresponded with all employees.

Within the first year, the adverse performance trends were reversed; consequently by October 1988, the organization was involved in a management buy-out. Turnover in 1989 amounted to £115 million with pre-tax profits of £9 million. At first glance, these results do not in themselves seem that remarkable, however they must be viewed against a backcloth of increasing debt and decreasing orders.

At the time of the study, exports, which were previously non-existent, had risen to 45 per cent of turnover and orders were up by 50 per cent. During the same period, debt had been consistently reduced by 20 per cent per year.

In many ways this case contrasts with the previous study primarily because in the former the emphasis was apparently heavily biased towards addressing culture and systems, and in particular learning systems, whereas in this case the emphasis was on strategic and systems factors. This is partly because in the former case, action focused on a specific problem, while in Sheffield Forgemasters Ltd the situation was less specific and broader based.

As in the previous case, the actions that had been taken can be classified as follows:

■ Systems—Simplification of organizational structure, improved communication, team effectiveness, reposition of training and specific and focused training
■ Culture—Development of trust and responsibility
■ Strategy—Influence of external recruitment, development (and communication) of mission, strategic intent and strategies, devolution of power and introduction of total quality management.

It is interesting to note that in both cases discussed above the changes were precipitated by a current or looming crisis, rather than being some part of a proactive strategic plan for the future.

Initially. these case studies seemed to suggest that in managing change and learning effectively there were at least three key variables which had to be addressed. These were:

■ Strategy
■ Systems
■ Communication.

These were consistent themes which were seen running through most of the literature we reviewed and it was primarily the identification of these three key variables (strategy, systems, culture) that led to the construction of the core research methodology.

Stage 3—Planning and implementation of research

It was decided to use the two specific techniques of structured interviews and questionnaires. It was considered that the contrast of these methodologies would enable the collection of both good quality and quantity of data. Both of these factors were felt to be important, the former to enable an expansion and increased understanding of the issues that were raised, while the latter would provide volume and give breadth to the study.

We therefore collected data around the following four key questions:

1. What are the factors that make learning and change experiences particularly powerful? Could these be contrasted against ineffective experiences, and are they transferable to the organizational context?

These questions aimed to focus on the complex interaction of processes which could include the individual, the job and the environment in which the person operates.

2. What are the specific skills that an individual needs in order to learn effectively and bring about personal change?
3. What kind of daily activities are helpful or beneficial in the learning and change process? How does an organization harness this individual learning for corporate benefit?
4. What could the organization do to develop organizational learning and the effective management of change?

These questions were explored through the research methods described and initial findings were collected from the following sources:

- 40 structured interviews
- 372 questionnaires
- 228 questionnaires (collected as part of the case study).

A detailed analysis of the respondents is provided in Appendix IV. This data represents respondents across 26 organizations and as can be seen there are representatives from a cross section of sectors including manufacturing, service and public sectors.

Having analysed the data it seemed that actually there were probably *four* major variables which embraced issues such as strategy, systems and culture:

- Direction
- Form
- Communication
- Adaptation.

The research appeared to suggest that in managing change organizations should address these four variable issues, which might be viewed as an amalgamated and integrated process. This basic model and cycle is shown in Fig. 4.1 and each of the four major factors are now described in more detail.

Direction
Direction comprises a number of management activities and includes strategic and tactical planning, as well as the mechanisms for objective setting and is the term used to describe the systems associated with business development. This involves the process of corporate analysis, problem solving and decision making. It embraces the way in which the organization strategically plans and the level and process of individual participation in such thinking and planning. Fundamentally, it is about the way in which the business aligns itself with the needs of its stakeholders. These processes often involve reflection and the need to observe things from different perspectives. Actions involve the process of

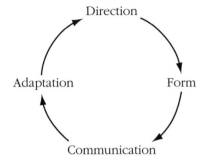

Fig. 4.1 Organizational learning and change cycle

managing information both internally and externally. In summary this is about:

The mechanisms by which an organization plans, controls, directs and organizes itself, in order to meet the business needs.

Form
Form relates to the way in which these plans are translated and designed into appropriate systems and structures to ensure successful implementation. It includes the ability to harness the conceptual and abstract thinking skills of the organization, as well as creativity and innovation. This is about more than just organizational structure, though; structure is important, but more important is the ability to adapt the organizational form to meet changing needs. In summary this reflects:

The structure and processes by and through which management process is achieved in the optimum fashion. It includes organizational design issues.

Communication
Communication is taken to include organizational culture and consists of a number of subsidiary activities aimed at gathering, sifting and collating information prior to utilizing it. Considerable emphasis is placed on the need to draw in information from the external environment, and the processes of synthesizing and disseminating such information for the good of the organization. This incorporates recognition of the need to adopt the relevant organizational culture. In the most effective examples this meant endeavouring to react quickly and operate with a minimum of restricting procedures. Behaviours are likely to be open and spontaneous, however it recognizes the need for a balance between formal and informal processes, particularly with regard to contact with the external environment. It is likely that equal weight will be given to the

communication of feelings as well as facts and figures. In summary this is about:

> The systems or means by which the organization transmits information, including thoughts, facts and feelings, both internally and externally.

Adaptation

Adaptation is believed to be the linking mechanism and is used to describe the practical application and consolidation of learning into tangible actions. This incorporates learning systems (the formal and informal mechanisms for delivering learning to individuals), adaptive behaviours (the skills undertaken by individuals to facilitate the process of individual learning) and learning processes (the enabling mechanisms for linking learning systems and adaptive behaviours together).

An important feature of this stage of the cycle is the recognition of the importance of individual learning and adaptation in contributing to organizational learning and change. In summary adaptation with respect to the model was taken to mean:

> The enabling processes, adaptive behaviours and mechanisms for the delivery of individual learning experiences which in turn facilitate organizational adaptation.

Detailed analysis of the data suggested a particular way of looking at the notion of the development of the learning organization and the management of change. It would appear that as learning develops through a hierarchy of levels, the character and volume of structured systems decreases. However, at the same time there is a corresponding requirement for an increase in learning behaviours. This can be demonstrated in the model shown in Fig. 4.2. Learning systems do not cease to have a place in the more advanced organization in terms of learning orientation, but as the organization modifies and adapts, the requirement for effective learning systems changes dramatically and there was evidence of an increased emphasis being placed upon effective behaviours and processes.

Our study also found evidence to suggest that there is an emergent organizational form which we have ultimately described as the virtual organization. This organization demonstrates strength and particular characteristics against each of the four factors identified in the model: direction, form, communication and adaptation. Paradoxically, the strength which the virtual organization demonstrates in these four areas is often based around a preparedness to take the traditional approaches and adopt innovative and radically different approaches. So, for instance, where a traditional organization might well spend much time developing a classical strategic and tactical plan covering a five-year

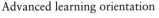

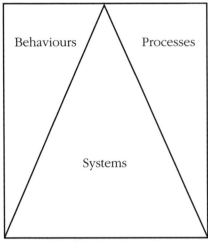

Fig. 4.2   Learning system, process and behaviours

period, the virtual organization would continually revise and review its plans in a remarkably fluid way. Similarly, whereas the traditional organization would expend a great deal of energy in defining the correct structure to meet its needs, the virtual organization would direct considerable effort into breaking down structural barriers and maintaining a loose 'form'.

The climate of the organization supports individual learning mostly through the process of encouragement.   Initiative is rife; the culture could be described as 'tolerant' in that it provides individuals with the opportunity to experiment, take risks and make mistakes. Such mistakes are treated as learning opportunities and challenging the *status quo*   is seen as the norm.

The word learning is used more frequently than training, and learning activities are individualized, with considerable emphasis being placed on self-insight and improving learning behaviours. Personal development and mentoring are standard; line management plays a crucial role in the development of people; and the organization assumes the role of enabler. Strategically, human resource management is integrated into the fabric of the business.

Contrasting the traditional and the virtual organization

Clearly it is unrealistic to allocate all organizations to two diametrically opposed categories—the traditional and the virtual. More appropriately, it might be considered that there exists a continuum of organizational status ranging from the more traditional to the virtual and that any organization could be seen as sitting in a particular place on the continuum at any point in time. Additionally, one might ask whether the organization is currently moving along the continuum, and indeed where competitors, customers, clients or suppliers are currently, and whether they are moving, and at what sort of pace. In order to bring the virtual organization into focus, though, we now contrast the characteristics one is likely to encounter in the traditional and the virtual organization; we will draw the comparison around the four key factors which we identified in our research. A visual summary is provided in Fig. 4.3.

Direction

In the traditional organization there is often evidence of well established approaches to strategic planning and organizing. Direction is provided by the most senior illuminati of the organization who formulate strategies, plans and policies which aim to steer the organization into the future. The underlying assumption is that the most senior people are the most enlightened, usually as a result of time-serving experience, and they know what is best. Others, including senior but not top managers, will tend to take their lead from what is often a fairly secretive cabal at the very top. Most people will follow either trustingly, ignorantly or with a degree of cynicism. In some cases there are attempts to involve others in the process of formulating local strategies and plans which dovetail with those of the organization as a whole; more often than not there is actually little real scope for the middle and junior ranking members to influence the direction of the organization. In the particularly institutionalized traditional organization people may have actually lost sight of its purpose or its purpose may have become confused; so, for example, it may confuse philanthropic with profit motives.

In the virtual organization there is clear evidence of direction and purpose, however it may manifest itself in different ways to those described above. There is likely to be a vision of how the organization can and will be in the future and this will tend to be shared by most if not all members of the organization. Such a vision may have been explicitly worked through involving people at all levels; even if there has been no formal vision building process then everyone will informally relate to, talk about and identify with the goals of the organization. Of course, this is easier where the numbers are low, but the virtual organization will retain the ability to communicate vision and involve others in formulating strategy even when the organization grows. Furthermore, while there is a clear vision of the future, this is counterbalanced by an ability to be adaptive and flexible. This will evidence itself by a tendency to continually monitor events and trends outside of the organization

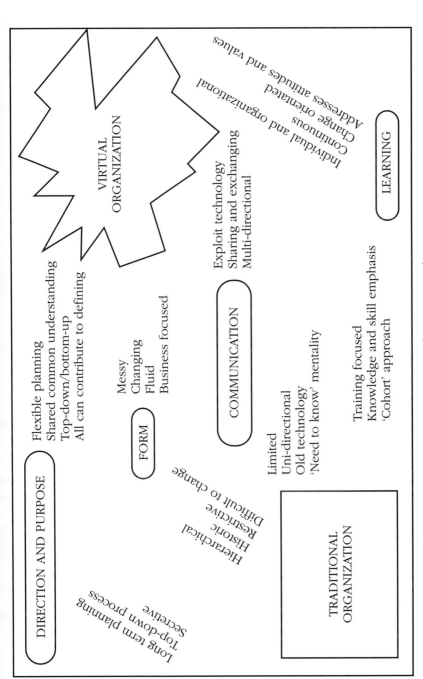

Fig. 4.3   A comparison of organizational status

and to develop new strategies and responses as considered appropriate. Strategic planning tends to be an ongoing, continual process rather than a once a year event. New ventures are embarked upon and this involves an element of calculated risk. Skunk works, think tanks and special project groups will contribute to identifying new directions and exciting opportunities; these will be managed and made real by those with strong business acumen.

Form

In the traditional organization the emphasis is on structure rather than form. There is likely to be evidence of clearly definined structures and ensuring that the *status quo* is maintained. There is a clearly defined hierarchy and often the organization is structured with its own internal interests in mind, rather than the interests of the business or the customer. Charles Handy provides a useful analogy when he talks about the role culture which can be pictured as a Greek temple: the functions or 'pillars" of the bureaucracy provide strength in the structure and there are strict controls over communication between different parts of the business. Interestingly, Handy (1976) suggested that where the environment is stable and the organization can control its environment, for instance in a monopoly or oligopoly, then this role culture will succeed. At the time, he quoted the civil service, the automobile industry, life insurance and retail banking as examples. In each of these sectors one has seen an accelerating change curve and it is now unlikely that organizations in these sectors will be able to survive much longer with this approach. Indeed, the evidence from our use of the Ch.A.O.S. instrument in the financial services sector would suggest that there is generally a sector shift towards the virtual organization end of the continuum. (This is supported by the case study of the Nationwide Building Society provided in Chapter 7.) Similarly, in our work in the automobile industry we have seen some fascinating examples of traditional organizations attempting to make a quantum leap to becoming virtual organizations (see, for instance, the case study of Allied Signal in Chapter 8). They are setting up cross-functional work teams, structuring manufacturing around production cells and *kaisen* groups and turning supervisors into facilitators. All this is being overlaid on years of tradition, precedent and structural rigidity: the culture clash can be profound.

  In the virtual organization, structure tends to be less clear to the outsider and can be difficult to understand. The organization changes its form to meet the needs of the business and, importantly, the customer. It is normal to find work groups centred around business projects, contacts and assignments; naturally this means that as the shape of the business changes so does the form of the organization. Additionally, it can be seen that in the virtual organization, members often possess an ability to adapt their style to meet the needs of different customers or clients; this we describe as a 'chameleon-like' quality. By contrast, in the traditional organization there is a tendency for members to be locked into particularly stylized ways of behaving.

Communication

Communication in the traditional organization tends to be restricted; such restriction is clearly related to the hierarchical and functional culture. Frequently there will be evidence of slow, uni-directional and even non-existent communication up and down the hierarchy. Communication between different functions will be limited and often there is evidence of suspicion of the motives of others outside of one's own area. There tends to be an emphasis on secrecy regarding information and people may talk of working on a 'need to know' basis. People at most levels and in most functions will tend to complain that communication presents a problem, but there is a tendency to look to others to blame. The problem is summed up by the approach taken by one manager of a bottling plant of a major drinks company. We were working with this organization to try to effect a major culture change. We had used the Ch.A.O.S. instrument in order to identify the health of the organization prior, during and after the change programme. The manager concerned was genuinely keen to improve communication and had instigated a briefing session where he gathered all of the shopfloor personnel in the staff canteen and read out the latest production figures and spoke of some of the changes to plant which were taking place. When we asked him what effect the exercise had had his response was discouraging. He said 'Well, they don't have any views or ideas—I know because I asked if there were any questions and there wasn't one person who had anything to say'. When we challenged this manager by suggesting that, while his intentions were good, his method was inappropriate he revealed the extent of the problem by saying, 'Well, if you want me to, I will carry out the same exercise again and we'll see if they have anything to say a second time'. It was as though he expected that by using the same method but maybe speaking louder he would improve communication.

By contrast, in the virtual organization if anything there will be over communication and often the same message will be presented in a number of ways. Communication is multi-directional and there is an emphasis on exchanging information. There is a willingness to use the technology which can assist communication and to break down potential communication barriers which might exist due to factors such as status and geography. Senior people are visible in the heart of the organization whereas in the traditional organization they may never be seen throughout the entirety of a person's career.

Adaptation

In the traditional organization there is more emphasis on formal training as the route to adaptation than on learning as such. Where the tradition of training is strong, it is common to find schemes to train new entrants to the business in particular younger members who may be processed through some form of apprenticeship. These people are essentially dealt with in cohorts and there is more emphasis on the scheme than the individual. Training for the more experienced members of the organization may be seen as remedial or will follow a fixed hierarchy of courses for different levels of personnel. Sometimes training is institutionalized with teams of specialist trainers providing syllabus-led skills and knowledge-based training year after year, often losing sight of the needs of the business. Where training is limited, this is often due to an underlying fear of developing people who will then leave the organization because they are more marketable.

The virtual organization will recognize the need to continuously develop its intellectual property through its people. Learning is seen as an ongoing requirement and essential in ensuring an ability to adapt, and opportunities are made available for individuals to develop new skills through both on- and off-job methods. There is a culture of learning and it is recognized that learning is in itself a skill which can be developed. Mistakes and negative experiences are reviewed and seen as learning opportunities. The organization shows evidence of learning so that when key personnel leave it is not vulnerable. The virtual organization encourages inputs from outsiders and sees this as a way of gaining fresh perspectives and identifying ways of continuing to adapt. Adaptation takes place in the area of not only knowledge and behaviours, but also addresses attitudes, values and beliefs.

In the next four chapters we work through the four main factors of the model in some detail and compare and contrast examples of approaches taken by traditional and virtual organizations. We draw the analogy of the move towards becoming a virtual organization as something akin to a journey. Organizations embarking upon this journey will move towards virtual organization status at varying speeds, depending on their current status and their ability to manage change.

In order to help organizations to assess their readiness for change we have designed the Ch.A.O.S. instrument and here we show ways in which it has been used in different organizations.

Using Ch.A.O.S. as a change management tool at Railtrack (formerly British Rail)

This case study relates to an area team within British Rail which used Ch.A.O.S. in 1991 to assess the perception of employees before their quality steering group implemented their change strategy. This was following a major change programme, cascaded down the organization.

The data collected from the use of Ch.A.O.S. clearly provided an indication as to which area of activity should be addressed as the initial strategic thrust in further managing change. This was to subsequently lead to a number of initiatives, all grouped around the issue of improving organizational communication.

Having completed an off-job organization development programme, one area team put together a strategy for quality which focused around three key issues:

■ Structure and organization
■ Manpower planning
■ Communication.

The difficulty that this team faced was to determine the extent of their problem. It was seen as essential to understand this in order to focus limited resources at the point of most impact. Likewise, measurement of the current situation was seen as critical, if they were to assess the contribution of any specific initiatives which they were to instigate.

The survey was given to 10 per cent of their population, which amounted to 131 employees. These employees were selected at random to ensure a cross-section of grades. This ensured a representative sample and the surveys were distributed anonymously and marked only with the grade of the recipient. They were returned directly to the authors for analysis. The return rate was 64 per cent and, interestingly, it was fairly well balanced across all grades.

On a macro level, the total area was compared to other BR norms and other businesses; while on a micro level, the seven different grades were contrasted with each other. This in itself produced some surprises, with some categories of employee expressing a desire for a focus on improving communication, while those in other job roles felt that training should be a priority.

Encouragingly, there was evidence to show that some initiatives which had already commenced were having an impact. This was detected through analysis of personnel from job grades where specific interventions had occurred, then contrasting them against those from grades not involved in such initiatives.

In addition, Ch.A.O.S. demonstrated (and dispelled) certain myths that existed in respect of the performance of the organization. For example, training systems were generally perceived as being superior to those provided by outside industries. However, evidence of learning behaviours showed that 600 individuals felt too inhibited to question the status quo.

Given the wealth of data contained in the survey results, the steering group repositioned their strategy to focus primarily on the issue of communication.

As with any strategy, the group worked through the survey planning to build on their strengths, while minimizing their weaknesses. The data provided served to confirm many of their perceptions of the problem, however, all agreed that there had been some surprises and that the measurement element enabled them to effectively prioritize activities.

It was also interesting that, in this case, the organization was trying to develop behaviours such as initiative through a traditional skills development programme. In reality such changes of behaviour required changes in other systems and processes in order to support the required changes. Effectively, there was a requirement for organizational learning as well as individual learning.

The group expressed a wish to repeat the survey after six months in order to ascertain the level of movement. Overall the use of this instrument was seen as valuable by the management team, consequently they circulated their experience and results of using this approach throughout the organization.

| CASE STUDY 4.4 | # Using Ch.A.O.S. as a diagnostic instrument in a major hotel group |

This was a major, prestigious, international hotel group, in which Ch.A.O.S. was used in part to diagnose a specific problem and the data from the analysis was subsequently used to determine the correct course of action, which then directly led to the introduction of a culture change initiative.

In this case the survey was used on the whole organization. Comparative and normative data was provided by random sampling of other hotels within the group.

The senior management team of a particular group had vaguely identified a problem of performance within a certain department of one of their major hotels. They assumed that this problem was the result of the development needs of the controller, who was responsible for the day to day operation of the hotel. They indicated that they felt this was a result of his limited technical (financial) skills. Their rationale was primarily based on his failure to deliver accurate work on time.

Initially, time was spent interviewing the senior team and as a result of this research it became apparent that a wider group of employees within the department were considerably disenchanted by a number of issues relating to how they were managed.

The survey was given anonymously to all 35 employees in the department and the results were discussed with the controller. By comparison with other organizations, the findings showed that the main areas for attention were related to direction. However, at this time, there was no normative data available from other organizations in the hospitality industry. Due to this fact, random sampling was undertaken elsewhere in the group. Nonetheless, the results still highlighted significant shortfalls in this particular hotel.

Detailed analysis of the data indicated that the issue appeared to relate very much to management style. Other supportive evidence suggested that the controller was highly autocratic, preferring to control and supervise the vast majority of tasks and activities completed in the department in a direct and overpowering way. Delegation was almost non-existent, the use of initiative was stifled and bureaucracy was rife.

This style of management was quite clearly inappropriate; it resulted in the controller mis-managing their time and this in turn manifested itself in their inability to complete requests from their corporate head office. Consequently, this gave rise to them appearing to be technically inefficient.

Different interventionist strategies were considered; these ranged from providing the controller with individual training and development, through to the use of a structured organizational development programme.

The latter option was selected primarily because the survey had indicated that some of the difficulties were so severe that it was felt that individual training alone would be insufficient to achieve the desired results within a pre-determined time. It was felt that an organizational level intervention would provide additional impetus which individual training alone could not achieve.

The direct result of the findings showed evidence of:

■ Inappropriate management style
■ Low employee involvement
■ High waste
■ Inhibited learning behaviours
■ Bureaucracy
■ Inflexibility
■ Poor role definition.

Initially the programme was designed in three tiers for the senior management team, the heads of departments and the non-managerial grades.

The authors had worked for the client for some time and fortunately an earlier assignment had researched the core competencies that would be required by controllers over the next decade. Among other things, this had shown the need for trust, responsibility and empowerment. Consequently, part of the programme focused on these competencies. The ultimate aim of this programme was to develop and foster a climate of involvement, participation and ownership by all staff.

Bushe (1989) defined systems transforming innovations (S.T.I.) as affecting more than a few social and technical sub-systems and directly affecting relationships among a large percentage of the employee population. Clearly this was the case in this group. He argues that if introducing strategies involving S.T.I., it is difficult to predict at the outset all the possible implications. Parallel learning systems are believed to be strategic interventions which take time and money and must be sanctioned by the authority in the system. They are probably most useful in empowering and fully utilizing an organization's human resources. Likewise S.T.I. can be contrasted to organizational innovation where the emphasis is on enhancing or improving some aspect of the business without changing the overall nature of how an organization operates. The data provided by the survey clearly suggested that a major culture change programme would result in the required S.T.I.

It was agreed that certain performance indicators would be used to assess the level of success. These would include both hard and soft measures, such as staff turnover and staff response. In addition the survey would be used as a tracking mechanism over a period of three years.

The overall programme was presented as a pilot for the whole Group.

CASE
STUDY
4.5

Using Ch.A.O.S. to address learning at Grand Metropolitan Brewing

In Grand Metropolitan Brewing, the instrument was used to diagnose an issue of ineffective learning behaviours. This was subsequently remedied through a specific skills development programme.

With hindsight it was recognized that without the use of this survey, the problem may not have been identified, and this could have jeopardized a considerable investment in the implementation of a major development initiative.

The survey was utilized in a highly focused way across this part of the group as part of the strategy for introducing and managing open learning.

Previously, the organization had committed itself to the introduction of open learning technology and had planned to establish three learning centres at different brewing operations. Originally the survey was used as a general diagnostic measure; however the results showed some significant findings, particularly related to the mechanisms of learning, which needed to be addressed as a result of this diagnosis.

Learning behaviours were found to be consistent with other normative data from other organizations, and learning systems were noticeably stronger. However, learning processes were significantly weaker than might be expected. Essentially learning processes are concerned with communication. These are the mechanisms by and through which an individual gains access to learning systems. An example of this might be an individual's awareness of what learning provision existed, and knowing how to utilize this resource.

This raised critical questions as to whether a strategy to introduce a major change in learning provision could be launched in an environment where learning processes (communications) were not as effective as they could be.

In a similar way the survey identified that there were a number of issues related to the underlying attitudes and beliefs that existed in the organization, some of these were seen as likely to inhibit the success of the development initiative.

To address these concerns two specific activities were initiated. First, a specific and detailed communication plan was put together in respect of launching the concept and the provision of open learning. Effectively the communication plan outlined the strategy by planning specific communication using multi-channel media through the following hierarchy:

■ Awareness
■ Knowledge
■ Liking
■ Preference
■ Choice/selection.

Second, the group training manager and senior line managers met to discuss and agree their vision of learning within the organization. This was followed by the development of a Human Resource Development Charter which effectively spelt out their values and beliefs in respect of training and development.

It was during these meetings that the role of the training personnel was explored and it was recognized that this clear movement towards self-managed learning would present specific challenges for the staff. Consequently the training community were provided with advice and support with regard to the redefinition of their own roles.

Specifically using Ch.A.O.S. in your organization

As previously suggested, the following chapters of the book each individually address the four key factors which will allow the reader to assess their organizational performance against our model of organizational development and against the characteristics of the virtual organization.

In particular these chapters are structured as follows: direction (Chapter 5), form (Chapter 6), communication (Chapter 7) and adaptation (Chapter 8).

Each of the above chapters discuss a separate critical factor in depth and then provide the reader with 10 focused statements against which readers can assess their own organizational or departmental performance. It should be noted that these 10 statements are not intended to provide a complete assessment; in fact, this probably represents less than 50 per cent of the research characteristics but more importantly does serve to act as a mechanism for further analysis.

Remember this assessment can be conducted on a departmental or organizational basis. The greater the number of individuals completing the instrument, the greater the reliability. Where the population is large, random sampling should be undertaken and care should be taken to ensure that the sample is representative.

Generic benchmarks are provided in Appendix II and specific company standards can be provided on request to allow an organization to assess itself against other identified organizations.

If subsequently the reader wishes to undertake the complete analysis then they are welcome to contact the authors at the address provided at the back of the book.

References

Bushe, G.R., Use of Parallel Learning Structure to Implement System Transforming Innovation, *Management Decisions,* 14(2) (1989).

Cunningham, I., Open Learning Won't Work Unless Learners Learn How to Learn, in *Towards Open Learning,* Open University Press, 1987.

Dolan, S., A Different Use of Natural Resources, *People Management,* October, 1995.

Grunlan, P., *Constructing Achievement Tests,* Penguin, 1968.

Handy, C., *Understanding Organizations,* Penguin, England, 1976.

Knowles, M., *The Adult Learner: A Neglected Species,* Gulf Publishing, 1973.

Preparing for the journey

There is no grand stroke that does it.
It's a lot of little steps

PETER A COHEN
(Chairman, Lehman Brothers, 1988)

In this chapter we focus on the first of the four critical organizational factors in the model previously described, *direction*. In particular we:

■ Look at approaches to strategic planning and suggest that a new approach is required in order to establish direction for the business in rapidly changing circumstances
■ Suggest the need to balance 'hard' measures of performance with 'softer' measures addressing the subject of human behaviour
■ Consider the changing role of management and the increasing need for leadership in organizations
■ Describe a way of defining an organizational vision and argue that there is an increasing requirement for leaders at all levels to unite followers behind such a vision
■ Provide examples of vision statements and belief statements developed by a range of different organizations
■ Consider a number of specific aspects of organizational performance particularly related to direction.

In the last chapter we introduced the organizational model which emerged from our research into the subject of change management in successful organizations. We stated that there appear to be four key factors which need to be addressed and these are:

■ Direction
■ Form
■ Communication
■ Adaptation.

Traditional and virtual organizations approach these four factors in significantly different ways and in the last chapter we briefly discussed some of the differences by way of introduction to the subject. Here, though, the book moves on to tackle the four areas in detail, starting naturally with the factor we have entitled *direction*.

Direction encompasses the strategic thinking and processes which are adopted in order to set the course for the organization. For the new organization in a start up mode this is often a question of agreeing the *raison d'être* and may be more obvious and less difficult to manage than in the traditional organization. Increasingly, traditional organizations are being challenged with the requirement to question their overall strategy; so they are asking questions such as:

- What really is our purpose?
- Are we in the right market?
- Who are our customers and what are their expectations?
- How are external factors likely to impact on our organization in the future?
- Who are the other stakeholders?

Clearly, such questions are strategic in nature. They are fundamentally related to the whole business and to its future survival or success—in a true strategic sense they relate to the whole campaign, not simply the immediate battle. For organizations which are asking these questions for the first time, such questions can lead to difficult discussion, conflicting views and, sometimes, self-doubt. Establishing the direction of the organization is by no means easy and it is certainly more than a desk-based exercise. It is about more than simply fixing the budget for the forthcoming year or financial plan for the next few years. In the best examples, these directional discussions involve members of the organization at all levels; it is recognized that those at the operational level, or at the customer interface, have just as valuable a contribution to make in considering the sort of questions outlined above as the most senior leaders of the organization.

Approaches to strategy

Strategic planning and forecasting was critical in the post-Second World War years until the late 1960s, while economic recovery meant that there was a need to expand production following a period of scarcity. Competition was less of an issue and there was room for most of the players in the market. The strategic skill was to be able to anticipate future growth and adjust the corporate strategy and plans accordingly. Organizations gained strategic advantage by being better able to forecast and anticipate the gradual changes and adopt the more appropriate response.

From the mid-1960s to 1990s the dynamics of competition became more apparent and strategies became more competitive. It was important to become proactive in order to survive and to tackle competitors and the changing market place. So there was more emphasis on competitor analysis. Given this scenario and the fact that the very term strategy has military connotations, 'strategy' in the classic sense was probably what was needed in order to think through ways of beating the enemy, or in a business sense, the competition.

Now, in the late part of the 1990s, there is an even less predictable and difficult scenario in terms of being able to formulate strategy, due to what Boisot (1995) refers to as the geopolitical upheaval whereby the size of markets, the players, the rules are even less clear. Clearly the rapidity of the changes which took place with the fall of Communism in most of the Eastern bloc states in the early 1990s is now really starting to have an impact on Western organizations. At the same time, changes taking place in the geopolitical map of Asia and the Far East are adding to the melee. One might ask how useful strategic planning and forecasting is in this sort of dynamic environment. Indeed, one has to question whether the sense of strategy, with its military connotations, remains appropriate; we now talk to those who used to be our enemies, we form alliances with them and collaborate, we both compete and work with them at the same time.

Boisot summarizes four types of strategic response and presents a useful model to help in considering the issue of strategy in the future. As we summarize these four approaches to strategy here, you might like to think of how strategic matters are addressed in your own organization; we will ask you to reflect on this with the 'Pause for thought' questions below.

Strategic planning

This is the term used to describe an approach based on a belief that the context of the organization is predictable and that we need to work hard at managing and collecting data and then applying the right strategic tools. Data would be collected at regular periodic intervals and there would be a top-down process of turning grand strategies into operational plans. As an approach this lent itself to situations where the data was not changing too fast for the strategists who were trying to understand it. This also assumes that any short term changes only cover up what are fairly predictable and definable longer term trends and patterns.

Emergent strategy

This is a concept popularized by Henry Mintzberg, which is rather different. Here, the organization makes gradual and regular changes to respond to the environment. There is a different assumption: that the environment cannot actually be predicted through the use of analytical processes and techniques. If one makes a strategic plan, then, by the time it is implemented, other variables will have emerged which cause it to be adjusted. Furthermore, there is an important role for those at a more operational level in being able to take action and respond as appropriate. Strategy in this sense is more fragmented and this is a more realistic framework when an organization is operating in a changing environment.

Intrapreneurship

This is the approach to strategy described by Pinchot (1985), which is appropriate where the rate of change is so high that neither of the two previously described approaches would work. This is much more of a responsive or reactive model where the best the organization can do is to tackle challenges at local and different levels in the organization rather than expecting to present a cogent corporate strategy. The emphasis is on action and it has to be accepted that there will be good and bad decisions taken by different people in the organization at different levels. This suggests structurally that there is a need for loose groupings and high levels of initiative on the part of the intrapreneurs; this is what we have seen evidence of among those organizations we would describe as virtual organizations. However, for this sort of approach to work there is a need for a particular set of behaviours to be prominent, not least of all trust. Later we look at the profile of successful members of the virtual organization and find some interesting commonality with the requirements for intrapreneuring.

Strategic intent

This is the term used to describe the strategy which draws on the vision for the future of the organization. This is often summed up in a vision statement or some sort of summary which encapsulates the purpose of the business; additionally such vision often serves to unite the members of the organization under one mission or banner. This is particularly important where individuals and different functions or teams within the business may be coping with different and diverse pressures. Such a vision needs to be sufficiently focused to have meaning and sufficiently broad to be enduring in the face of rapidly and often dramatically changing circumstances. Later in this chapter we pursue this strategy in more depth and provide some examples of how different organizations have approached vision building. We also argue that there is a place for vision building at all levels of the organization; it is just as relevant to build a vision for an operational team as it is for the senior executives. With strategic intent there is an element of intuition which balances with the analytical dimension. This approach to strategy lends itself well to the decentralized organizational form which is predominant in the virtual organization.

So, these four approaches to strategy provide some help in considering the most appropriate approach for the organization given its circumstances. Clearly one of the critical factors is the rate of change which we looked at in Chapter 2; if the organization is having to cope with the accelerating change curve then the strategic intent and intrapreneurship models are likely to be more appropriate. It is actually less realistic to expect to be able to look back to the past and identify patterns based on information from the external and organizational environment. In the virtual organization there is more to be gained from looking forward to the future.

PAUSE FOR THOUGHT

How would you describe your organization's approach to strategy?

■ Which model does it fit best with:
  –Strategic planning?
  –Emergent strategy?
  –Intrapreneurship?
  –Strategic intent?
■ How does this become evident?
■ How appropriate is this given the circumstances and context of the organization?
■ To what extent are members of the organization at all levels truly involved in having a say regarding the strategic direction of the business?

In the past, if one was to look at the subject of strategy from an academic perspective the main emphasis would have been on financial measurement; so the strategists would track financial trends, study ratios, make financial forecasts and formulate appropriate plans. In the classic sense, the strategy would define what the organization intended to achieve and the tactics would take these strategies and look at how they should be achieved. Financial targets would be established based on an assessment of what was realistic given all the information available. Directors would work to financial plans agreed at the top and these would then be cascaded down through the organization with whole layers of managers being accountable to their seniors primarily on the basis of financial performance. Traditionally, in organizations such as The General Electric Company (GEC) in the UK this is how captains of industry such as Arnold Weinstock have managed and grown extremely successful businesses. Undoubtedly, one of Weinstock's major strengths was his ability to define, read, understand, interpret and act appropriately upon a hard core of financial ratios.

The emphasis on what we would call hard measures has increased up until the 1990s. The principle which said that the route to success is achieved by setting clear, hard and definable targets might even be tracked back to the Management By Objectives (MBO) movement of the 1970s. Such schemes formalized the setting of hard goals and in principle were sound but faced difficulties in implementation; often there was an over emphasis on bureaucratic form filling and an emphasis on hitting numerical targets almost regardless of how they were achieved. Then, through the 1980s, there were many attempts to iron out the difficulties of the MBO approach with a move to establish targets for most organizational members as opposed to just the managers; there was evidence of an effort to take a more collaborative approach. Nonetheless, the same problem of an over emphasis on the hard targets, often at the expense of the method or process used, was frequently seen. This often meant that some people who achieved their objectives did so in such a way as to cause more overall harm than good. Paradoxically, those who may have been adopting the correct approach and behaviours in the long term might fail to meet their short term objectives and this would be reflected in their assessments and ultimately the way they were rewarded.

The Institute of Personnel and Development (formerly IPM) (IPM, 1992) published the results of a major research project into the subject of performance management in the UK. This study included over 1800 employers with a 46 per cent return, covering 20 per cent of the UK workforce. There were some interesting recommendations regarding the actions organizations should be taking if they are to ensure that individual and organizational performance improves. Among these suggestions were the following:

- Organizations should define the goals of the organization and communicate these effectively to teams and individuals at all levels.
- Organizations should consider the intrinsic needs of employees, such as opportunities for development, as well as extrinsic needs such as remuneration.
- 'Reward-driven integration' which emphasizes, for instance, performance related pay, is of limited value in isolation. There was no conclusive evidence of a causal link between performance related pay and bottom line business results.

■ 'Development-driven integration' which addresses such developmental issues is just as important.

The findings of this report were consistent with the observation that the pendulum had swung too far in the direction of hard measurement, hard assessment and hard reward. Some organizations have now recognized the need to define both hard business measures such as sales, profit, return on capital employed or new business gained, as well as what have sometimes been described as softer measures. Such measures would include recognition of the skills, knowledge and behaviours which the individual needs in order to achieve a successful output. One way of looking at this is to consider the concept of inputs and outputs as shown in Fig. 5.1. Here we suggest that any performance related output can actually be tracked back to certain behaviours or competencies which the individual inputs. If it is possible to define the critical behaviours then it is possible to use this information to create a behavioural profile for any job, role or task; once this has been defined the next logical step is to recruit, train and measure performance against these indicators. Throughout the 1990s organizations like Esselte, Motorola and Cellnet have used this approach to develop standards of performance.

This is different from the classic approach of drawing up job descriptions. Job descriptions tend to describe in task terms the activities which need to be carried out. Such an approach is quite appropriate where there is a reasonable level of stability and it is known that the tasks which have to be completed in a job today will be just as relevant in the future. Where there is a high degree of change in the requirement of the job and the job holder needs to carry out varied and changing tasks then

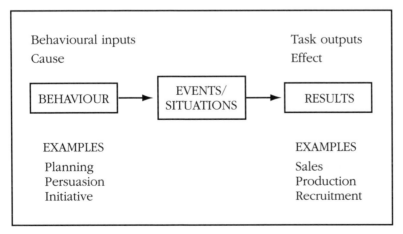

Fig. 5.1   Defining successful performance (*Source:* Hale, R.I. and Whitlam, P.J., *Target Setting and Goal Achievement*, Kogan Page, 1995)

describing the role in terms of tasks becomes less meaningful. This probably explains why organizations we encountered which fit more with the virtual organization model either do not have job descriptions or, if they do, then they are highly flexible. In traditional organizations the job description tends to be interpreted in a literal sense and this, combined with other cultural norms, mitigates against flexibility. Ironically in such organizations the role of the job description often comes into its own when an individual is perceived not to be performing at the appropriate level. It is questionable whether in the virtual organization individuals even have jobs in the traditional sense; they tend to talk about their current 'role', 'the brief' or 'project accountabilities'. This is a subject we will look at in more depth in the next chapter, where we look at the *form* of organizations. We will look at the argument that actually the 'job' as such is fast becoming a thing of the past and we could be entering a period where organizations operate without jobs in the traditional sense.

To the uninitiated, the absence of job descriptions may appear to be a recipe for disaster. However, in the virtual organization an individual's job is both contextual and situational; that is to say that the individual circumstances describe the job requirements. In such organizations 'generalists are king' and where specialists are employed they are small in number or are expected to take on generalist responsibilities and contribute to the overall purpose of the organization.

CASE
STUDY
5.1

Improving responsiveness through outsourcing at Cola-Cola Schweppes Beverages

When Coca-Cola linked with Cadbury Schweppes in the late 1980s to form the new large joint venture bottlers of Coca-Cola Schweppes Beverages, despite having in excess of 5000 employees in over 13 different locations, the organization employed only one training and development specialist. It was envisaged that training and development activities would in the main be supported by external resources, people who would be employed on a contract basis as required.

Naturally, on its own this approach to the provision of training would be insufficient, however when combined with the implementation of a strategy to re-skill line managers as generalists, as well as shifting the responsibility of learning onto the individual rather than this being seen as the sole prerogative of the organization, then these approaches appeared to work.

In particular, this approach of incorporating off-shore personnel to support the small number of personnel in the organization provided flexibility and speed of response. Undoubtedly this provided a real competitive advantage for the organization.

What is also interesting in this scenario are the implications for line managers who may historically have seen their power base as being derived from their number of direct reports and as a consequence of these changes may have felt that their power had been eroded.

If one is operating in a rapidly changing environment which might be affected by internal and external factors then a more relevant question to ask, rather than what tasks are required, is 'What are the critical and relatively enduring behaviours or skills which are needed for success?'. Some of these behaviours will be relevant to many or even all of the people in the organization. Some will be more relevant to specific functions or roles. Either way, it will be possible to then think of each of these critical skills or behaviours in the following terms:

■ Is this skill trainable?
■ Is this behaviour more personality related?

Clearly, if it is possible to develop a certain skill with training then, so long as one is confident about a person's potential to develop such a skill, it may be acceptable to recruit someone who does not currently possess the skill. This might be the case with, for instance, skills such as planning and organizing, financial analysis or computing skills. If, however, it is felt that the skill is really more of a personality related behaviour, say, for instance, initiative, integrity or risk-taking, then it will be more important to recruit people who have been identified as already possessing these behaviours.

Our evidence clearly suggests that often when individuals are selected for specific roles, insufficient attention is given to the competencies that may be personality based. Consequently, when an individual does not perform at the necessary level it becomes extremely difficult to tackle such problems in a constructive way.

In a similar way, where new employees are required to learn new skills in a short period of time, some organizations seem to fail to assess the individual's ability to acquire these skills in the optimal time. As a result often such individuals fail to contribute to their full potential within the business.

Leadership and followership

The role of the leader in developing, changing and providing direction and purpose for the organization is critical. We believe there is evidence that the very nature of management and leadership is changing with great rapidity. It appears, for instance, that the very word manager is being used less in organizations today than it was in the past and is being replaced by titles and words such as: facilitator, leader and adviser. Surely this is more than a cosmetic change to satisfy the latest fad or copy the approach taken by others. Much is revealed by looking at some of the major shifts in thinking about the subjects of management and leadership.

Management thinking has clearly moved on since the concept of Taylorism in the early part of the 20th Century, where management was based around the assumption that tasks should be systematically analysed and workers should be instructed, monitored and strictly controlled. In practice, though, it seems that some of the original concepts have simply been reworked possibly with some enhancements and updating. Business Process Re-engineering, for instance, albeit more customer focused, is surely similar in concept to some of the original approaches taken to analysing tasks, which may have gone under the heading of Time and Motion or Work Study in the past. While one might assume that due to social changes, the way in which employees are managed has advanced, there is still much evidence of the remnants of Taylorism and McGregor's Type X manager in existence in many traditional organizations today.

In the virtual organization, however, it is quite different. It is accepted that the classic role of management, that is one of planning, organizing, directing and controlling, is changing. Yes these roles may still be important, but their very nature is changing.

One can see why each of these roles is of less significance than it was in the past. It is difficult to plan with any degree of certainty and in many cases it is less realistic to expect to be able to produce detailed long term plans for the business than it was in the past. In the past, a 10- or 15-year plan might have been produced and could actually help the organization in terms of giving direction and a route forward. Management in the classic sense is the most appropriate approach when one is adopting a 'strategic planning' approach as defined in the previous section; where there is order, a high degree of predictability and where change is at such a pace that one can relatively easily keep pace with it. Now, however, with the accelerating change curve scenario, a detailed plan drawn up today may simply become redundant tomorrow because of factors which are simply unpredictable; this could be a major technological breakthrough, the advent of a new competitor or a political or economic factor.

Similarly, to organize resources in a detailed and future focused way is less easy. Personnel who are required for an immediate project may not be required in the near future and there may be a need for a high degree of flexibility in being able to adjust staffing numbers accordingly. As for the role of the manager in monitoring and controlling, again while the basic skills are still needed, there is a requirement for a new mind set; flexibility and open mindedness are essential. Plans of course still need

to be monitored but they are monitored, and adjusted on a more frequent and regular basis. People are controlled but their expectations are
different from those in the past; it is expected that there will be a spirit
of participation and consultation. Furthermore, people who may not be
the most senior are likely to hold more of the answers and expertise, as
well as being more inclined to question the way things are done.

Given such changing trends in the role of management, it is worth considering the critical skills or competencies required. Clearly the trends
identified above call for increasing flexibility and open mindedness. It is
unusual for such qualities to be developed in people as specific skills or
traits, however the virtual organization tends to attract people who possess such qualities and certainly fosters an appropriate spirit.

There have been many attempts to produce a profile of the successful
manager in the hope that having formulated the definition it would then
be possible to identify potential and develop managers who meet a
required and consistent standard. Perhaps unsurprisingly, given the
diversity of management roles and organizations, attempts to draw up a
generic list of skills or behaviours have proved inconclusive.

In the UK, the Management Charter Initiative (MCI), a body compris-
ing a number of leading corporations, have defined management competencies under the following headings:

■ Managing operations/services
■ Managing people
■ Managing finance
■ Managing information.

The work of the MCI has made a significant contribution to thinking in
this area throughout the early 1990s. While this approach is highly analytical, in that it takes each of these four areas and breaks them down
into units and elements of competence, the difficulty one faces in trying
to create a picture of the management role which applies on a broad
basis is that if it is defined too broadly then it loses any real meaning or
usefulness, and if it is too specific then it becomes inappropriate or irrelevant in individual cases. Some organizations have overtly spurned such
attempts to define management, while others taking a pragmatic
approach have used such frameworks in order to help in drawing up
their own company related definitions. Working to generic lists of skills
and competencies may be helpful when there is a high degree of consistency in the nature of the role across the organization, as has been the
case in the retail sector, or where there is a low rate of change. Where
there is more diversity and the rate of change is high, however, it may be
necessary to accept that there are no longer any generally applicable
definitions of management which are of practical help to the organization.

We are seeing, however, at the same time as the declining emphasis on traditional management, an increasing interest in the subject of leadership. Many organizations, for instance, are establishing the role of *team leader* in place of supervisory or junior management roles. Increasingly there are different levels of leaders such as team leader, group leader and project leader. It appears that leadership is no longer the preserve of those at the top of the organization. There is a strong case for leadership where the environment is fast changing and where there is a need to help others to contend psychologically and physically with uncertainty regarding the future. There is a real need for strong leadership in the case of the 'intrapreneurship' scenario described above, and in particular for leadership at all levels of the organization. In this scenario, individuals in diverse and often specialist areas need to show initiative, the ability to take risks and to self-authorize themselves to take decisions; they need to lead others and to empower others to lead in their own areas of expertise.

It is worth considering at this stage how leadership actually differs from management. An interesting comparison is provided by Kotter (1990), who proposes that management is about:

- Planning and budgeting
- Organizing and staffing
- Controlling and problem solving

and as such aims to produce a degree of order and consistency of results. Leadership by contrast is seen as being concerned with the following:

- Establishing and communicating direction though a vision of the future
- Aligning people behind the vision
- Motivating and inspiring people

and as such produces useful change.

It is this picture of leadership as a transformational force which is particularly appropriate in the virtual organization. We have seen many examples of large traditional organizations which have survived, even thrived, in the past due to a major strength in terms of management, but where there was little evidence of leadership. Ask a number of people in these organizations who they would identify with as their leader and you will find they struggle to give a convincing answer. If you then probe a little deeper and ask what the vision for the organization is then you may be met with blank faces or some cynical remark about the corporate mission statement which they had no part in defining and do not really understand. It is the visionary aspect of leadership which relates particularly well to the 'strategic intent' model presented earlier in this chapter.

As a subject, leadership is often treated with more mystique than management; it is as though it is considered less easy to define and to teach—you either have leadership ability or you don't. The lack of a practical approach to leadership and the relationship between leadership and change is reflected by the comments of leadership guru John Adair (1989), who has said:

> There is much more need for leadership nowadays, mainly due to the upheavals in the economic system creating a much wider sense of change and the need for it. Change tends to create leaders, and leaders tend to create change—the first of those tendencies being much stronger or more effective. But continuity reasserts itself in that most British managers are still not leaders—they are not actually doing it; they have learnt only to talk about it ...

The perennial debate regarding the development of leadership qualities has mostly centred around the argument of whether effective leaders are born or can be 'made' through the development of leadership qualities with effective training. Many of the traits-based approaches to studying this subject have identified widely different characteristics in the effective leader. Some of the traits identified have included:

- Risk taking
- Enthusiasm
- Integrity
- Understanding of people
- Communication skill
- Flexibility
- Industriousness
- Tenacity.

Studies of the backgrounds of great leaders have suggested some interesting biographical patterns. For instance, many great leaders have experienced lonely, isolated childhoods, often having lost a parent in childhood, usually the father, or there is evidence of contrasting relationships with their parents.

Interestingly, it seems that most of the major leaders in history tend to possess two qualities: first, they tend to be either very large or very small people physically and second, they have a strong sense of vision. While it is possible, of course, to find exceptions to these generalizations, it is the issue of vision which we want to address in more detail here because we believe that there is a particular need to unite members of the organization or team behind a vision especially when operating in a climate of change and uncertainty.

In most entrepreneurial organizations there is a strong requirement for leadership qualities and for at least one person at the top or in the centre who possesses a clear vision of how things can, even will, be in the future. In many cases these leaders might be described as visionary; they are both comfortable and excited when talking about the future. They will describe how things might be in the future often in a high degree of detail; sometimes it is actually difficult to determine whether they are talking about something which currently exists or which could exist in the future. In the words of one great satirist: 'Vision is the art of seeing things invisible' (Jonathan Swift, 1667–1775, *Thoughts on Various Subjects*).

Our own research into the characteristics of successful leaders in industry has suggested that they will often harness the powers of mental visualization and imagery in order to create pictures of success. They will do this to help in the achievement of both short term, more immediate goals and to move towards the achievement of longer term objectives. While we found that some people tended to be able to do this more naturally, that is without formal or structured training, we also found that techniques of visualization can be taught and developed.

Successful leaders are likely to possess the ability to formulate a vision of the future, often with little help or assistance from others. They then have the ability to convey this vision to other people in such a way that others become more comfortable in looking ahead and are more cohesive in their understanding of the goals of the team or organization. Usually the vision can be summed up in a succinct, interesting, even exciting way and it is behind this statement of the organization's vision that the organization's entire value and belief set can be identified.

Increasingly, organizations are attempting to define their vision, values and beliefs so that they provide a unifying force for the benefit of both internal members and external stakeholders. Actually producing the words can be a very difficult and time consuming exercise and there is a danger here of confusing clever word play with powerful vision building. Effective leaders, though, are able to formulate and crystallize the picture of success; it may be that the marketeers or public relations wordsmiths then help summarize this. The statements which are most powerful, however, are often those which are short and to the point: Coca-Cola aimed to 'Put a Coke within arm's reach of every consumer in the world' and Komatsu to 'Encircle Caterpillar'. Steve Jobs at Apple talked about a goal of 'creating the world's friendliest computers—computers that empower the individual and aiming to transform the way people do things'.

If such statements are able to distinguish the organization from others then they are likely to hold more meaning than if they simply regurgitate the buzzwords and power-words of the day. Some leaders will support the overarching statement or picture with statements which seek to summarise the values, beliefs or aspirations of the organization.

Some go further in providing guidelines on the behaviours and attitudes which should be encouraged. So Levi Strauss, which underwent major organizational change in order to survive the turmoil of the 1980s, under the leadership of CEO Robert Haas (1990) developed an 'aspiration statement' which spoke about being a company which members are proud of and committed to, where they have an opportunity to contribute and learn. He mentioned the importance of fun and suggested this called for a particular type of leadership which emphasizes:

■ directness
■ openness to influence
■ trust
■ accountability

and the ability to model and develop such behaviours in others. Here, there is a similarity of approach to that taken by Motorola in defining the qualities of effective leaders and followers under the banner of its 'individual dignity entitlement' initiative. In this initiative, the rights of the individual are made explicit and management is held to account for its performance against these rights.

Gardner (1995), in his study of great leaders, suggests that they achieved effectiveness through the stories which they convey to their followers. Here, stories could refer to their key theme or drama which is seen as a dynamic process embodying key messages. He draws an interesting distinction between those who are leading on a general basis rather than in an expert area. So leaders of nations seek to lead a diverse range of people and it is considered important for such leaders to actually embody and live the principles which they purport to believe in. This is considered less important for leaders in specialist fields, where more emphasis is placed on their professional specialism. Indeed there is a difference between the direct leader who needs to be visible and seen to be leading and the indirect leader who may lead in a particular field without having a high public presentation profile. Another useful categorization which Gardner defines is the difference between the ordinary leader, the innovative leader and the truly visionary leader. The ordinary leader does not necessarily stretch the consciousness of the followers, whereas the innovative leader takes a latent story and raises its profile; examples of innovative leadership approaches would be those taken by Ronald Reagan or Margaret Thatcher. The real visionaries, however, actually create new stories: Gandhi is a good example of this type of leadership.

While it can be fascinating and instructive to look to the great world leaders for guidance on the qualities of leadership, it is important to recognize that it is neither realistic or even necessary to expect organizations to be led by public visionaries in the above sense.

Undoubtedly, there are certain characteristics of leadership, though, which are of relevance to the successful corporation of the future and which the virtual organization demonstrates. First, there is the importance of being able to convey a strong vision of how things could be or will be in the future. This in itself suggests the need for certain communication skills and we have recognized that many successful business leaders will, through their conversation and presentation, paint rich and colourful pictures, often drawing on the powerful use of analogy, storytelling and anecdotal examples. However, linked to this is the ability to establish certain down to earth, specific and measurable goals to work towards: this is the task focus aspect of the organizational leader. Often such people will be able to motivate others through their sheer commitment and infectious enthusiasm, and they will model the behaviours they seek to encourage.

In addition to this they will create a sense of urgency as they go about their business and they will expect the same sense of urgency from others. When one enters the doors of an organization led in this way it is possible to literally see the sense of urgency; people move quickly, talk quickly and communicate passionately. This is not to be confused with fire-fighting approaches where people rush around simply reacting to events; there is actually a balance between reactivity and proactivity. The leader takes action and moves the business forward and expects others to do the same albeit at their own level. By contrast, in some of the more traditional organizations we have worked with we have seen a notable lack of urgency: people are focused only on their own area of work, they are reactive, there is a 'good enough' attitude to completing tasks, there is no evidence of personal pride, tasks which could be completed immediately are simply left or deferred, people are referred on to others rather than dealt with personally.

Additionally, the qualities of leadership which are increasingly required in the organization of the future suggest a need to listen to the views and opinions of others and a willingness to empower them to make decisions and take risks and to make mistakes without a fear of recriminations. The days of the omniscient leader, if they ever truly existed, are over; as the body of knowledge is changing so fast it is quite possible that the followers will be more knowledgeable and better informed than the leaders. In fact, one of the qualities which we have seen among successful leaders is their willingness to accept responsibility for their own decisions, even if they prove to be wrong ones. There is an acceptance that with the increasing number of unknowns, and the corresponding need to make decisions, there will be mistakes; the key thing is to be able to analyse them and learn from them intelligently.

The subject of flexibility is worth briefly mentioning in looking at leadership. It has been recognized that the qualities of great world leaders of the past, and following the 'great man' approach are not necessarily so appropriate in the organizational setting of the future. Many of the great leaders of the past were true leaders of their time and given the circumstances in which they had to lead. However, if one looks at their nemesis it is possible to identify the fact that they often fell from power because of an inability to adapt or change their approach when there was a need to; one thinks, for instance, of the demise of Winston Churchill after the end of the Second World War and Margaret Thatcher at the end of the 'get rich quick' 1980s. In contrast, organizations are increasingly calling for their leaders to strike a difficult balance between steadfast vision, determination, tenacity and belief and the ability to adapt and flex in different situations and circumstances. In our study of the characteristics of successful chief executives we identified that one of the key qualities which was commonly found was that of adaptability (Hale and Whitlam, 1995). This refers to the chameleon-like quality which some people display in being able to adapt to the styles of other people or organizations.

In the next chapter we look at how the virtual organization demonstrates the ability to change and adapt its *form* according to differing needs; here we are looking at the individual manifestation of this, where effective leaders are sensitive to the demands of different situations and can adapt their behaviour accordingly.

Finally an often neglected area of concern when organizations address the subject of leadership is that of the followers in the organization. There is sometimes an arrogant assumption that if you get the right kind of leadership in place then the rest will fall into place accordingly. This is a mentality which may have worked in the traditional organization based on leadership through the wielding of position power, coercion and force. This approach to leadership was once described by Harry Truman in the following way:

'A leader is a man who has the ability to get other people to do what they don't want to and like it.'

This is clearly less appropriate in the organization of the future. Furthermore, the behaviours which are required from the followers nowadays are not enforceable; they tend to come through coaching, influence, encouragement and persuasion. In attempting to encourage behaviours such as risk taking, initiative, enthusiasm, tenacity, responsibility and empowerment among the followers, there is a need to actually spell out what is expected and to then contribute to the development and realization of such skills and behaviours. Something more subtle and challenging than the instructing or telling approach is required. The leaders and the followers will inevitably share a number of the same qualities and in many cases members of the organization will have dual roles—as leaders and as followers. It is important to listen to the followers regarding their expectations of the leaders.

In one organization we were working with the new dynamic and enthusiastic leader was criticized by his senior managers for not being sufficiently visible in the organization; they were simply relaying the perception of the majority of company members who felt he was not visible enough internally. His reaction was to deny that there was a problem; they just needed to cope without him. Logically he was right; he was frequently away from the organization, building contacts and developing the business, and they were quite capable of managing without him on site. There was a real expectation, however, that their leader should be seen more frequently—this was a need of the followers and it could have been met with little extra effort. All he needed to do was brief people on where he was going, what business he was involved with and when he would return and to publicly recognize the progress which the followers were making back at base. As well as being sensitive to the needs of the followers, some organizations will overtly define the skills and behaviours they wish to encourage.

PAUSE FOR THOUGHT

How would you describe the style of leadership in your organization?

Is it more of a managed or a led organization?

To what extent is your organization led by a direct leader or an indirect leader?

How visible is the leader?

To what extent does he or she demonstrate the behaviours which are expected of others?

To what extent is there a vision of where the organization is heading?

Is this vision known, understood by all employees and reinforced by actions?

Is leadership confined mainly to the top or is there evidence of real leadership at the middle and lower levels?

How clearly have the organization's values been communicated ?

Developing a vision—a practical approach

Despite the continuing popularity of the belief in leadership as a mystical, hidden quality which people are born with or at least develop very early on in life, we believe it is possible to develop certain leadership skills in a pragmatic way, and our experience with some organizations has focused around the importance of developing a vision. This is produced as a means of uniting and motivating teams of people ranging from the senior management team to more operational level teams. This process of building a vision might be likened to the analogy of scattering iron filings on a table top and then stroking a magnet under the table. What will happen is the filings which were dispersed and pointing in different directions both pull together and align in the same direction. In the same way the individuals in the group who may have held different beliefs regarding the objectives of the team or organization pull together and align behind a common vision of where they are heading.

Here we suggest an approach to building a vision which can be adopted for both broad strategic purposes which may cover the period of say one to three years; or equally, the same approach can be used in working with project or functional teams which have been required to pull together and to define or redefine their objectives for specific and more short term goals. As was mentioned before, leadership is not the preserve of those at the top of the organization; the need for vision can be applied to any group of people who are required to work together towards a common goal.

The difficulty that a group of individuals face when they are pulled together and expected to function effectively as a team, is that if you were to interview each person separately regarding the objectives of the team the chances are that you would hear as many different versions as there are team members. People will come to the organization, team or project with their own unique perception, which will be based on factors such as their previous experience, preferences and beliefs. At this stage it would be inappropriate to categorize any one person's beliefs regarding the vision or mission of the group as right or wrong; what you would be hearing from them is their personal perception, which is their reality. In order for the team to define a common purpose or vision, though, the following approach might be taken.

The team needs to come together off of the job for a predetermined period of uninterrupted time. Clearly the objectives of the session, and an output statement, need to be agreed and it is helpful if someone performs the role of facilitator in order to co-ordinate the process. Each member of the group reflects on their own perception of the objectives of the group and privately commits these thoughts to paper following the format suggested below.

'We want to ...

> (an overall statement of the reason for the team's existence)

in a way which ...

> (a further statement which builds on or qualifies the first one)

in order to ...

> (a declaration of the outcome which is required)

as measured by...'

> (how it will be known when success has been achieved).

It should be stressed that this is simply a template to ensure that each member works to a consistent format. The members of the team work through this process privately so that their personal perception and views are not distorted or influenced by others before they are expressed. Each person then lays their individual statement out before the group. Once they are all displayed alongside one another, members circulate looking at the statements of others. Where clarification or explanation is needed, individuals offer this. If a person is particularly attracted to the comments of another he or she may underline it to reinforce its appeal. At this stage the team members are wandering, perusing, reflecting and engaging in thoughtful discussion.

This then progresses into an attempt, through a process of consensus building, to agree the wording of a statement which expresses the vision or mission for the team. The critical point to emphasize here is that every member of the group must wholeheartedly support the ultimate statement. Usually what ensues is a discussion which might to an onlooker appear to be based around semantics and detailed definitions. In truth, though, it is a critical stage in the process of vision building whereby the real objectives of the group are defined and agreed. It is important for the facilitator at this stage to emphasize that before any wording is actually agreed by the group all members must be absolutely committed to such wording.

Simply working through this process is in itself a tiring and demanding task; most people under-estimate the time needed in order to do it properly and the debate around the groups' purpose can be both illuminating and frustrating. It should be recognized that there is a bonding effect which comes from the group working through the discussion and it is frequently found that the more difficult the discussion, the stronger the ultimate effect.

Below we see some examples of corporate vision statements which have been developed by using this process in three very different organizations.

This first example shows the output of a vision building session which involved the senior directors of the mineral water company, Perrier (UK), part of the Nestlé group. As can be seen in the first line of the mission statement, the words are carefully chosen to define exactly what the direction of the organization is. There were a number of strategic options here and there was a need to agree which markets the company was operating in. It can also be seen how specific comment is made regarding progress towards the achievement of the vision by assessing against business objectives and customer satisfaction. Clearly the measures which are built into the vision need to be realistic and, as in this case, they may refer to other more detailed documents or assessment criteria. Here, the vision is underpinned by a number of beliefs which were agreed at the same session. These provide more detailed information about the expectations with regard to how the organization and the people within it are expected to behave; they are guiding principles and in many ways they spell out the culture of the organization. The overall time taken to achieve this output was in excess of two days, involving the whole board of directors.

The Perrier (UK) group mission statement

CASE STUDY 5.2

The mission

We will be the best, single focused bottled water company in the UK, consistently providing quality products and services.

This will be achieved by maximizing potential market opportunities in order to ensure a profitable and successful future, and will be measured by the achievement of business objectives and total customer satisfaction.

Our beliefs

Integrity is paramount in everything we do.

Although profit focused, we will continuously challenge overhead costs.

We will make the optimal use of all resources in the business.

Teamwork is critical, however we will foster interdependency and co-operation across the group.

Our communication style will be open and participative.

Employee involvement will be encouraged and through demonstrating respect for the individual we will increase job satisfaction and ownership.

We will actively encourage all employees to develop their full potential.

Innovation will be highly valued, likewise the use of entrepreneurial skills.

Measurement will be built into everything we do, hence providing the basis for continual improvement.

Our over-riding goal will be to ensure we get things right, first time every time.

In this example we looked at how a vision statement can be developed to provide overall understanding of the direction of the organization. In this next example we look at the approach taken by a specific functional team in the European Division of Coca-Cola.

This was developed by senior management responsible for management development across Europe and sought to provide others with an understanding of both its direction and purpose, as well as its overall way of operating. Once again, you will see that the vision is followed by a series of statements relating to the beliefs which underpin the vision.

CASE
STUDY
5.3

A vision for developing people at Coca-Cola

We will build a systematic and integrated framework for the development of all our management;

in a way which equips our people with the necessary knowledge, skills and attitudes;

in order to ensure that we can meet business needs both currently and in the future; and

our success will be measured by our knowing that we have the right managers, in the right jobs, at the right time.

We believe ...

- That all managers have the potential to consistently improve both their current performance and future potential.
- The role of the European Group is to enable or facilitate the development of a system of integrated activities, and that this system should be done in partnership with the stakeholders, and aimed at achieving the overall vision.
- All the constituent activities in the system must become institutionalized and owned by line management as well as the individuals.
- To ensure ownership, central tasks and activities will be designed in a collaborative manner. Special emphasis will be placed on being flexible, with particular regard to recognizing regional, cultural or business differences.

- The emphasis in the system will be on outputs rather than activities.
- Where specific actions are required, these will be focused at meeting identified and defined business needs.
- The approach will essentially be practical and pragmatic and will always embrace the principles of best practice, rather than be influenced by current fads or fancies.
- In the delivery of specific development activity, the focus will be on learning rather than training, we will seek to exploit the use of technology.
- Performance improvement, using accurate measurement will be built into everything that we undertake.
- Finally, that our ultimate goal is to move towards a business culture that supports the notion of our being a learning organization, where organizational and personal learning (and change) are inherent in all we do.

We believe that the above examples are evidence of good practice and they provide the reader with some real examples of how leaders of either organizations or business functions have worked through, with their teams, the development of a shared common vision in order to provide direction and a focus for future efforts.

In none of these cases was there a need for a visionary leader in the sense described. What was found, though, was evidence of committed leaders who were willing to work alongside their team and recognized the benefits of involving them in defining their purpose.

Finally, having formulated a statement of the vision it may be helpful to cross check it against certain quality criteria as a statement:

- Are the words exciting?
- Does it explain what is really important to us?
- Is the language simple?
- Does it provide understanding of our way of working?
- Does it conjure up positive images?
- Is it unambiguous?
- Does it clearly define success?
- Does it avoid comparisons?
- Is it equally of value to all our stakeholders?

Of course, some organizations go to great lengths to develop a vision statement, then fail to utilize it to the optimal benefit. The success in all of the above examples was the efforts which were made to publicize the statement both internally and externally to customers, clients and suppliers.

Where the statement has been formulated by a senior team and the goal is to harness the energy of the entire organization then it is critical that the same process is cascaded down through other teams and functions. In this case, each team or function would formulate its own vision while ensuring it is compatible with that of the organization as a whole.

PAUSE FOR THOUGHT

Does your organization or business function have a vision statement?

Is it a living statement which is often referred to, or a sterile document rarely known and seldom used?

Do individual functions/departments have their own vision statements which contribute to the vision of the organization as a whole?

In what way were individuals involved in developing the statement?

How effective is the statement when compared to the quality criteria above?

Are core beliefs clearly identified and communicated to all employees?

Assessment of direction

Finally, we provide you with an opportunity to consider your own effectiveness against the critical factor of *direction*.

The statements below are designed to assist you in identifying ways in which you can focus on your organization's approach to direction. Essentially, this is seen as a prerequisite for helping you move towards becoming a virtual organization. These questions should not be seen as a test; there are no right or wrong answers. However, their effectiveness relies on the frankness of your responses.

Listed below are ten focused statements relating to our research findings about the virtual organization. You may use this brief questionnaire to assess your own department or organization. This is a forced choice questionnaire requiring you to respond against each statement.

Please read each statement carefully and respond by answering either Yes (agreeing) or No (disagreeing) to each statement. There is no time limit; it will probably only take two minutes to complete.

1. We use team objective setting/targets across our business. Yes/No
2. Performance measurements are based mainly on hard quantifiable targets. Yes/No
3. We are highly customer focused, we constantly strive to improve our products or services. Yes/No
4. Our vision is known to all employees as well as our customers and suppliers. Yes/No
5. There is no genereally understood vision for the future. Yes/No
6. Once our business strategy has been set we tend to stick closely to it. Yes/No
7. Leadership skills are apparent at most levels in our organization. Yes/No
8. We involve almost everybody in the process of business planning. Yes/No
9. Access to financial information is strictly controlled. Yes/No
10. We rarely reward staff by virtue purely of their actual contribution. Yes/No

Scoring

If you answered Yes to any of the following statements, give yourself 10 points for each Yes.

1 ....
3 ....
4 ....
7 ....
8 ....
Total ....

If you answered No to any of the following statements, give yourself 10 points for each No.

2 ....
5 ....
6 ....
9 ....
10 ....
Total ....

Grand total ....

Consider the above grand total as a percentage relating to performance against the factor of *direction*. Those organizations which we believe measure up as effective virtual organizations tended to score in excess of 80 per cent.

In this chapter, then, we have spent some time exploring in detail the subject of organizational direction. In many ways, direction is about defining the purpose and goals of the business and we have looked at different models relating to strategy, suggesting that an increasingly dynamic approach is called for in the virtual organization.

It was also explained how there is likely to be a move away from just defining hard quantitative measures in looking at successful performance. It is increasingly appropriate to define the key behaviours or competencies which are required in an organization, particularly in an environment of accelerating change.

The other critical issue we have looked at under the heading of direction is that of leadership. It appears that leadership is set to replace management as one of the keys to organizational success in the future and in more advanced organizations there is evidence of effective leadership and followership at all levels, not just the top.

Effective leaders are likely to formulate a vision behind which followers and other leaders in the organization can unite. Furthermore, they will tend to involve other members of the organization in defining and crystallizing the vision. This need not be a mystical process—we looked at specific ways in which vision can be created.

In the next chapter we will proceed through the model of organizational development to look in particular at the factor which we describe as *form*. If setting the direction for the organization can be likened to preparing for the journey—the equivalent of deciding where to go, obtaining the map or overview and then planning the steps to move towards the destination—then the issue of organizational *form* can be likened to selecting the vehicle.

Form addresses issues such as organizational design and shape and we question many of the long held assumptions about organizations. No longer is it really necessary to have one permanent base or corporate building, nor is it, for instance, essential to have a permanent staff waiting to be allocated work. We even question whether the job as we have known it is appropriate as a concept in the virtual organization. To use the analogy of the journey, when deciding on the nature of the journey, the terrain and distance to be covered, we decide on the appropriate vehicle. And it is often the case that we will choose to change the vehicle or means of travel during the journey as appropriate. Successful organizations in the future will be able to adapt and change according to the different situations they encounter on their corporate journey.

References

Adair, J., Personnel management 20 years on, *Personnel Management* 1989.

Boisot, M., in *Developing Strategic Thought*, (Ed. B. Garratt), McGraw-Hill, Maidenhead, 1995.

Gardner, H., *Leading Minds*, Harper Collins, USA, 1995.

Haas, R., Values make the company: an interview with Robert Haas, *Harvard Business Review*, September/October, 1990.

Hale, R. and Whitlam, P., *The Power of Personal Influence*, McGraw-Hill, 1995.

Institute of Personnel Management, *Performance Management in the UK—An Analysis of the Issues, 1992.*

Kotter, J., *A Force For Change—How Leadership Differs From Management,* Free Press, 1990.

Peters, T. and Waterman, R.H., *In Search of Excellence*, Harper & Row, New York, 1982.

Pinchot, G., *Intrapreneuring*, Harper & Row, New York, 1985.

Selecting the vehicle

*The dinosaur's eloquent lesson is that if some
bigness is good, an overabundance of bigness
is not necessarily better*

ERIC JOHNSON
(President, US Chamber of Commerce, 1958)

In this chapter we move on to explore the subject of organizational
shape or *form*. In particular, we:

■ Suggest the requirement for a new paradigm in looking at how organizations shape and define themselves, which we describe as organizational form
■ Propose that there is a need for a new mind set in considering the
position of jobs and employment
■ Review the implications of the virtual organization from the perspective of human resource management and the management of people
■ Look at changes taking place with respect to how organizations physically set up and explore the innovative approaches taken by organizations which are experimenting structurally with the virtual organization concept
■ Track the development of concepts such as virtual business parks,
hot-desking, teleworking and telecottages and suggest that such
approaches are now being taken seriously by leading organizations
■ Finally, consider a number of specific aspects of organizational performance, particularly related to improving form in your organization.

Defining organizational form

In this chapter we look in depth at the subject of organizational *form*.
This is taken to mean more than just the organizational structure. Indeed
the very word organization may in itself be restricting. Perhaps a better
word would be 'organism'—at least this implies that the form is in a
constant state of evolution and change. Form may include structure, but

it is a lot more. In the past, organizational development specialists have placed a major emphasis on the importance of ensuring the correct organizational structure is in place when managing organizational change. Structurally this often led to a clear demarcation of roles and responsibilities and an emphasis on professional, job and management functions. This might be said to apply in the obvious sense in the hierarchical, traditional organization or bureaucracy and to a large extent this was even the case in the project or matrix environment, where admittedly more imagination and creativity was applied. In the world of the virtual organization, though, structure in the classic sense is only part of the story; there is a need to rethink our concept of structure and to think about how the organization should best adapt itself for given situations or challenges and how it should respond to changing social expectations and technological capabilities; hence the use of the term *form*.

So, form is taken to incorporate such themes as the shape of the organization, how it adapts to different situations, how roles are defined and where, how and with whom people work. In addressing the subject of organizational form and reviewing some of the truly innovative experiments which organizations are engaging in, there is a need for a new mind set. We need to think in terms of portfolios instead of jobs and careers, overlap instead of boundaries, and virtual organizations instead of solid business empires. Rather than working to the rule book there is an increasing need to support anomalies and paradox, to tolerate inconsistencies and to work flexibly. We are witnessing the emergence of a new organizational language which is driven primarily by these changes; so we talk of a jobless society, telecommuting, hot-desking and hotelling.   These are concepts which were unheard of as little as 10 years ago in the business world and the labels have emerged as a minority of companies have been pushing back the boundaries and redefining the concept of the organization.

Such radically different ways of organizing suggest a genuinely new approach to developing, motivating and supporting the human resource of the organization. Trying to progress on the journey towards becoming a virtual organization and selecting the wrong vehicle, or organizational form, will inevitably lead to a stuttering start, while others who have selected correctly move on at a pace.

Here we look specifically at the implications for the human resource specialist, who for the latter half of the 20th Century has in many cases had a key role in defining the shape and workings of the organization.

We also suggest that there are new categories of worker emerging in the world of work and we look in particular at the mind set needed by the 'professional portfolio workers' and the 'white collar labourers' in the changing social and corporate environment.

Additionally, we consider some of the truly innovative approaches taken by organizations which have been consciously experimenting with the virtual organization concept, in terms of the physical aspects of the organization. Here we look at organizations which exist without necessarily having a permanent physical base and which may be extremely dispersed physically but maximize their use of technology in order to overcome geographical constraints.

First we will consider some of the major developments which have taken place through the ages which have affected the way in which organizations manage their shape or Form.

The changing organizational landscape

If we were to track the development of the commercial organization in history we would see that it is a relatively recent concept. While it is recognized that human beings have organized themselves in one form or another since as far back as hunting and gathering days, the commercial organization and the establishment of jobs are recent innovations of the last 200 years or so. In the western world with the industrial revolution there was a move from the land to the cities and into the factory environment. The nature of industry as it evolved lent itself to structured approaches to organization; raw materials could be harnessed, people organized and told what to do, they would apply relatively consistent processes, skills or techniques and produce reasonably consistent products. Development focused around creating more consistent and reliable products by refining and systematizing processes and practices.

As the service sector developed the same logic was applicable, only in more of an office than factory environment; people could be given administrative and commercial tasks to do and they would deliver known outputs in the form of services for clients or customers. Despite the negative experience of organized labour and the controversy regarding exploitation and the reinforcement of a social and economic class system, this became firmly established as the norm right up until the late 20th Century.

Only now are we seeing another revolution in how people organize themselves and how they work together to add value in order to contribute to the economy. Previously the predominant way of working was for people to come together and organize to add value to materials through the use of manufacturing processes. The newly assembled products would meet external customer demands and would be purchased at a market rate depending largely on supply and demand. Now we have found, through the application of technology, the means to mass produce certain products with less emphasis on human labour. Machines, robotics, complex processes, software and hardware systems have come to the fore. In the field of production the real value is now added through the application of brain power. Organizing brain power and intellect among groups of disparate people is proving even more challenging than organizing labour.

Additionally, we have seen the unremitting growth of the service sector as society has developed increased expectations with regard to services. This again has increased the need to develop professional skills in order to tailor products and services to meet the bespoke needs of clients and customers.

These trends, combined with demographic and social factors, have wreaked havoc with the relative post-war industrial stability we once knew and which, despite the moderate ups and downs, we felt comfortable with.

Concepts as profound as the job, the career and the organization as an institution are being turned on their heads; and the effect is evidently divisive. Handy (1994) points to the paradox whereby those who have time to spare do not have the money or the means to earn, whereas those with the ability to earn are so busy that they have little spare time.

Other figures support the fact that there is no longer such a thing as the normal working pattern or routine: it is believed that less than half the UK workforce is in full-time employment and in the UK of those aged over 55 only 33 per cent are in any paid work; in France the figure is 27 per cent and it is 11 per cent in Italy. One-third of UK workers now work the nine to five day. Syrett and Lammiman (1994) describe a Cranfield School of Management research project which suggested that less than 50 per cent of the labour force in the European Community are permanently employed full timers. Schor (1992) found that the average American now works the equivalent of an extra month per year compared to 20 years ago, because organizations really want less people and more work to be done and individuals actually want the money.

So is it possible to make some sense of this confused picture? What lies behind the apparent contradictions?

We have technology which can carry out most manual and many intellectual tasks and despite the fact that in the 1980s we predicted more leisure time by the end of the century, workers are working longer and harder. Those who are working are working harder, and increasingly people experience real stress due to the demands of their work—yet unemployment remains a world-wide problem in the developed world. Long established patterns of work are breaking down; many people are clinging on to the hope that things will return to 'normality' as we once knew it—but it is not happening. Organizations are delayering, downsizing and right-sizing despite increased demand—and still this does not guarantee an improvement in their earnings. In an American management survey of companies making major staff cuts in 1987–1992,

Bridges (1994) found that less than half improved their earnings and one in four actually saw earnings drop.

It is questionable whether there are any definitive answers to these paradoxes; the picture is not becoming any clearer and it seems that we will need to try to cope with the contradictions and confusion rather than hope for a resolution. Organizations which fit with our model of the virtual organization certainly appear to be more comfortable in their ability to adapt to a constantly changing environment; some of them even talk about 'institutionalizing change'. In these organizations they accept that they cannot possibly understand all the variables in the organizational world and recognize and accept that change feels uncomfortable. They are prepared to live with and work around contradictions, illogical situations and support anomalies. Such organizations may:

- Have people who are part of the organization and independent at the same time
- Collaborate with their competitors
- Launch products before they fully understand them or their potential
- Have employees without bosses
- Have junior people paid more than their bosses
- Allow multiple reporting structures.

The following case study summarized from Ricardo Semler (1989) shows the approach of just one organization.

Redefining the organization at Semco

Semco is a manufacturing company with five factories and 800 employees, who are involved in the manufacture of a range of sophisticated products ranging from marine pumps to digital scanners. The company saw a turnaround from near collapse in 1980 to becoming one of the fastest growing companies in Brazil. The head of the organization, Ricardo Semler, puts this down to a tight focus on three values: democracy, profit sharing (23 per cent of profits after tax are distributed to the workers) and information.

The size of production units is also important and these are not allowed to increase over 150. The structure is described as three concentric circles, a middle one with just five Counsellors, in the next one there are the eight heads of divisions called Partners and all the rest are in the outer circle and are called Associates. The associates make up the majority of employees and cover functions such as research, design, sales and manufacturing. Some have either permanent or temporary team and task leaders' responsibilities and as such are called Co-ordinators. So, there are just four titles and three layers of employees.

In terms of pay, anomalies are supported and it is common for associates to earn more than partners. In fact, employees are encouraged to determine their own pay based on published information from salary surveys. They are paid what they think they should be paid and there is a major emphasis on trust combined with the importance of individuals ensuring they are contributing to the well being of the business. There is a twice yearly upward appraisal where the subordinate evaluates the boss.

Decision making aims to be particularly democratic on the basis that to get the best out of people they need to feel committed to their work. Often there are company wide votes on decisions which in a traditional organization would be taken unilaterally by the management. For instance, there was a company wide vote on where to buy a new factory and effectively where to relocate to.

Rules and regulations have been abolished and civil disobedience is viewed as a sign of commonsense at work. Expenses are not checked—again there is an emphasis on trust and there are no time clocks; people can work when they please as long as they achieve the output.

There is a programme in operation for new entry managers called 'lost in space' where managers join with no job description for 12 months and can do anything they want as long as they try working in 12 units.

There is a focus on teams as the primary working unit and these are self managing.

Clearly in this case study it can be seen how one organization has actually redefined the organization and where one visionary leader has questioned many of the generally held assumptions about organizations and the management of people. It appears to be characteristic of many of the organizations we would describe as fitting more closely with the virtual organization approach that they question long held beliefs or 'givens' about organizations. We would go so far as to say that in the near future there will no longer be a place for the job or for that matter the actual workplace, the factory or office, as we have known it in the past.

Death of the job

The job as a concept is something that emerged with the industrial revolution; the advent of industrial machinery and the industrial organization lent itself very much to the compartmentalization of tasks into clearly definable groups or 'jobs'. In the main, when the unskilled job was conceived it was routine in nature and people carried out jobs in many cases almost as human extensions of the machinery. As the demand for production increased, over time the job became seen as something which people did on a full-time and permanent basis.

Of course, not all jobs were unskilled. There emerged a number of new skilled jobs associated with new inventions and machinery and there was still a place for some of the old crafts; people would learn such skills by being apprenticed to a 'master' who would effectively take on a guardianship role and over a period of years impart the relevant skills of the trade. In some traditional organizations today, employers continue to view their role in taking care of their apprentices as in *locum parentis*. Traditionally, the apprentice would work under the master for a period of time after which it was assumed that he would then be sufficiently skilled to receive his indentures or mark of having arrived. This then served as the passport for the skilled man's job security for the rest of his life. It was assumed that he would work in a job using this skill until the end of his working life and any variation by moving into another field of work would be seen as very much the exception to the rule. Interestingly, the emphasis was focused on being a time-served apprentice; this very term suggested that experience and skill came with time and only in recent years have some organizations come to question this principle by seeking to train to minimum standards rather than fixed time periods.

With the development of the professions there was a similar emphasis on the importance of learning one's profession over a number of years through guided experience and more academic education. In a similar way to the skilled trades described above, professions were specifically focused, compartmentalized and considered as a chosen route for life.

As organizations began to grow and with the advent of the large industrial corporation the compartmentalization and specialisation of work only became reinforced. So, within the organization specialist functions evolved which called for specially skilled and trained person-nel; some of these were directly related to the business but there was also the growth of the 'staffer', who contributed less directly often by giving support to the line. And as the size of the organization increased, different layers in the hierarchy were created, and even here there was a mentality of specialization and segmentation; first line managers were considered different to second line, directors different from managers.

It is this logic, structure and order which is being thrown into disarray with the emergence of the virtual organization. Some would argue that we are returning, albeit in a new age form, to a mentality which actually existed before we had jobs; where people worked when and where they could and wanted to and ultimately took care of themselves, rather than being looked after by their organization or profession. Bridges (1994) talks of the death of the job:

The modern world is on the verge of another huge leap in creativity and productivity, but the job is not going to be part of tomorrow's economic reality. There still is and will always be enormous amounts of work to do, but it is not going to be contained in the familiar envelopes we call jobs. In fact, many organizations are today well along the path toward being 'de-jobbed'.

In looking at the argument for de-jobbing it is helpful to consider the original argument in favour of jobs. Jobs were geared to reasonably predictable and measurable environments where people and the businesses were best organized by being co-located and given a clear unambiguous remit. They could be overseen, figuratively if not physically, and they were held accountable for achieving certain tasks and outputs. Many people found security in the routine and the predictability of it all, and the fact that the organization was often large and institutional meant that people invariably became reliant on it and institutionalized. Jobs came with hierarchical position or recognition as a specialist expert and this gave a sense of purpose and for many led to public or social acceptance and status. Value judgements would often be made about people based on the job they held, their level, title and organization. This helped people outside the organization understand something about those within it and it helped those within the organization to see where they fitted into the broader social picture. Indeed in many traditional organizations, the hierarchical structure internally might be seen as a microcosm of the broader social hierarchy.

Many of the original arguments supporting the old picture of the job have now been swept away by the social, economic and technological changes we have previously discussed. No longer is there a need to co-locate and in fact there are many advantages to be gained from geographic dispersal of the organization, which we will look at in the next section. Working within a fixed time window is also an anachronism; the nine-to-five job and the clock watching mentality which comes with it will only constrain the ability of the organization in the future to meet the needs of the customer or client. As organizations increasingly operate on the world stage there is a need to be available to talk to others in other parts of the world when they are available. More than this, there is a strong resource argument supporting the idea of time-sharing office, factory and computer facilities. Equally there is a disadvantage associated with generating a sense of job permanence with mechanisms such as job descriptions, career structures and salary grading. Such systems mitigate against flexibility; flexibility in a practical sense when the organization needs to change its strategies and plans and flexibility of mind when the individual is required to adapt.

Then there is the human argument which recognizes that in order to get the best out of people it is more effective to allow them to work in the way they prefer to work: this calls for open mindedness in terms of, for instance, location, rewards, time issues, and environment and trust that given sufficient choice the individual will ultimately produce the required results. Furthermore, people now expect to be treated differently.

Social expectations have changed dramatically throughout the 20th century: people expect to have more control, to be given choices and to be treated with individual dignity. This is in stark contrast with the common view of employment in the past where even into the 20th century we have seen the legacy of the master/servant relationship, where key behaviours were obedience, loyalty, respect for seniors and where the employment contract was built upon the concept of 'a fair day's work for a fair day's pay'. Whereas in the past it was assumed the most senior people in the organization were more knowledgeable than their juniors, to apply this thinking today would be a dangerous approach; in many cases the real expertise is held lower down the hierarchical structure.

The fact that in the future jobs are unlikely to exist in the form that we have known them, does not, of course, mean that work will cease to exist; as suggested earlier in this section all the signs are that, despite advances in technology, the potential for work is actually increasing. It is just that the way work is organized is changing and this calls for a new mind set on the part of most of the key players in the organizational environment. Here we will look specifically at the new mind set required by the human resource specialist, by the 'professional portfolio worker' and by what we describe as the 'white collar labourer'.

The human resource specialist

Increasingly the human resource function is having to tackle issues of organizational design, structure and form. There is also a challenge presented by the need to manage organizations where the real value and power lies in the expertise and talents of its knowledge workers. Furthermore, the distinctions between those who are part of the organization and those who are outside of it are rapidly blurring. In the 1980s, the first tentative steps were taken in redefining the job; early experiments in job-sharing and job-splitting were then seen as quite adventurous. Part-time work used to be predominantly the domain of the clerical or support worker rather than the professional, and such part-timers were not taken as seriously as their full-time colleagues. Part-time working, though, is increasing in many developed countries, including the UK, Germany, The Netherlands and Sweden. The variations in types of part-time or full-time work are many. The following list is only partial:

- Temporary labour
- Temporary professional
- Fixed term contract
- Consultancy
- Retained experts
- Contracted-out services.

The workers who were once described as peripheral are fast becoming part of the mainstream. Handy (1994) reinforces the fact that the demarcation is fading when he says:

> I can see a situation in which it will no longer be possible to draw the distinction between full- and part-time work, when 'retirement' will become purely a technical term, indicating an entitlement to financial benefits, and when 'overtime' as a concept will seem as outmoded as 'servant' does today.

Such variety in the way in which people work in or for the organization means that there is a key role for the human resource professional in co-ordinating a disparate, diverse and increasingly geographically dispersed working population.

Historically in many traditional organizations, the human resource function has been focused on establishing rules and regulations, monitoring or 'policing' the workforce through policies and procedures relating to the management of people. In essence the human resource team were there to maintain the *status quo*. Admittedly there were some exceptions where more enlightened human resource teams operated more as change masters, contributing ably to organizational development and the development of people, but these have tended to be in the minority.

Given the changing organizational map, with its complex web of contributors, members and semi-members, there has never been more of a need for the human resource professional to contribute to the success of the business. This sentiment is echoed by Snell (1994) who says:

> In the virtual organization, HR's focus will expand to unite the needs of the individual with those of the organization. This is a major shift, demanding HR to become agents of change, preparing management and employees for the virtual organization.

The virtual organization calls for a different mind set compared to the traditional organization human resource role. There is a need for more tolerance of individuality as opposed to a constant search for uniformity, an ability to cope with ambiguity and there is a role in understanding the needs of the business at a strategic level and providing expert advice on the human resource implications of such issues. In many of the organizations which we assessed as being closer to the virtual organization model we found that there was a tendency for more interchangeability of personnel between line and human resource functions. Often in the traditional organizations the human resource staff had developed their own empires and specialist expertise and in doing so had lost sight of the real needs of the business. Interestingly, in these organizations individuals often developed as generalists rather than specialists which seems contrary to the traditional model.

In resourcing the business the traditional approach has been to fill vacancies, usually based upon job descriptions. As we have suggested in previous chapters, the classic job description is becoming redundant. The job description tended to describe key tasks and activities, often for everyone in the organization. It is less easy to do this in an organization where tasks and activities are changing daily due to changes in the market place or specific customer requirements or developments in technical capability.

The new imperative is to try to identify and define the key behaviours and competencies which are required for success in the role or organization. The emphasis should be on role rather than job. To some this may appear to be an issue of pure semantics; but the need here is to stress a holistic, flexible and evolutionary view of activity at work rather than a fixed statement of activities. In a similar way the shift is away from inputs (what needs to be done) to outputs (what success looks like). The individual is effectively enabled to use his or her unique human talents, including judgement to decide 'the 'how' component of the job.

At the Intel Corporation, they define roles around sets of competencies rather than traditional jobs. Many organizations find that such competencies tend to be more enduring in terms of the business need and they are often transferable from one organization or business sector to the next. Having identified the essential behaviours required in the business it is then possible to use this as a framework for resourcing, developing and managing people.

The relevance of the old territory of the human resource specialist can now be questioned. Who really needs job evaluation when there are no jobs in the old sense, when roles, tasks and responsibilities are changing frequently and where it is impossible to predict quite what people will be doing in three or six months' time? Bridges (1995) describes parts of Hewlett Packard where managers use ranking as a way of evaluating people; people are ranked based on their value to the company regardless of their level in the hierarchy—it is contribution to the business which counts.

At Microsoft, software design teams often will start a project with engineers working all the hours they can to get things going. The focus is on output, no-one monitors hours as such but everyone is very conscious of their level of output and performance. There are no bosses in the traditional sense; new team members are allocated buddies/mentors to offer help when needed. There are no standard career routes; people move from one project to the next depending on their expertise and the needs of the business. In doing so they build up expertise and a reputation; they develop their own personal portfolio with the large corporation.

It is interesting to reflect on the fact that this is a culture which is no doubt strongly influenced by the founders of the organization who worked in this way when they were driven by the technical challenge of developing the personal computer among the interest groups of Silicon Valley in the 1970s.

In an organization which is constantly adapting and changing its structure in this way, and which is so focused on the needs of the business, there are new pressures and demands upon the members which the human resource specialist needs to oversee and help manage. There is clearly a high risk of employees experiencing stress due to factors such as overload of work, conflicting roles and particularly ambiguity where there is possibly little formal direction and the onus is placed on the shoulders of the individual to define his or her role.

There is a critically important role in helping members of the organization to develop the necessary skills and knowledge required to succeed in the organization. Continuous training throughout a person's life is more likely to be the norm rather than the exception, as people are driven to update in order to exploit new technologies. While the core members of the organization will require training and development there is a need for the organization to consider the needs of those workers previously considered peripheral and to make some provision available. Arguably employees will probably be capable of successfully pursuing several different careers during their working lives. We will look in more detail at the place of learning in the virtual organization in Chapter 8.

In many large organizations in the past there was a well-established approach to career planning and development. It was possible to predict with reasonable accuracy the position and responsibilities which a junior manager might be commanding in 20 years' time, having climbed the corporate ladder. In the virtual organization there is no corporate ladder as such; members of the virtual organization often find it difficult to express the structure visually, because more important than structure is the ability of the organization to adapt its form according to business needs. Writers on organizations over recent years have wrestled with words and pictures to try to find the right analogies for the future in organizational design; we have heard of the 'clover-leaf' organization, the 'do-nut' and the organization as a series of 'eggs'. Indeed, our own research Whitlam (1990) suggested the death of the traditional organization to be replaced by a series of 'fluid cells', each with a finely balanced combination of independence and dependency.

For those responsible for managing the human resources of the organization this means a different role to that of traditional career planning and development. Rather than being able to advise people with any real degree of certainty of their future prospects, there is a role in helping them to consider a range of options, to make sense of their previous experience and to build up their portfolio and be able to present or sell themselves, whether within the organization or outside of it.

The professional 'portfolio worker'

Just as there is a need for a new mind set to be established among human resource managers, there is a need for all workers in the organization to rethink their *modus operandi* whether as employees, managers, leaders, professionals, experts, or entrepreneurs. Handy (1994) has provided a useful model in talking of the growth of portfolio workers, who behave in the way professionals have historically operated, by charging a fee for their work which is based on their level of experience and quality of work. We are seeing a significant growth in this way of working. Once you were either unemployed, employed or self-employed; now there are shades of grey—some people are employed part of the time and self-employed and unemployed other times. A number of individuals and organizations have caught on to the fact that this is possible and have developed the right mind set to cope with such ambiguity and plurality of roles. Others, including a number of governments, are finding this difficult; regulations for eligibility to state benefits, for instance, are focused on the unemployed with little mainstream support being available for the semi-employed or the occasionally employed. Individuals who may be pressed into portfolio working as the casualties of corporate down-sizing will tend to fall into two main categories: those who adapt to the change and for whom it becomes a major opportunity and revelation and those who fail because they apply old style traditional corporate thinking to the portfolio role. Approaching portfolio working with the traditional organization mind set will mean that the individual's business may never move beyond the drawing board or will ultimately hit rocky ground. The traditional corporate mind set says you need corporate budgets before doing anything, you develop products and market and sell them, you need to invest heavily up front before business starts working and there are teams of support personnel to help and assist you. Successful portfolio workers, however, succeed because of their understanding that the reverse is true in the small virtual organization: you need to act and generate income and use this as a way of funding investment, meeting immediate customer and client needs. Demonstrating responsiveness and flexibility is of tantamount importance and you take personal responsibility for both the broad picture and the detail.

Of course, there are tremendous benefits for the portfolio worker, not least the independence of, once established, being able to choose within reason who one works with and for. There are disadvantages too, such as the need to be able to balance workload, to find some way of usefully filling the time during periods of non client or customer based activity. This could be used to continue to build the business, to work on administrative tasks, for personal education or even to pursue a second vocation or profession.

So, what are the qualities required to be a portfolio worker? It is of vital importance for the portfolio worker to be able to market him or herself. This means being able to recognize the strengths of one's portfolio and being able to present these in a cogent and impressive way to potential purchasers. This suggests a need for classic sales and marketing skills as well as the need to be able to build strong long term relationships. An element of personal judgement is required in order to be able to judge who to work with and for, and indeed with whom to form strategic alliances. Simply possessing the technical ability will no longer be sufficient: even the long established professionals, such as the solicitors and accountants are having to adopt more of a marketing and business minded approach. Also, the portfolio worker needs to be able to manage the business itself. This may not be a big business in terms of headcount but there is a need to co-ordinate people and organizations, to project manage, to sub-contract assignments and non-core activities and to manage finance. There is a need to exploit the technology in order to be able to move swiftly at the behest of the customer or client.

The 'white collar labourer'

At the same time as seeing the rise of the portfolio worker we are seeing an increase in another type of independent worker, which we describe as the 'white collar labourer'. This may sound like a contradiction in terms, but as large organizations reduce their permanent employees to the hard core of co-ordinators and project managers and seek to operate more like the small companies in responding to business needs as and when required, they will seek to reduce unnecessary overhead commitments. This means buying in portfolio expertise at a premium when needed, rather than carrying the cost of such personnel all year round. Working on the same principle, it is often more cost effective to reduce the organization's reliance on in-company administrative support for routine, repetitive and bulk tasks. Many organizations out-source such work to be dealt with by specialist agencies or sub-contracted labour. As a result it is now possible to find substantial (in terms of turnover) organizations which take care of such tasks for the corporation; there are organizations which specialize in managing telephone calls, mailing, cleaning, documentation, computing facilities, to name but a few areas where we have seen growth of the white collar labourer. People working in this way need to be prepared to move swiftly from one project to the next and to work often with routine and major chunks of workload; if they are prepared to live with the lack of intellectual challenge, then the potential rewards are high.

It is interesting to briefly ponder the fate of the secretary in this age of virtual organizations, portfolio workers, white collar labourers and core staff. As we anticipated the coming of the technological revolution there was much speculation that we would move towards the paperless office. Certainly the technology now exists for organizations to communicate effectively without the need for reams of paper and gradually organizations, even some of the more traditional, have come to accept the value of the intranet, if not the internet, for communicating within the organization and beyond it. In the traditional organization the role of the secretary was institutionalized; often one would encounter a hierarchy of secretarial staff related to the status of the managers they were supporting. The role historically has been a supporting one, particularly focusing on the provision of administrative services, especially written and telephone related. The basis for the role was that the manager's time was better spent focused on directly relevant activity than on administration and typing. The skills of the secretary became specialized; there were and still are qualifications in typing, shorthand to help with dictation and in administration. The specialization of the role only served to reinforce the divide between the secretarial and the managerial role. Advances in technology and scrutiny of overhead costs, however, have led to a blurring of these boundaries. The technology is now much more user friendly and managers are more easily able to acquire keyboard and computing skills. There has also been a breaking down of the preoccupation with status which meant that it was considered wrong, even demeaning, for a manager to perform a secretarial role. Unfortunately, it seems to be taking longer to break down the stereotype of the secretary which has inhibited the development of much untapped potential.

There are two trends which can be identified. First, many more organizations are blurring the boundaries, so professional people have administrative responsibilities and secretarial staff are moving into professional roles. Indeed, in the virtual organization the full time dedicated secretarial personnel are likely to form only a small part of the core staff and direct personnel will take care of their own day to day administrative needs, while delegating major or specialist assignments to the centre or to sub-contracted white collar labourers.

Second, it can be seen that many secretarial and administrative workers have decided to continue to enhance their skills and have moved outside the organization to become professional portfolio workers or white collar labourers.

PAUSE FOR THOUGHT

How would you describe your organizational structure?

How have you arrived at this structure?

Do the employees in your business have 'jobs' or 'roles'?

Is successful performance clearly defined?

To what extent does your business make use of multi-disciplinary teams?

To what extent is your organization committed to the notion of the 'portfolio professional'?

What functions of your business are not core activities and therefore likely targets to be considered for sub-contracting or out-sourcing?

To what extent is your organization becoming paperless? Is this a realistic proposition?

How is the role of the secretary changing?

How do you ensure employees feel loyalty to and ownership of the organization?

Innovations in organizational form

So far in this chapter we have looked at the concept of organizational form, suggesting there is a need to think beyond organizational structure. We have identified that there are some major changes taking place outside the organization which are clearly impacting on the nature of roles within it. There is a need for a fresh approach to thinking about organizational form and this calls for particular competencies on the part of those who are responsible for organizational design and the human resources, as well as from those who have hitherto operated within the organization in line, professional or administrative roles.

Next, we will move on under the heading of organizational form to look at the physical implications of the virtual organization and we explore in more depth alternative methods of managing the employees who may be itinerant and geographically dispersed. However, before we do that, let us just reflect on how form is typically represented in the virtual organization.

The virtual partnership

We are describing a small specialist consulting business employing a small number of partners each of whom reside in different parts of the UK. Each partner receives a percentage share of the profits but, unlike traditional partnerships, these sums are paid out when the money is received as opposed to on a six-monthly or annual basis. This is seen as an important motivator, because members see the rewards for success shortly after the event and, of course, have to manage in times of organizational hardship with less reward; making the connection between individual success, organizational success and rewards is easy.

Capital items like cars or computers are purchased by the individuals, consequently the principle is that each can purchase to meet their own requirements. The partnership does, however, take care of issues related to health insurance and public liability.

The partners all work from their respective homes, each having a dedicated part of their home as their office. They are technology driven, using e-mail, fax and telephones to keep in touch. Communication depends on the needs of the immediate project. When working at home, it is not unusual for them to be in contact with each other 20 times in a day; conversely there may be periods of up to a fortnight without contact.

Members of this organization would claim that their office is where their laptop computer is; frequently this is within arms' reach even on vacation. This in itself is an interesting phenomenon, because the boundaries between work and leisure are themselves blurred and this clearly has implications in terms of personal organization and time and stress management. A major potential source of stress which has to be managed is that which comes from role conflict and role ambiguity.

The partnership prides itself on gaining competitive advantage due to the personal level of their service; this includes being available 24 hours per day to clients and providing a speedy response to client needs and requests. To date this has resulted in an organization that is nibbling away at the larger consulting businesses and equally importantly has a higher level of productivity and income per employee.

The partners are knowledge workers, often they are engaged to expose others to best business practice. They pride themselves on the way in which they keep ahead of their competitors by their use of technology. They exploit the use of the internet, particularly to access data primarily relating to their clients or their competitors and to keep up to date with developments in their specialism. Where they work with organizations which have embraced developments in communications technology, they will often communicate electronically.

They are loosely organized, with different partners taking responsibility for different clients and these responsibilities are allocated on a situational basis. Some partners have responsibility for 'leading' certain aspects of the development of their business, for example marketing, but all major issues are discussed and decisions made in a timely manner.

Decision making is swift; day to day financial accountability is delegated to one of the partners and the business is monitored by the weekly reporting on a few critical ratios. Debt is rarely a problem due to the personal relationships that are developed with clients.

Vision building takes place all the time, with the partners often thinking aloud about how to develop the business and once a year this process is formalized in an annual partners' meeting.

Anything that is not their core business is sub-contracted. This includes their accounting, legal services and marketing. In such circumstances the people or organizations responsible for this sub-contracting are seen as allies and part of the team, rather than as suppliers. It is interesting to note that in selecting individuals to work with a critical issue appears to be that the other person shares similar values and beliefs and that there is an element of personal trust and liking for the other party.

Their general relationships with clients are somewhat special, often these will be sustained over many years and the partners will effectively act almost as one of the client's employees. Informality is the key to their relationships.

Most new business is generated through network marketing, however they also engage in the use of some mailshot activity which is a constant source of new leads and enable an organization which is small in numbers to achieve a profile as significant as that of the international giant consultancies with whom it competes.

Associates are employed on a contract by contract basis and great care is taken in their selection to ensure best fit. Usually such individuals have a long standing relationship with the partners and a key issue is integrity: the partners must be able to trust the associates and vice versa. This actually is a factor which is considered more important than ability: it is felt that one can give training to develop the relevant skills and knowledge but if there is no real basis for trust then the relationship simply will not work. Bearing in mind the fact that this organization is founded on its intellectual property, this is a particularly sensitive issue and one which the partners are always aware of when forming new relationships.

The business is supported by a secretarial resource who is themself a self-employed person working for numerous clients, but who over the years has developed a special relationship in terms of providing a reliable service to the partnership. Their business is also located approximately 150 miles from the nearest partner, but with a high reliance on the use of technology the service level is high.

As the partners may not necessarily meet very often, each year there is an informal opportunity to pull the partners and their families together to review the previous 12 months and to consider the future. This is seen as an important annual event as it reinforces the organizational identity and enables the families of organizational members to appreciate the work of the partnership and equally for the partnership to recognize the sacrifices made by family members coping with the pressures of life with a virtual organization partner.

In principle, the above case study describes how our own organization operates. The particular features include the lack of recognized structure, restrained control, individual accountability, personal responsibility and 'no sacred cows'.

Having identified some major trends in terms of patterns of employment and ways of working, it is appropriate to turn our attention to some of the practical opportunities which are presented by the technological advances affecting the workplace. Many forward thinking organizations have now established virtual offices and workspaces and some organizations now have a bigger presence in cyberspace than in factories and offices. It might be considered that the technological capability has now advanced beyond the psychological ability of the manager or worker to cope with working at the leading edge of technology; hence the attention now given by many organizations to addressing the psychological impact of new ways of working before and during the implementation of many initiatives. Nevertheless, we are witnessing a revolution in working practices and many of our previously held assumptions about the physical requirements of the organization are being questioned.

If we were to track the history of the organization from a physical perspective, an interesting cycle of development emerges which is clearly related to a variety of macro trends.

Prior to the industrial revolution, organizations, where they did exist, tended to be local and often centred around the family, whether in the form of a particular craft or in rural communities. We used the term cottage industry to suggest a small, co-operative and community based organizational pattern. With the industrial revolution, we saw a migration to the cities as the factories were established. Clearly efficiency was gained from having personnel grouped in one place in order to make use of capital equipment. Control was made easier due to the fact that you could literally oversee workers. In its heyday, the factory came to represent a sense of permanence, industry and the work ethic. In the worst examples ecologically, though ecology was less of an issue at the time, it was a dirty, unhealthy, noisy environment where the working underclass were exploited by the industrial aristocracy.

With the development of the large corporation, led by the captains of early industry, there was a move to build large, impressive institutional buildings—the bigger the better; size was an effective demonstration of the organization's success. This is a mentality which is still seen in many of the organizations we would categorize as traditional, but it is an approach which is challenged head on by the virtual organization.

As early as the turn of the century we saw the development of the garden city movement, which aimed to create a new living environment and to attract commercial organizations and to provide a suitable alternative to the unpleasant working environment of the factories in the big cities. Also there was an attempt to incentivize organizations to set up on industrial estates and many of the early estates majored on visual impact, on the basis that such places were to be visited and admired. Some aimed to provide a 'nest' facility whereby larger organizations would encourage the development of smaller businesses through being located in the same area. Following the Second World War there was an emphasis on modernization and the previous emphasis on the importance of grand facades was replaced ultimately by a recognition of other more environmental criteria.

In the 1970s the concept of the business park evolved; this was really the high technology version of the industrial estate and again the idea of the organizational nest facility was encouraged. Here, though, we saw the collaboration of universities and local government, encouraging a link to education and research. The business parks were the forerunners of the science parks which stress this issue of educational, research and commercial integration even more proactively. These are usually established on a greenfield site and tend to be categorized as either spontaneous, as in the case of Boston, or managed with amenities, as in the case of Stamford. Science parks have developed in rather different ways in different countries: in the UK there is a major emphasis on the education to industry link and the importance of the transfer of technology is emphasized. This might be seen as recognition of the need to contribute to the management and growth of the knowledge based sector. In France, with the technopoles, there are a number of nation wide networks, some of which are run by large consortia.

Now. with the advances in telecommunications and computing technology, there are some fascinating developments on from such physical organizational groupings. These are sometimes described as virtual business parks or virtual science parks. Hewlett Packard, for instance, was instrumental in establishing the Avon Internet Business Park in the UK. This brings together, free of charge, a number of organizations which wish to advertise their products or services or provide information, by using the Internet as the means of communication. The business park is very real, as the case study below suggests, but it has no physical presence apart from on a couple of computers linked to the Internet.

CASE STUDY 6.3

Avon Internet Business Park

The Avon Internet Business Park (AIBP) is an experimental exercise being run by Hewlett Packard Laboratories, Bristol, UK and is designed to help HP and local businesses understand trading conditions on the Internet.

The AIBP is host to a number of UK businesses which are interested in exploring the marketing potential of the internet. The metaphor of a 'virtual business park' allows us to use everyday terms when talking about the technology which underpins the Internet.

An HP workstation acts as the business park's reception area, presenting a directory of services with clickable links to all of the hosted businesses and handling all the traffic between the Internet and the virtual offices.

Some of the businesses occupy offices on the main machine, while others have offices on separate machines. In the terms of the metaphor—within reason, you can make all the noise you like without disturbing the neighbours. A separate office also brings higher confidentiality by allowing businesses control over who has access to their Internet web pages. You don't have to allow all and sundry into your office.

Just like an ordinary business park, the AIBP provides businesses with a range of ancillary office services.

Occupiers of virtual offices in the park connect via the Internet to their virtual office in the AIBP. They can create advertising and publicity material or simply business information they wish to share (in their real offices) and then, when satisfied, transfer this across the Internet to their virtual office. One of the interesting results of this experiment will be to see how effective the Internet is as a marketing opportunity.

As a business, Hewlett Packard are involved in order to increase their understanding of how organizations which could ultimately be their customers use technology. By working with the local business community they are experiencing at first hand the demands of an electronic commercial environment. Since it was set up the number of organizations establishing a presence on the virtual business park has grown steadily and includes public and private sector organizations ranging from financial institutions to consultancies.

Similarly, there are some interesting experiments taking place in developing the virtual science park. The distinction between the virtual business park and the virtual science park are similar to those of their physical predecessors, the latter focusing more on educational and research links. An example of the virtual science park is being run by the University of Leeds in the UK. The Virtual Science Park allows researchers to keep in constant contact with industry while travelling no further than the nearest computer. This includes software which automatically searches out colleagues and video conference calls them using a number of networks and webs.

Such advances are often given front end funding by forward thinking large organizations. This can be seen in the example of Hewlett Packard above and British Telecom in the telecottaging work which we discuss below. These organizations clearly recognize the advantages to be gained by trying to understand the potential of the technology in providing new ways of working. Effectively they are pushing back the boundaries in a very pragmatic way, where there is clearly no known or accepted approach or body of knowledge. Contrast this with the approach taken by some traditional organizations which seem to make a concerted effort to deny that such advances are yet being taken seriously or are of any relevance to them.

Virtual business parks and virtual science parks may be somewhat difficult to conceptualize because of the lack of a physical presence and admittedly it may be some time before they become common. Not so, however, with regard to the range of flexible working options which organizations are experimenting with. It has been acknowledged by many leading organizations that there is much to be gained, both in terms of motivation of people and in hard financial terms, by adopting innovative and flexible working practices. In many of the company examples we see large organizations operating in a similar way to smaller businesses.

In the virtual organization there is a recognition that there is no logical or business reason why staff should be co-located at all times and why offices should allocate unique and separate places of work for each person. Interestingly, some of the innovations in the use of space have come out of disaster recovery, for example following devastation caused in the London city terrorist bombings and Californian earthquakes. Digital Equipment (DEC), for instance, decided to adopt a hot-desking approach following a fire which burnt down their Basingstoke offices in the UK. With hot-desking employees have no permanent workspace of their own; they have a lockable trolley for their personal possessions which is wheeled to a preferred or available space; from such a space employees are able to access computers and telecommunications systems which are just as, if not more, effective as in the traditional office environment. People carry cordless telephones and computer consoles are pulled down from the ceiling. Otherwise employees set up their office in their car, hotel or home depending on their preferences and the logistics of the task (Kinsman, 1994).

A similar hot-desking strategy has been adopted widely by IBM in both their UK offices and in the USA. Workspace is divided into four categories: managers' offices, permanent administrative workstations, hot-desk facilities for consultants and 'touch-down' desks for short visits from staff. At IBM's marketing headquarters in the UK all employees have a personal moveable telephone number, a 'virtual number', and they book into workstations for the period of their stay. This is referred to as their SMART (Space, morale and remote technology) initiative and the ratio of employees to workplaces is four to one.

Interestingly, it has been found that apart from the cost savings there has been a 36 per cent increase in time spent with the customer (Wilson, 1994). Such approaches cause some of the traditionalists to stand back in horror, particularly where it seems that the manager's status symbols and hitherto visible trappings are abolished. In the traditionalist culture people tend to be more concerned with issues such as the size of their desk or the type of executive chair they have, and often these concerns actually take precedent over the business need. In the virtual organization, though, there is a recognition that the key thing is to meet the needs of the business. Why, for instance, should a computer terminal be allocated to just one individual who only uses it for a few hours a week when it could be made available in a common area for access by anyone who can make good use of it? The managing director of Rank Xerox, a £3.6 billion business, has abandoned his office and now works alongside his colleagues, sharing an oval shaped desk with three other people. By creating an open working environment the size of a tennis court it is believed that there will be faster decisions, better communications and more accessibility.   The advertising agency Bartle Bogle Hegarty has introduced what it calls 'nomad' meeting tables, which employees actually move around the building (Woods, 1996). In Cellnet's new UK premises tables and chairs are informally clustered around the central atrium for meetings; reasonable confidentiality is maintained but informal communication improves as passers-by occasionally engage those meeting in discussion—even directors work in open plan areas and a 'clear desk policy' is encouraged.

Equally there is no reason why the organization should view itself as a discrete physical entity and some innovative approaches have been taken which actually blur the physical boundaries between the organization, partner organizations, the customer and the supplier. Ernst & Young have a 'hotelling' system where consultants are out working with clients most of the time and the clients actually provide a desk and technology as a working base. In New York and Chicago they have reduced office space by 25 per cent and ultimately expect savings of up to $40 million per year. Consultants book into their own organization's base for short blocks of time and are allocated a working space by a central administrator (Barnatt, 1995).

Most organizations which have adopted such approaches recognize the real value which comes from savings in capital equipment and overheads. Effectively such costs are either passed on elsewhere, such as to the hotel, the client or the home and in many cases savings simply come from more efficient use of existing resources or shrinking of permanent facilities. IBM claims savings of up to 30 per cent in office space and architects DEGW survey the utilization of space before recommending redesign and typically find that organizations only achieve 40 per cent occupancy at peak points. They use the term 'intensification" in looking at better use of workspace and view organizational buildings as sponges: they can absorb increasing numbers as and when they are needed (Wilson, 1994).

Linked to the questioning of traditional assumptions about the physical workplace, there has been a dramatic increase in the level of teleworking. This is a term used to describe working at a distance from the organization, often from home, and exploiting technology, in particular, computing and telecommunications, in order to make such arrangements viable. Many organizations are reaping the financial benefits of operating in this way.

Of course, there are potential barriers which need some consideration. For instance, Rank Xerox (Barnatt, 1995) experimented with these approaches as long ago as the early 1980s and found difficulties due to people feeling socially isolated. This tends to support the argument that one of the significant reasons why people attend work at a common workplace is to satisfy social needs. The figures suggest, though, that telecommuting is on an upward trend: it is estimated that there will be a rise from 7.6 million in the USA in 1994 to 25 million by the end of the century (Greengard, 1994).

Some of the arguments in favour of such approaches are related to environmental factors and the advantages which accrue from teleworking and telecommuting with reductions in travel, transport and pollution. At a political level there is considerable interest in such ways of working and the European Union has set a target of there being 10 million teleworkers by the year 2000 and sees advantages in bringing employment opportunities to remote, often rural, areas (Panucci, 1995). One should recognize as well, the advantages here of also being able to meet the needs of those who have a considerable contribution to make to commercial organizations but have no desire or need to relocate to a central office location.

There has been a growth in the formation of telecommuting centres where people can visit a local or conveniently located centre which provides a range of technological and office services to enable them to work at a distance from the main site of the organization. Some of these centres have been set up on commercial terms and some have been positioned as community projects with support from public, charitable or co-operative funding. This has been the case with advances made in the telecottage movement which supports the creation of telecottage facilities. In telecottages people, usually from remote and rural areas, attend a local centre in order to train and work. They are provided with access to technology and to date many telecottages have emphasized the provision of training to help the development of appropriate business and technological skills. While there has been, to an extent, a voluntary sector emphasis in many of the recent experiments, there is a recognition of the value which comes from exploring the potential of such approaches commercially. This is seen by the involvement of organizations such as British Telecom and Apple Computers in helping to support initial funding of certain telecottaging initiatives.

The case study below is drawn from a summary of speeches made at a seminar on telecottaging and published in *Telecottages* (Dengigh, 1992).

Telecottages

The emphasis in telecotttages is on access. Originally telecottages focused on rural areas, but it is recognized that they have a place in urban settings too. The main point is that access is provided to training, learning, information and work. There is a range of types of telecottage: some are commercial, some community focused and some mixed. A European Commission report (Current Experiences and Perspectives for Teleworking 1992) makes three recommendations regarding telecottages: the key development tool should be the telematic centre at a community level, such centres should be multi-purpose in order to be viable and there should be a local focus.

Colin Craig spoke for the Association of Community Enterprises in the Highlands and Islands in Scotland and described a project which started in 1989 with a major invest-ment aiming to bring the most up to date technology to the most remote communities in Europe. Some time was spent studying the Danish experience and four projects were set up including The Isles Telecroft, which is part of a community co-operative and sup-ported by British Telecom with a serious investment by way of funding. All of the pro-jects were set up in areas where there was little by way of technology previously. The challenge has been to achieve demanding targets in terms of revenue and qualitative matters. Also, it is difficult to combine community and commercial objectives and there is a need to ultimately ensure that commercial revenue growth replaces grants. There is a need to generate a local pool of talent. There is evidence of some resistance of com-mercial companies to put out work to teleworkers.

Information on The Shetland Isles Telecroft was presented by Laura Baisley, Manager. This telecroft is situated in the most northerly island in the UK. Crofts are small, exten-sive and part-time agricultural units. There is a strong motivation within the telecroft for people wanting to play a part in the wider community, despite the rustic image which may exist. The parent company of the telecroft is a community co-operative owned by 200 shareholder residents. For a successful operation of this nature it is seen as critical to have a mix of local enthusiasts, an existing business structure and local training with access to technology. This telecroft provides services including design and printing for local businesses and groups, producing stationery for the community, doing word pro-cessing jobs and providing business services to small businesses.

So we can see from the above case study that some of the innovations in ways of working, and effectively in redefining organizational form, bring together an interesting blend of community and commercial interests. It is interesting to note in the telecroft case study the comments regarding the continuing resistance of some commercial organizations to put their work out to workers at a distance and it is worth considering why this might be the case. There is no doubt that such approaches can work on a very commercially viable basis. Witness, for instance, the examples of New York Life which runs a claims office in Ireland using technology to make managing at such a distance work. Similarly, Saztec, a Californian company, has data entry clerks working in China at $2 per day; their work is transmitted electronically and effectively the organization is able to work around the clock and across time zones. It tackles the issue of quality control by employing three people who work independently on the same tasks and data is only accepted when all three give the same response. This might lead one into an argument about the ethics of drawing on cheap labour and human exploitation, but the telecottage examples reviewed in the case study above are seen by their creators as providing valuable employment and personal development opportunities where they would not otherwise exist.

To summarize, we are seeing a breaking down of the traditional picture of the organization as a physical entity, located in one or just a few places. We would suggest the organization as a monolithic structure will soon become a thing of the past. The picture painted in the quotation below (Rogers, 1996) may seem rather futuristic, but it clearly provides food for thought:

> Networks of small companies are emerging as the driving force of the future. Multimedia technologies and industries could end the division of the city into zones of housing, offices and factories. Indeed the distinctions between office and home, work and play, education and entertainment are themselves set to dissolve ...
>
> As homes, schools and workplaces come to centre on a common communications network, buildings themselves will become less and less defined by a single function: the same fundamental structure will serve as a school, an office and a 'factory' ...
>
> In the future buildings will become dematerialized. It will be an age not of solids but of transparency and veils—of indeterminate, adaptable and floating structures, which respond to the needs of users...
>
> As structures become lighter, buildings will become more permeable. There is no reason why pedestrians should not walk through, rather than around them. The street and the park may be part of the building or the building might hover above or below them.

Assessment of form

Finally we provide you with an opportunity to consider your own effectiveness against the critical factor of *form*.

The statements below are designed to assist you in identifying ways in which you can focus on your organization's approach to form. Essentially, this is seen as a prerequisite for helping you move towards becoming a virtual organization. These questions should not be seen as a test; there are no right or wrong answers. However, their effectiveness relies on the frankness of your responses.

Listed below are ten focused statements relating to our research findings about the virtual organization. You may use this brief questionnaire to assess your own department or organization. This is a forced choice questionnaire requiring you to respond against each statement.

Please read each statement carefully and respond by answering either

Yes (agreeing) or No (disagreeing) to each statement. There is no time
limit; it will probably only take two minutes to complete.

1. We work mostly in our teams, often mixing with other parts of the business.	Yes/No
2. All employees have clearly defined job descriptions.	Yes/No
3. For most roles we have identified skills/competencies for achieving successful performance.	Yes/No
4. We are often encouraged to change roles/functions in our business.	Yes/No
5. Our organizational structure seldom formally changes.	Yes/No
6. We seldom exploit the use of technology to manage information.	Yes/No
7. We have few policies and procedures.	Yes/No
8. There is quite a lot of ambiguity about our reporting relationships.	Yes/No
9. Our structure is very well defined.	Yes/No
10. We organize around business processes rather than customers.	Yes/No

Scoring

If you answered Yes to any of the following statements, give yourself 10
points for each Yes.

1 ....
3 ....
4 ....
7 ....
8 ....
Total ....

If you answered No to any of the following statements, give yourself 10
points for each No

2 ....
5 ....
6 ....
9 ....
10 ....
Total ....
Grand total ....

Consider the above grand total as a percentage relating to performance against the factor of *form*. Those organizations which we believe measure up as effective virtual organizations tended to score in excess of 80 per cent.

In this chapter we have looked at how some of our traditional assumptions about the nature of work, the job and therefore the workplace are being questioned. Some organizations are really taking the virtual organization concept into uncharted territory by experimenting with really innovative approaches.

Such changes are being driven by a combination of factors. Clearly technology now permits us to operate in the same organization or team but at a considerable distance. Also people are now starting to question some long held assumptions about the need for people to be in the same location in order to be supervized and managed. Such developments are in many ways potentially liberating and some of the leaders in this area are realizing both the financial and the human benefits of virtual working.

To make such changes does, though, mean letting go of some of the traditional thinking and freeing up one's mind-set; there is a strong need for 'unlearning' of old habits, attitudes and beliefs. The truly virtual organization will be flexible enough to be able to adapt its form to suit its environment.

To innovate in terms of organizational form means that there will be a consequent need to adopt new approaches to communication. Just because new technology makes communication more easy this does not necessarily mean that, unless they work at it, organizational communication will improve. In fact, there is an argument which says that due to the increased reliance on technology there is a need to compensate by ensuring human relations do not suffer as a consequence.

In the next chapter we will move on to look in detail at the next factor in our model of organizational development, *communication*. Effective organizations in the future will focus on effective communications both within the business and outside of it. In fact in the virtual organization the boundaries between the organization and other organizations are often blurred. We will look at the approaches taken by a number of different organizations, some which might be seen as more traditional but which are bringing about major cultural change and some which are evidently operating at the leading edge.

References

Barnatt, C., Office Space, Cyberspace and Virtual Organization, *Journal of General Management*, 20 (4) Summer, 1995.

Bridges, W., *The End of the Job,* Fortune, 1994.

Bridges, W., *Jobshift: How to Prosper in the Workplace Without Jobs,* Nicholas Brealey, 1995.

Dengigh, A., Telecottages *The UK Experience,* Report of the 1992 Seminar, ACRE.

Greengard, S., Making The Virtual Office a Reality, *Personnel Journal,* September, 1994.

Handy, C., Post-industrial Paradoxes, *The Independent,* 20 February, 1994.

Handy, C., *The Empty Raincoat,* Hutchinson, London, 1994.

Kinsman, F., Now You See It Now You Don't, *Human Resources,* Spring, 1994.

Panucci, D., Remote Control, *Management Today,* April, 1995.

Rogers, R., Building the Cities to Move the Spirit, Reith Lectures, *The Independent,* March 13, 1996.

Schor, J.B., *The Overworked American,* Basic Books, New York, 1992.

Semler, R., Managing Without Managers, *Harvard Business Review,* September/October, 1989.

Snell, N., Virtual HR: Meeting New World Realities, *Human Resource Management,* November/December, 1994.

Syrett, M., and Lammiman, J., Developing the Peripheral Worker, *Personnel Management,* 1994.

Whitlam, P., 'The Future of Human Resources', Lecture to Carlsburg Conference on Managerial Competencies, The Netherlands, 1990.

Wilson, S., The Virtual Office at Work, *Human Resources,* Autumn, 1994.

Woods, R., Free-range Bosses Lose Trappings of Office, *The Sunday Times,* 30 June, 1996.

The fuel for the journey

*How well we communicate is determined
not by how well we say things but by how
well we are understood*

ANDREW S. GROVE
(CEO, Intel Corporation)

In this chapter we focus on the way in which organizations approach the subject of *communication,* which we believe is a critical factor in becoming a virtual organization. In particular we:

■ Consider how communication within the business is handled, and show how a spirit of open and prompt communication is encouraged in all directions
■ Explain why deliberate attempts to improve communications through the introduction of systems often fail because they do not address cultural issues or the need to manage unlearning
■ Relate the subject of communication and culture change in a major case study of Scottish Hydro-Electric plc, a traditional public sector utility organization making a successful transformation with privatization against a background of accelerating change
■ Look at how the subject of trust and integrity is addressed in effective organizations and contrast this with organizations where communication is based on fear and suspicion
■ Propose that the team will be the primary working unit in the future and look at how teams communicate effectively and consider the characteristics of 'dysfunctional' teams
■ Discuss how organizations are exploiting technology as a way of communicating both internally and externally and in order to harness the increasing mass of data which is readily available outside of the business
■ Examine a case study of a major project carried out by Andersen Consulting and the Nationwide Building Society which entailed redefining the way in which the organization communicates with its customers, and which has created a competitive edge

So far we have considered in depth two of the four factors which need to be addressed by organizations in order to help them cope with the accelerating change curve, namely *direction* and *form*. We now move on to look at the subject of *communication,* which is the third factor in our model. In many organizations people are quick to label communication as the key factor which needs to be addressed. It is as though this is seen as the common barrier to organizational effectiveness. In contrast, though, few individuals, when probed about communication, are able to realistically pinpoint exactly how such communication difficulties can be resolved. Often if one asks those at the top of the organization 'Where does the problem lie?', one is pointed towards the middle or junior levels; conversely if one asks the same question of those in the lower ranks the finger is pointed firmly upwards.

Furthermore, the graveyard of failed communication initiatives which we have witnessed bears testimony to the fact that simply imposing what is considered to be good communication practice on top of a lagging corporate culture is a guarantee for failure.

We would view the issue of communication as providing the fuel for the journey towards becoming a virtual organization. Having established the route (direction) and being able to select the right vehicle (form) according to the circumstances, it is necessary to be able to move forward on the journey and to keep moving. Successful organizations will establish good communication systems and processes and this effectively will enable the organization to keep moving, to keep progressing and to adapt to changing circumstances. Communication in the context of the model needs to run in all directions and should be continual.

In this chapter we compare and contrast the approaches taken in terms of communication by traditional and virtual organizations. We also look at how certain organizations are attempting to make the transition from traditional to virtual organization. We would suggest that in the virtual organization the overriding characteristics of communication are as follows:

- Communication is tackled simultaneously both through formal and informal mechanisms
- The focus is on ensuring that the business faces the external environment, considerable use is made of customers and suppliers as sources of information
- Communications related technology is exploited
- Efforts are made to establish the right climate and culture for a free flow of communication
- There is an abundance of communication.

As with the issue of organizational form, members of the virtual organization sometimes find it difficult to explain exactly why their approach to communication is effective and often communication seems to be informal and messy. Paradoxically, we have seen many traditional organizations which have implemented formal systems of communication but these have proved less effective than the original publicity hype associated with their launch might suggest.

Internal communication

Since the early 1980s with the publication of *In search of excellence* by Peters and Waterman (1982), the importance of organizational culture and communication has been well publicized. This interest in improving communication has led to a proliferation of organizational communication and culture change initiatives, many of which have been short lived and which have since fallen into disrepute. Unfortunately, such attempts to specifically focus on communication have often been met with scepticism because they have attempted to tackle inherent communication difficulties. Such difficulties in communication are often ingrained in the organization and inextricably linked to the cultural or organizational norms. Cultural norms are often unwritten, however they are extremely powerful and tend to exert tremendous pressure on members of the organization to conform with them. So in the traditional organization where formal and written communication might be the norm, for a new manager who decides to communicate in a different way by, for instance, using informal and verbal approaches, there is a real risk of being ostracized and viewed as a maverick. Similarly it is often noticeable how some people are so inhibited by restrictive cultures when working within the traditional organization that they do not realize the extent of such inhibitions until they actually leave the organization. Only when working in a more liberating environment do they find they are communicating more freely and openly in all directions and they describe a feeling of emancipation or release. This is often the case when people move from a large traditional corporate environment to a smaller more entrepreneurial environment. Conversely, there are examples of some people making this sort of organizational move and finding it difficult to cope with the informality of the 'virtual' way of communicating. This is demonstrated most clearly in the brief case study below.

Making the transition

CASE
STUDY
7.1

In early 1995, Jan joined a small specialist consulting business having previously held senior managerial roles in three major Fortune 500 companies, all of which were in the leading edge of technological innovation. Jan had a strong scientific educational background and his appointment in the consulting business was seen as building up the organization's strength in terms of its scientific expertise. In addition he was assessed as having strong communication and influencing skills.

From the very beginning it was evident that Jan was experiencing some problems in his new role. First, he seemed confused particularly by the lack of structure for communicating with his colleagues. Jan showed a preference for putting things in writing and in many ways would have preferred to have had some sort of manual that would clarify processes and procedures. On one occasion, a few weeks after he had joined the business, he was gently rebuked for his over reliance on e-mail. He was advised that across the business individuals tended to communicate informally relying heavily on verbal discussion.

In a similar way Jan seemed to want to operate in a more formal way in his relationship with both his manager and others in the business. This was the exact opposite of how things tended to work in the organization where there were only really boss–subordinate relationships as such in order to satisfy the needs of client organizations to see some sort of hierarchy. In actual fact the main priority within the business was the individual's specific technical expertise and their ability to generate business.

After one particular meeting which was held over dinner in a restaurant and without a formal agenda, Jan wrote to his colleagues to record what he felt were the agreed action points. His colleagues were surprised at this response, indeed they felt his style was somewhat contractual and this prompted a further meeting in which Jan was provided with an opportunity to express openly the difficulties he was experiencing. At this time Jan expressed the fact that he did not really understand the reporting relationships within the business. He felt he needed greater supervision and support, he also stated that he was unsure as to how to communicate, for instance when to telephone or when to put things in writing. His colleagues did their best to explain how they saw things but found some of these issues difficult to explain. They concluded by explaining that there were few absolutes as to how things worked and he would need to keep 'feeling his way'.

Over the next few months Jan undertook a number of different assignments. It was noted that the content of his work was good, however he was continuing to have problems in terms of how he communicated across the organization. Ultimately Jan was so dissatisfied and frustrated with the situation that he left the organization and returned to another blue chip company and a more traditional corporate environment to which he was clearly more suited.

This is an interesting case study for a number of different reasons. First, it so clearly illustrates that in the absence of formal communication there is a high need for trust. Second, the climate or culture within which communication takes place is also seen as a significant factor and finally this case shows how individuals need to be aligned with the communication philosophy of the organization; where there is a mismatch this is likely to lead to considerable misunderstanding and not a little frustration.

From an organizational perspective, where communication initiatives have failed the problem seems to stem from an assumption that it is possible to tackle communication as a discrete factor in isolation from other issues; often there is a failure to recognize the importance of the history of the organization and the relative place of the current initiative.

We have seen, for instance, a number of organizations attempt to create a Total Quality Management (TQM) culture and in doing so they have tried to open up communications and break down barriers across functions and between different levels of staff. Logically they have understood the argument of the internal customer/supplier relationship and the need for more openness in communication, however they are unable to simply tear themselves away from entrenched behaviours. This was seen in an amusing, if not rather sad, way in the case study of the organization discussed below.

Trying to force communication improvements

CASE STUDY 7.2

We had been working with a major international organization who were committed to a TQM initiative and they had set up a number of workshops to enable employees at all levels to understand the principles of TQM and to try to convince them that they were embarking on an opening up of communication. This was an organization where most staff at the more junior levels were inhibited by their senior management in presenting ideas upwards for fear of saying the wrong thing and the ensuing recriminations. Some of the more enlightened directors realised there was a need to genuinely address this issue. Unfortunately, though, some of the more traditional directors were effectively going through the motions of attempting to encourage more upward communication.

This became most apparent when we were running a session at the end of a workshop which was designed specifically to provide junior staff with the opportunity to raise questions which had been concerning them but which they had previously been fearful of asking. The mechanism used was what we described as an 'Askit basket', whereby employees would write down their question and anonymously put it into a basket along with questions raised by others in the workshop. Such questions could relate to any issue of concern to the employee and a senior director would then attend the session and as questions were picked out of the basket he or she would attempt to answer them as openly and honestly as possible.

On this one occasion, a traditional time-served director was due to field the askit basket questions and he was clearly rather anxious about his ability to answer them. This anxiety was clearly increasing as he saw the basket filling up with questions over the period of the day.

Eventually he became so concerned that he privately approached the facilitator of the workshop and asked if there was any possibility of quietly drawing the basket to one side and reading the questions beforehand, with a view to editing out those questions which he considered too difficult to answer or too threatening.

Apart from the fact that this would have raised serious questions over managerial integrity, it also demonstrated the high level of suspicion and distrust which existed in both directions up and down the organization.

To have taken his proposed course of action would have been a totally self-defeating action and the fact that this particular director was able to think in this way only served to highlight the fact that trying to force a change in behaviour among those who had a clearly entrenched mind set would not work. Forcing this director to be open in communication when he had been used to 30 years of secrecy and suspicion would simply not work. There was a real need for a process of unlearning before new behaviours could be developed, and there was even a question in this case as to whether this person would ever make the transition. One of his major concerns was that questions would be raised which represented a personal attack or an attack on senior management. Also he was concerned that he would not be able to answer some of the questions which might be raised. For someone who came from a school of management where it was assumed that those in authority should have all the answers, to have to admit publicly 'I don't know' would have been too much to bear.

So we see here an example of one of the key findings of our research into the subject of organizational learning and change: the fact that, in order to bring about major organizational change, there is a need to address the matter of unlearning, rather than assuming it is possible to simply overlay new approaches on the existing organization.

Interestingly, organizations such as 3M operate a similar system to the 'Askit basket' which is aimed at opening up communications; however, it might be considered that the climate is more conducive to such approaches than in the case study organization above. In the 3M system, called 'Answer Please', employees ask any questions, by completing a written form, and posing the question to senior executives. Such questions are processed by a co-ordinator who ensures confidentiality is maintained and employees are encouraged to raise any questions or make comments they may have relating to working in the company. 3M stress, though, that this is not to be seen as a replacement for normal working relationships between the supervisor and employee, and staff are encouraged to consider whether their remarks could be better addressed to their own supervisor. This approach specifically demonstrates how the organization recognizes the need to consider not only the system for improving communication but also to address the behaviour of employees and managers. While anonymity is guaranteed if the employee wishes it, there is also a facility for interesting 'Answer Please' letters and replies to be published: employees have the choice. This can be seen as an effective way of asserting the fact that the organization is truly attempting to encourage open and widespread communication in both directions and recognizes the need to both encourage the right culture as well as to establish formal systems which will open up communication.

In contrast, there is a tendency in some organizations to punish the messenger or carrier of bad news. In the words of an Ancient Greek 'None love the messenger who brings bad news' (Sophocles, *Antigone*). Such organizations do not exactly extend their punishments to include cutting off the hand of the bearer of bad news as in Ancient times, but the individual employee may be labelled as disloyal or not committed to the organization. In such organizations the danger is that these businesses do not take the opportunity to really learn what others believe to be true and as a result these organizations may at best miss opportunities or at worst be under threat of extinction. Indeed there is evidence of this phenomenon in a number of different organizations and industries.

Some more forward thinking organizations, like Motorola, have recognized the importance of this issue and as a result have positively published statements which explain as a principle of effective communication 'We do not shoot the messenger'.

Clearly where there are formal attempts to implement effective communication without the cultural issues being addressed there is less chance of success.   Attempts to formally improve communication which have seen widespread failure in many organizations that have failed to address contextual issues include, for example, the use of suggestion schemes and team briefing initiatives.

The origins of suggestion schemes can be traced back several decades and to a period when it was considered exceptional for members of staff, particularly those at a more junior level, to have ideas and suggestions regarding the business outside of their own area of personal responsibility. In some organizations when it was recognized that there was probably a wealth of latent ideas which needed to be drawn out from such employees they would be encouraged to volunteer their ideas to the suggestion scheme. Such suggestions would then be considered, often by a panel of 'worthies', invariably senior managers, who would reward good ideas with a token offering, while taking such ideas and implementing them for the greater good of the business. Companies running suggestion schemes tended to view bright ideas from the lower ranks of the organization as exceptional rather than as the norm. In the worst examples many people would not even hear a response from their organization regarding the suggestions they had made; this in itself would have a very demoralizing effect on such contributors and ironically, considering the motivational intent of such schemes, would cause more dissatisfaction than having no scheme at all.

In the context of the virtual organization the very nature of the suggestion scheme is an anathema. It is assumed that everyone will want, as a part of their everyday job, to contribute to the success of the wider business; why is there a need for a special scheme to encourage people to do what they should be doing anyway? In the virtual organization members of the organization are always looking for and recommending ways of doing things more effectively or differently. Rather than such behaviour being seen as exceptional it is seen as normal. Increasingly traditional organizations which are recognizing the need to change are removing formal suggestion schemes altogether.

In a similar way team briefing initiatives, which have historically been introduced into organizations in an attempt to improve communication, have become more and more out-moded. The principle of team briefing is remarkably simple. Those at the top of the organization develop a core brief regarding developments in the business and this is briefed down through the organization on a regular basis with those being briefed given an opportunity to raise questions they may have upwards. This as a process is meant to improve the flow of communication up and down through the organization. In many of the traditional organizations we have worked with or studied, the success of team briefing has been very limited. This has been related to a number of limiting factors associated with the constraints of a traditional culture. For instance, even where downward communication has been improved through the implementation of team briefing there have been difficulties associated with upward communication. Again, attempts to formalize communication have proved difficult; it appears that there is more of a need to create the right environment so that effective communication can take place naturally. This is likely to be a more effective strategy than setting up a system with rules regarding how communication should and should not be conducted.

Evidently in the traditional organization communication tends to be formalized, structured and is often carried out in accordance with a protocol which is often overtly declared in rules and regulations regarding who should communicate with whom. There is an emphasis on written communication over and above verbal communication and it is common to find an overly detailed approach being taken to, for instance, writing up minutes of meetings and following up verbal discussions with letters or memoranda of confirmation. It is as though there is a contractual requirement to record conversations which take place internally due to an underlying mistrust or suspicion of others.

Also, such written communication is often seen as a way of ensuring that a common picture of what was discussed verbally is arrived at. It seems there is a need to compensate for the fact that the verbal communication is not as effective as it might have been and hence the different parties are likely to have different impressions of what was agreed.

In the command and control hierarchical organization the emphasis is placed on top-down communication, whereas in the virtual organization people communicate in whatever way and with whoever they need to in order to move the business forward. Interestingly, there will be a high level of cross department and cross functional communication and this will lead to people either consciously or sub-consciously acquiring new knowledge about the business. This helps in the development of an environment where knowledge and expertise are shared as opposed to guarded in a protective and jealous way.

Virtual organizations are known for their speed of communication. If you communicate a key message to one member of the organization you can be assured that within a very short period of time other relevant members of the organization will have received the same information, without a great deal of distortion due to the 'Chinese whispers' effect. In the worst examples of the traditional organization, however, there is a tendency for communication to be considerably distorted because of selective listening, perceptual distortion or deliberate attempts to re-interpret messages. It is believed that this is related largely to the fact that in the virtual organization there is more openness in communication and trust in the intentions of others. Also, there is less demarcation of roles and responsibilities due to the fluid form of the virtual organization and people tend not to become so entrenched in their own parochial mind-sets as they each have a strong vested interest in success.

In the virtual organization there is a genuine spirit of openness and access to information. Also, people are told of the reason for doing what they do and the impact this has on the business. What is more, they are actually interested in the impact of their work on the business as a whole. In smaller organizations this, it seems, is an easier issue to address. This does not mean it is not possible in the large organization, but, as with many matters of communication, it is something the large organization has to really work at.

Jack Welch, Chief Executive of General Electric, consciously worked at breaking down the barriers to effective communication which arose in GE. He recognized the way such barriers were inhibiting the business and he worked to establish the concept and reality of a boundaryless organization. In defining this term we are told 'Boundarylessness is Welch's term for breaking down the barriers that divide employees— such as hierarchy, job function and geography—and that distance companies from suppliers and customers' (Tichy and Sherman, 1993).

In the case of Scottish Hydro-Electric plc, which is discussed in detail in the case study later in this chapter, again there is evidence of a conscious effort to break down barriers which had evolved internally for various reasons. Here it was considered there had been an over emphasis in the past on sub-cultures which had developed within the organization and were related to matters such as geographical location, the nature of the business or history and tradition.

Similarly, it has been reported that British Aerospace is planning a corporate transformation aiming to increase efficiency by 30 per cent in a decade and Dick Evans, Chief Executive, notes that in order to deliver on such an ambitious plan 'we have to remove all the barriers between the different pieces of the business and create a single British Aerospace identity and culture—something this company has never had ... If structure is a barrier to delivering what we want, then we will change the structure' (Lorenz, 1996).

Of course, it is not necessarily possible to simply tear down the barriers to effective communication by announcing that they should no longer exist. Where the organization is large and where there is a strong history and culture of functional demarcation of responsibilities and interest then it takes time to establish a spirit of openness; one of the key issues to be addressed is the need to build trust, particularly where there may have previously been suspicion of those who may be physically and functionally located in other areas of the organization.

Trust and integrity

The importance of developing a climate of trust cannot be underestimated and this is something which is apparent in the virtual organization. This quality of trust and integrity which is vital, is, as with many of the qualities of the virtual organization, difficult to define. It might be considered even more difficult to develop in organizations where it evidently does not already exist. Nonetheless, there are some useful indicators which might be considered by those seeking to move toward the virtual organization model.

One of the key issues in the virtual organization which has an impact on the whole subject of trust is the fact that people are often physically split up from their colleagues or managers. This is particularly the case in organizations operating approaches such as teleworking and telecottaging which were discussed in the previous chapter. Here there is a particular need to be able to trust members of the organization who are operating at a physical distance from their managers or leaders. Equally, in organizations where members are separated geographically due to the nature of the business, for instance because it is meeting the needs of customers in different parts of the world or where business functions are carried out in various locations, again trust takes on a special meaning.

With increasing globalization it appears that the trend is away from co-location and that organizational members will have to contend with the stress and insecurity which can accompany working at a great distance from the centre of one's team or organization.

Effective teams and· organizations which are geographically dispersed do tend to compensate for the time apart by ensuring that there are occasions for coming together. The coming together, it should be emphasized, is not always to conduct operational activities. Technically many of these activities can be conducted at a distance by harnessing the power of telecommunications and computing technology. Often, however, in the virtual organization the coming together is evidently designed to address some of the social human needs which may not be met through everyday eye-to-eye contact. So conferences become festivals and occasions for fun, leisure or even celebrating success. Families are often invited to get togethers as a way of developing the sense of belonging and the fact that the organization is really a special kind of family in its own right. To the onlooker from the traditional organization such activities may appear frivolous or irrelevant but they have a real purpose in meeting a basic human need for social contact.

Handy (1995) raises the question of how to manage people you do not actually see and he emphasizes the special need for trust—a factor which does not sit comfortably with the traditional organization which is used to control. Handy refers to the virtual organization as a concept without a place and quotes the fact that we have for some time seen the success of sales forces working without a physical place and the Open University in the UK which has for some time pushed back the barriers as an educational institution without a place. He emphasizes the particular need for trust in the virtual organization and suggests there are certain principles of trust which need to be recognized. Included are the following:

■ Trust is not blind; there is a need to develop relationships of trust over time and it is difficult to really develop trust with more than say 50 people.
■ There is a need when building an environment of trust to be able to constantly adapt and change. (This is a theme which we pursue in more depth in the next chapter.)
■ There is a need to accept that you can create an environment of trust but at the same time be ruthless if people are not shaping up in terms of job performance.
■ There is a need for the leaders in the organization to actively embody the values or mission of the organization.
■ There is a need to ensure that there is still a level of personal contact: Handy noted that 'Paradoxically, the more virtual an organization becomes, the more its people need to meet in person'.

It is this final point which the virtual organization manages effectively by reaping the benefits of distance working and physical flexibility, while recognizing the requirement to develop a sense of belonging.

In the virtual organization there is also a genuine sense of trust and respect for the specialist knowledge and expertise of one's colleagues. This is an environment where individuals do develop real expertise because the body of knowledge may be relatively small due to the high rate of change. People acquire knowledge and new skills quickly—the virtual organization will normally pride itself on factors such as speed of response and in the knowledge based sector this means acquiring and using information more effectively and speedily than your competitors. The organization is also likely to be working under considerable time constraints which means that there is a particular need to be able to trust your colleagues to do what they know how to do best or at least where they may not know the answers, to apply good judgement. At the same time it is important to stress that trust is not to be confused with tolerance of anything other than best possible performance. Colleagues in the virtual organization tend to set high standards for themselves and for others and those who fail to perform tend to be quickly exposed and confronted.

In the case study below we see how a traditional organization is attempting to embrace many of the principles of the virtual organization and it is interesting to note the particular focus placed on the importance of the cultural aspects of communication.

The case study has been drawn from the work of the senior management of Scottish Hydro-Electric plc, who have been successfully involved in implementing a major culture change programme. This has been introduced in the light of the privatization of the electricity supply industry in the UK and with the advent of a more competitive market in which electricity supply organizations need to ensure they deliver an excellent service to customers while reducing internally inefficient and often historical practices. It is recognized in the industry that the future will be competitive, uncertain and performance focused.

In many ways it shows how a traditional organization is managing the transition as it commits to operate in a more future focused way. The culture of the public sector in this industry traditionally emphasized the importance of public service with no performance motive and no competition. For staff this meant stability and security of employment and what has been described as an 'entitlement culture'. They knew what their job was, what it would be in the future and could plan their careers with confidence. Organizational change would be very slow and then only after protracted discussion, consultation and agreement with staff and their trade unions. Furthermore, there was a low level of accountability for most people and the effort put into the job would be minimal.

Clearly this industry, as with many of the utilities, is currently in the midst of an accelerating change curve and in order to manage this it can be seen that there are a number of structural, human resource and industrial relations issues which need to be addressed simultaneously.

There follows a more detailed explanation of the organization's culture change initiative under key headings as summarized from an internal review of the organization's approach.

Managing culture change at Scottish Hydro-Electric plc

Scottish Hydro-Electric is an expanding energy group supplying both electricity and gas and serving customers throughout Britain. Its prime objectives are to give customers exceptional products, service and value for money. The company's roots are in the north of Scotland and 69 per cent of the electricity sales volume is in Scotland, where electricity is generated and delivered through the power system network and supplied to domestic, commercial and industrial customers.

There is a recognition that staff deliver performance of the organization to other stakeholders and there is a need to increase their level of satisfaction and performance while maintaining their commitment. It is seen that there are a number of key issues to address:

- Management competence
- Staff motivation
- Devolution of power and authority to the front line
- Succession planning.

Management competence

Until privatization of Scottish Hydro-Electric most managers had joined the industry as graduate engineers or with craft skills and the emphasis was on technical competence and procedures. Staff had guaranteed jobs and automatic salary increments linked to length of service, and remuneration was agreed at a national level; therefore there was no real need for managers to tackle issues of motivation or to deal with change. Managers were selected against technical criteria without there being any structured approach to selection. Poor performance was rarely dealt with, except by offering generous severance terms.

In the future, managers will have to be highly developed people managers and this means they need to:

- Deliver outstanding performance from their staff
- Have excellent interpersonal skills
- Exhibit leadership at all levels
- Have coaching skills
- Be good listeners
- Have the ability to give and receive feedback to ensure the removal of fear
- Regularly practise performance management
- Respect the value of their own staff
- Realize that all staff have a contribution to make given the opportunity
- Demonstrate the company's values.

The first stage in attempting to move towards the achievement of these goals has been to develop a set of 10 managerial competencies for all managers in the organization. These reflect the company's values and are:

- Leadership
- Developing people
- Planning and delivering results
- Commercial awareness
- Flexibility
- Judgement and decisiveness
- Organizational awareness
- Team working
- Impact and influence
- Customer service.

These qualities form the basis for assessing and selecting managers, for developing them in their current roles and for identifying those with potential for the future. There is a link in to the company's performance management system by using these competencies for giving feedback and coaching managers.

Assessment centres have been introduced to select managers at all levels and this has involved a significant investment with over 150 assessment centres being run over a two-year period.

Some managers clearly continue to have difficulty in changing their perspective as they do not regard people management as a critical issue, nor do they possess the basic key skills and attitudes needed to get the best from their staff. However, efforts continue to improve management skills against the key competencies that have been defined.

Staff motivation

In the past, staff were motivated by a sense of pride in maintaining the electrical supply to all customers, many of whom were based in remote locations. Cost was not an issue, more important was the need to provide a service to the community and to respond to faults quickly. There was also a sense of staff rallying round to solve problems and the main focus was on technical excellence. Staff were well paid and so long as they moved around, had the opportunity to progress.

In the future, there is a need to channel the motivation which has always existed when dealing with emergency situations into everyday work. Staff will be expected to be valued for their contribution and the company must focus on building the self-esteem of staff. At the same time there is a need to retain the unique commitment to service to the community and pride in the job at all levels. Underpinning this will be a performance management system which rewards the contribution of the individual and the team both financially and non-financially. They will also be given opportunities to develop their skills and career and there will be concerted efforts to break down the 'them and us' attitude. Internal communication needs to be outstanding so that staff feel they know what is going on and have the information they need to do their job better.

Activities to bring this about include the development of a grading structure for all staff which is perceived as fair and competitive in the external market. A bonus system is to reward individual success against important short-term targets and the performance management system will reward sustained performance.

The performance management system has been introduced with the provision of full training for managers, so that all staff have a personal development plan which will help them achieve their aims for career development.

Ultimately, the incremental salary system will be replaced by a performance-related pay structure. A flexible benefits scheme will give individuals choice and remove some of the status barriers which exist.

A communication strategy is being introduced based on an extensive audit of staff and trade union officials' views.

It is considered that the main challenge here is to overcome the fear which employees may feel regarding the security of their jobs, given the high rate of change in the industry and uncertainty in the economy. It is recognized by staff that the power base of the trade unions is becoming weaker and many staff feel vulnerable. It is also recognized that the company should seek to develop a committed rather than a compliant staff. In order to manage these barriers the company is developing a security agreement with the trade unions which, while not guaranteeing jobs for life will set out best practices for avoiding compulsory redundancies wherever possible.

Devolution of power and authority to front line staff

In many areas in which the company provides a service, such as in the more remote Islands of Scotland, there are examples of staff fulfilling a wider and more responsible role in an effort to deliver excellent service to the customer. This has been seen where team working initiatives have entailed the establishment of teams which have taken on extra responsibility without extra financial reward. Also, there are a number of well qualified staff who are in a position to take on additional skills.

The intention is for each front line member of staff to have the skills, authority and desire to act in any situation on the way that is in the best interests of the company and for all to understand the importance of customer loyalty.

Efforts are continuing to introduce team working and the introduction of a new performance management system has led to individual performance development plans for front line staff.

New business negotiating committees are to focus on their own business requirements within the company and there is a joint commitment with the trade unions to jointly train managers and local trade unions on how to deal with and introduce change.

There has been a major shift in the relationship with the trade unions towards a joint problem-solving partnership. This has meant sharing information with the trade unions and a joint project management relationship in the introduction of initiatives such as the company job evaluation scheme.

It is expected that the introduction of a single pay structure will highlight the anomalies that have existed for many years and which have been exacerbated by changes in job roles due to recent structural and technological changes which have not been reflected in job grade or pay. A real challenge is to resolve the situation of under and over payment. Difficulties will include the fact that some of the managers may not have the necessary interpersonal skills to achieve the best level of internal communications and the trade union representatives are generally untrained beyond the requirements for basic industrial relations. It is for these reasons that the company is running joint managerial/trade union training programmes in employee relations in order to upgrade skills and knowledge.

Succession planning

Historically progression through the company has been through a hierarchical chain of command, depending on seniority and length of service rather than job performance. Furthermore, movement in and out of the company was nearly always within the electricity supply industry for engineers and professional staff.

Many senior and middle managers did not have the required skills and understanding required to operate in a private sector company.

The removal of management layers has reduced the number of managers at all levels. It is planned to only recruit high calibre managers in the future with the potential to take on more responsibility and bigger jobs.

There has been a special effort to identify those managers with potential to reach executive and board level positions. Potential candidates for such office have been through a development centre process and assessed against the competencies required for such future job roles. Each attendee is provided with feedback and individual development plans are developed. These managers are referred to as 'developers'. Additionally, a group's 'feeder' managers have been identified and provided with their own development centres in an effort to prepare them to develop into the roles currently held by the 'developers'. This approach to identifying potential and preparing managers for further development is seen as an ongoing process.

In tandem with this initiative there is a review of the compensation packages on offer in order to ensure that such staff are competitively rewarded.

To summarize, it can be seen that in the case study above the organization needed to contend with a number of challenges and paradoxes which might well be applicable to any organization seeking to make the transition from a traditional culture towards the virtual model:

■ A need to move fast in changing the culture, but to recognize the history and be sensitive to the requirement of encouraging people to change rather than being able to force such change.

■ A new approach to industrial relations with a true sense of partnership between management and unions sharing in responsibility for learning about and managing change; this contrasts with the traditionally adversarial relationship.

- A recognition that not all staff would be able to make the change required in the new form of organization, but also to manage their departure from the organization with respect and dignity.
- The importance of relating rewards to contribution to the organization and redressing inconsistencies.
- The increasing importance of considering the future of the organization and developing and identifying the leaders and managers of the future.
- A need for measurement, with clarification, of the organization's values and key competencies against which staff should be selected and developed.

So far in this chapter we have identified the fact that there is a need to manage communication within the organization by both informal as well as formal processes and systems. We have suggested that due to the special nature of the virtual organization there is a particular need for people to be able to develop a high degree of trust and integrity is clearly a key quality. We will now look at what we believe is set to become one of the biggest organizational issues in the future, given the level of flexibility and ambiguity which many will have to contend with—this being team working.

Synergy through teamwork

For some time organizations have recognized the value which comes from developing effective teams in organizations. It may be the case that synergy is one of those over used words in the corporate world. However, in the virtual organization there is a recognition that if one takes the subject of team development seriously then the output from a team of people can truly be greater than the sum of the parts.

In the best examples of team working, organizations are able to bring together people from diverse backgrounds with a range of behavioural skills and create a climate where they can work effectively together.

Working in teams is nothing new and indeed many traditional organizations attempt to draw strength from team working. However, there are many examples of such organizations failing to maximize the potential of team working. As well as there being a number of potential benefits to be reaped from working in teams, there are a number of dangers or downsides which become apparent if an effective team environment is not created. It is not difficult to identify the behaviour of dysfunctional teams; this is best demonstrated in the following case study.

A team in decline

In 1996 we were asked to work with a major functional department within a major financial services organization. Our understanding of this department was that the team was not working well together. These were the qualities we observed which we came to associate with dysfunctional teams.

Introspective

Whereas successful teams manage their relationships with the world outside the team effectively, this team tended to put up barriers and become more introspective. Often they deluded themselves that their introspection was actually a strength due to their special relationships internally and the failure of external people to understand them.

In truly effective teams, however, outsiders are very much welcomed into the team and made to feel part of it. Outsiders are seen as valuable resources who can offer new and different expertise and perspectives. In fact, in many teams in successful virtual organizations the boundaries between who is part of the team and who is outside it become somewhat blurred.

Intimidated by their leader

In this team there was evidence of the team members feeling intimidated by their leader or others whom they assumed had special expertise or personal power within the team. This resulted in people who had valuable inputs holding back and failing to offer their contribution. Equally, the leader deliberately sought to intimidate others in the team by supposedly controlling them and establishing authority in overt and obvious ways. Sometimes this showed itself by the leader victimizing and publicly humiliating one member of the team; this individual, who might be described as a 'kicking dog', tolerated such bullying and served as an example to others in the team of what could happen to them if they fell out of favour with the leader.

In contrast, effective teams tend to encourage all members to contribute either by way of their technical ability or their ability to address process issues.

Failure to challenge

In this team there was a failure to challenge the assumptions and views of others. This is to do with the fact that groupthink occurred, whereby the group developed a sense of invulnerability and decisions were made as members felt obliged to conform with what appeared to be the accepted wisdom of the team.

Successful teams, however, will create an open climate where individuals feel they can challenge and counter challenge one another without people taking personal offence. In this way issues are examined thoroughly from different perspectives and this leads to a higher level of understanding.

Blame culture

In this dysfunctional team, where the level of operating had deteriorated beyond straightforward repair, there was often evidence that there existed a blame cul-ture—where individuals pointed their fingers of blame at other people, bodies or organizations in order to explain their lack of performance. They were quick to suggest that the problem lay anywhere else than at their own door.

A useful analogy can be drawn here between what psychologists refer to when they talk about individuals having an 'inner locus of control' where they take personal responsibility for their own ability to actively influence events. In successful teams there is also evidence of such an inner, albeit within the team, locus of control. Such teams tend not to normally blame external factors or bodies for their difficulties, but will look to their own performance and critical-ly evaluate themselves. Such behaviour is also seen in sporting teams; super teams, for instance, will critically review their performance even when they are doing well in order to find ways of continuing to improve. Equally they will not dwell on negative experiences for longer than is necessary to pull forward learning points for the future.

Escapist behaviour

Again, when the team's ability to function had deteriorated chronically, then we tended to see examples of escapist behaviour. As with many team issues, there are parallels with individual reactions. The team over indulged in comfort behaviours such as drinking, discussing trivial issues or mocking of others.

In contrast, successful teams will socialize and mix well both internally and with others, but they remain focused on moving towards the achievement of their goals or mission.

Functionally focused

In this team there was an over emphasis on strict demarcation of functional roles. This was based around the different skills of team members and clearly it is logical that people should be selected for different roles based on their expertise. However, when demarcation becomes territorial then it can have a restrictive effect.

In successful teams people are encouraged to learn about issues and develop skills outside of their own natural field of experience. This will lead to the creation of a learning culture as individuals benefit from the broad range of experience and skills in the group. Successful teams will also pay particular attention to behavioural and process related issues; so they will take care of matters such as levels of involvement, feelings and emotions and achieving the right balance in terms of key team behaviours.

Clearly the above case was a somewhat extreme example of how ineffec-tive teams tend to present; nevertheless, it does serve to highlight the dif-ferences between highly successful and unsuccessful or what we came to describe as dysfunctional teams.

In the virtual organization there is much evidence of team working and individuals are often members of more than one team; so they may be on their local work team which is customer focused, on a special projects team and on an international function focused team. The permutations are many; the key issue is that in the virtual organization people are able to cope with the ambiguity and stress which comes from multiple team membership.

Furthermore, in the virtual organization team membership is seen as something which is dynamic and constantly changing. One's role in one team may be in a support capacity and in another it may be as a leader. In one team your role may be increasing, whereas in another it may be fading. In fact, many virtual organizations recognize the fact that a team of the same people only has a finite life span or period in which it can be truly productive. This has led us to adapt the model of group development as proposed originally by Tuckman (1965), who suggested that groups tend to form by progressing through the first four key stages of development shown in Fig. 7.1. Forming tends to be seen as the quieter more reflective early stage of formation. Here, members are trying to understand the task and the roles of other people in the team and where they might fit in. Next comes a more vocal period referred to as storming, where conflict often arises as people start to assert their views and establish their roles. Eventually certain norms are established: these reflect the culture of the group and the agreed, albeit often implicitly, *modus operandi.* These stages are normally the prerequisite to effective team performance. We have suggested that many teams also go on to a

Fig. 7.1   Stages in team development
(*Source:* Tuckman, 1965; adapted by Hale, R. and Whitlam P., 1996)

'dorm' stage where they become tired, their sense of purpose diminishes and their behaviour often is ritualistic. In successful virtual organizations this is avoided by moving people around teams, changing the membership in order to reinvigorate the team or simply abandoning the team. To this end many teams exist only for a fixed period of time. It is interesting to see that the behaviour of many individuals within teams will suggest that they actually tend to move into 'mourning' stage after they have been disbanded. This is particularly the case where the team members see themselves as having been part of a particularly cohesive and strong team or where they have faced difficult challenges. This stage is often evidenced by the team coming back together again for reunions and reminiscing about old times and recounting stories from their previous existence.

In successful teams there is an ability to move through the key stages of team formation and to face up to difficult stages such as those often experienced when the team is storming. Ineffective teams will often become stuck at the storming stage, or even accelerate through the stages too quickly without really addressing key issues which need to be worked through at each stage. In the latter case it is not unusual to see, for instance, the team exhibiting unusual levels of politeness (often associated with forming) whereas there are real undercurrents of tensions and conflict (associated with storming).

For some time in the field of team building there has been an emphasis placed on the importance of achieving the right balance in terms of behavioural preferences. This line of thinking has clearly been significantly influenced by the research and writing of Belbin (1981), who defined a number of key behavioural roles and has suggested that we all have preferred roles we like to assume in group situations. His profile of successful teams has added greatly to the body of knowledge in this area and has contributed to many business teams thinking more about process and behavioural issues than they might otherwise have done. Interestingly, however, recent work published by Katzenbach and Smith (1993) has suggested that in fact a demanding performance challenge tends to create a team. Their studies of organizations such as Motorola, Hewlett Packard, McKinsey and Pfizer suggest the following key points:

- Team basics, for instance team size, purpose and process are often overlooked.
- Top teams are the most difficult to develop because of the time issue and the individualistic nature of many people at the top of the organization.
- Most organizations intrinsically prefer individual over team accountability.

- Teams with strong performance standards tend to spawn more real teams than company promoted teams.
- Teams naturally integrate performance and learning.

Perhaps most significantly in terms of the future of organizations they note that:

> In fact, most models of the 'organization of the future' that we have heard about - 'networked,' 'clustered,' 'nonhierarchical,' 'horizontal,' and so forth—are premised on *teams surpassing individuals as the primary performance unit in the company.* According to these predictions, when management seeks faster, better ways to match resources to customer opportunity or competitive challenge, the critical building block will be at the team, not individual, level.

PAUSE FOR THOUGHT

Which are the major teams in your organization? Consider full-time and part-time membership of teams and temporary and permanent teams.

How were they compiled?

Who are the sponsors or stakeholders?

How were the individuals selected—by task skills or behavioural characteristics?

How well have the teams defined their goals, objectives or mission? What is your evidence?

How well does the team interact with the world outside the team? What is your evidence?

How well does the team receive outside intervention or contributions? What is your evidence?

How is the team performance measured and rewarded?

External communication

In the virtual organization there is a recognition of the need to break down barriers and distinctions between different functions and teams within the organization and outside.

We have previously referred to the fact that increasingly organizations are finding themselves collaborating with their competitors and forming networks in order to share knowledge and expertise. This is especially important where the body of knowledge is changing rapidly and where no one organization holds all the answers. Evidence suggests that in the virtual organization the relational gap between customers, suppliers and the organization is becoming less easy to predict and therefore to manage. Today I may find myself as the customer whereas tomorrow my role may be that of the supplier. These relationships are increasingly difficult to manage and will involve the organization in using both customers and suppliers as regular and valuable sources of information.

Of course, traditionally we have recognized the importance of feedback from customers; however, this has tended to be retrospective often asking customers to provide feedback on our products and services. More progressive organizations will also communicate with their customers in a more proactive manner, for example using customers as a source of information both prior and during product development. In a similar way some organizations develop their relationships with their suppliers, regularly using them as a source of information in providing comparative data as well as general background information. One particular organization in which we provided training asked the participants to complete the usual course evaluation forms, but also asked us to provide feedback and evaluation to the client regarding how we rated them as 'customers'. This was an interesting approach which yielded good quality data and dramatically improved the expectations between both parties. Ultimately we extended this approach to many of our customers and clients.

To the uninitiated this may seem somewhat threatening, but evidence suggests that those organizations prepared to take the risks associated with these types of approaches are likely to reap the rewards.

Another characteristic of external communication relates to the potential communication (and indeed collaboration) between apparent competitors. Increasingly organizations collaborate in order to seek solutions to specific problems or as a defensive gesture against outside competition that may be threatening them. As a result, today we may collaborate and tomorrow we might be in direct competition.

In these cases trust and integrity are notoriously difficult concepts to develop and although one could argue that there will always exist some sort of latent threat, this might be described as the development of an 'I won't hurt you, if you don't hurt me' relationship.

A final consideration with respect to external communication is the use of technology for finding data that may be of value to the virtual organization. Such approaches are usually supported by an organizational culture that encourages individuals to network, network and network!

The following case study is drawn from a summary of the work carried out by Andersen Consulting in the UK in working with a major financial services organization, Nationwide Building Society. It is shown how, by reconsidering the approach to the service of the organization around the needs of the customer and by harnessing the capabilities of advances in communications technology, it has been possible to redefine the nature of the customer's relationship with the organization. It is considered that this project reflects the pushing back of the boundaries in defining the organization.

Creation of interactive banking at Nationwide Building Society

Nationwide is the UK's fourth largest mortgage lender and eighth largest retail financial service organization, with assets in excess of £38 billion, 7 million customers and nearly 700 branches.

Nationwide has a history of innovation in what has historically been a slow moving industry. Its merger in 1987 with the Anglia Building Society was the largest completed merger in the UK financial services industry.

The challenge

Competition within the retail financial services market is putting ever greater pressure on UK building societies to improve both sales of products and services to their existing customers.

New entrants such as Marks and Spencer, a food and clothing retailer, are using their own reputations for trust and quality to move into and gain market share in financial services. Additionally, organizations such as Virgin are threatening to strike at the heart of the traditional financial services organization by offering responsive and less expensive services. Existing financial services institutions are taking advantage of new delivery channels, particularly the telephone, to sell and service their products. Despite Nationwide's own attempts to redefine products, the public perception is of increasingly commoditized products to be chosen on price. Increasingly retail financial services companies are having to compete on price and accessibility.

Automation, as illustrated by a fully automated branch implemented by Nationwide, brings its own problems. Automation can reduce costs and improve service but it also risks weakening the depth of relationships with customers. To succeed, Nationwide needs to sell customers high value products such as investments and mortgages, not just process transactions more efficiently.

To respond to these pressures while building on its own competencies and reputation in the marketplace, Nationwide wanted to improve sales effectiveness by:

- Allowing customers to spend time with Nationwide exploring their financial needs, without incurring high costs.
- Establishing a new level of service and trust in terms of the quality of information made available to customers.

- Enabling staff to concentrate on the customer not on remembering the details of every product or on administration.
- Finding ways to deliver services to customers in places they previously could not reach.

The solution

In 1993 Nationwide asked Andersen Consulting to help it explore the potential use of emerging multimedia technologies as a sales and marketing tool within its existing branch network.

Initial work with Andersen Consulting included development of a prototype of a 'virtual branch' employing a wide range of multimedia techniques and technologies. The impact of this prototype on senior management, and subsequently on customers through market research, was enormous. It offered an apparently simple way for customers to understand and explore their financial needs and how they can be satisfied. More than that, it offered a vision of how the organization could present itself to its customers in an increasingly virtual world dominated by a wide variety of electronic delivery channels. Work began in January 1994 on turning the concept into reality.

In January 1995, Nationwide went live as planned with the production system which was implemented at a pilot branch. Subsequently, the system, known as Interact, has been installed at a further six branches and three at non-branch locations.

Innovation

Interact represents the most innovative use of new multimedia technologies within the UK financial services industry and beyond. The system's initial performance confirms Nationwide's view that Interact gives it an important business advantage.

The project drew on Andersen Consulting's multimedia research in the UK and took technical advice from Andersen Consulting's Infocosm Multimedia Factory and the Institute of Learning Science in the US. This included two significant pointers: that the solution should be 'non-technical' (the Interact system is contained within custom designed wooden furniture and has been described by customers as being like a 'television fitted into a desk') and that it should use everyday metaphors (screen symbols are doors and posters not PC icons).

The system truly makes effective use of multimedia technologies—30 minutes of video, audio, extensive animation and full three-dimensional graphics.

The system is a 'virtual branch', yet can be installed inside a conventional building society branch, in a building society lobby or in any non-branch based location. It is a multimedia kiosk, but looks like a stylish piece of office furniture. It is referred to as a self service system, though strictly speaking it is a self sales system or a self buying system. And the most obvious paradox is that while it is credited with a list of technology firsts, it is 'un-technology like'.

What do customers experience?

First, they see a typical high street and a Nationwide branch pictured on screen, complete with street noise. They enter the branch pushing—touching—its doors. Once inside they are welcomed by a 'receptionist' who answers any general enquiries. They can then go to savings and current account areas, or to a homes and mortgages area, a loans area and so on.

The system allows its customers to find out about, experiment with and apply for Nationwide's products and services. They can talk to staff in a central call centre (Nationwide Direct) using a discrete video conferencing link, or print quotations and application forms on the spot.

Perhaps most importantly, the system gives customers the sense of being in complete control. The interface is so intuitive that no one needs any training and customers feel the system is theirs.

To deliver this overall experience, however, the project had to adopt a host of untried technologies and integrate them for the first time.

Project management

A joint Andersen Consulting–Nationwide team built a disciplined and intimate working relationship, developing an innovative approach including a pioneering iterative design, build and test procedure. Both business processes and technology were designed in partnership with real customers. The project team conducted over 150 interactive usability sessions with a combination of Nationwide's current customers and potential customers asking people what they thought and allowing the development to be driven by their views.

Business requirements were analysed along with setting out standards for the look and feel of the system. Simultaneously, work started on specifying the technical requirements and developing a table-driven multimedia architecture which would deliver these requirements to customers. The keys to the successful development were:

- Getting multi-disciplinary teams, containing business experts, designers, programmers, copy authors and graphics artists, to work together productively.
- Developing prototypes to allow senior management, staff and customers to comment on the designs early. The earlier issues are identified the better the final system and the less the wasted effort.
- Taking tough decisions about which design ideas were working and which should be dropped.
- Being willing to re-engineer or completely reinvent processes that did not seem to make sense to the customer.

This development strategy was supported by a full change programme. The programme identified which job groups would be affected by the system, and devised both communication and training strategies for these job groups within Nationwide. But more importantly, it created a sense of enthusiasm and demand from staff for the system. At first sight Interact might have seemed a threat to the relationship between staff and customers, and even to the staff's very jobs. Through involvement in the development and the clear commitment of senior management, staff actively wanted the system, talked proudly of it and even tried to find ways to use the system which had not been envisaged in the original design.

The benefits

Systems installed on a pilot basis served to test the business case for a potentially ambitious national roll-out.   Usage is exceeding original expectations, particularly in locations where the terminal is available 24 hours a day or where the terminal is not located in a branch. Customer feedback is enthusiastic and supportive. Sales at branches with Interact have increased. Branch managers report that all staff now feel confident in helping customers find the right product for them on the system, even if they have not been trained in selling or in the specifics of the product.

Based on the initial positive results from the pilot, Nationwide expects a roll-out could deliver:

- Increased sales to existing customers
- Gains in terms of new customers
- Greater effectiveness in the use of branch staff time
- Enhanced staff confidence in their ability to help customers select the right product
- Improved customer satisfaction, retention and cross sell rates.

The future

In the Nationwide's 1995 Annual Report, the chief executive describes Interact as having the 'potential ultimately to be made available in customers' homes'.

Nationwide views Interact as part of a new personal banking experience which could transform the financial services industry. It is a 'virtual branch', allowing customers to do almost everything that they can do in a physical branch.   Ultimately, this will help Nationwide to refocus its distribution strategy—and to take the services directly into the home, the work place and public spaces.

The Nationwide hopes the system will encourage more people into its branches. It hopes to generate more high quality sales leads. It believes Interact will make Nationwide's products more accessible to more people so that it will sell more—and it wants to create a new banking experience which reinforces Nationwide's image as a highly innovative, creative organization.

This is evidently an innovative project in the financial services sector and it is being implemented at a time when this sector is experiencing an accelerating rate of change. It is interesting to learn from this example that by redefining the organization's customer interface and by harnessing new technological capabilities, it has been possible to take an organization based in what has long been held as a traditional sector and thrust it into being the vanguard of virtual organization experimentation.

Furthermore, as with Scottish Hydro-Electric plc, there was a recognition of the need to make such changes alongside a full change programme with appropriate communication and training strategies.

(Summarized with permission of Andersen Consulting
and Nationwide Building Society)

Assessment of communication

Finally, we provide you with an opportunity to consider your own effectiveness against the critical factor of *communication*.

The statements below are designed to assist you in identifying ways in which you can focus on your organization's approach to communication. Essentially, this is seen as a prerequisite for helping you move towards becoming a virtual organization. These questions should not be seen as a test; there are no right or wrong answers. However, their effectiveness relies on the frankness of your responses.

Listed below are ten focused statements relating to our research findings about the virtual organization. You may use this brief questionnaire to assess your own department or organization. This is a forced choice questionnaire requiring you to respond against each statement.

Please read each statement carefully and respond by answering either Yes (agreeing) or No (disagreeing) to each statement. There is no time limit; it will probably only take two minutes to complete.

---

1. We have strong formal and informal methods of communication across the business.   Yes/No
2. We have a strong 'grapevine' which alerts us to rumours.   Yes/No
3. We systematically use our suppliers as a source of data.   Yes/No
4. We communicate verbally where at all possible.   Yes/No
5. There is a clear demarcation between us, our suppliers and customers.   Yes/No
6. We work as individuals more than teams.   Yes/No
7. We have access to considerable information as to how our business is performing.   Yes/No
8. Customers are seen as vital in providing us with information about both our services and that of our competitors.   Yes/No
9. Our communications are highly organized and formalized.   Yes/No
10. Decisions tend to be taken from the top and then implemented down through the organization.   Yes/No

---

Scoring

If you answered Yes to any of the following statements give yourself 10 points for each Yes.

```
1 ..........................................................................................
3 ..........................................................................................
4 ..........................................................................................
7 ..........................................................................................
8 ..........................................................................................
Total ....................................................................................
```

If you answered No to any of the following statements, give yourself 10 points for each No.

```
2 ..........................................................................................
5 ..........................................................................................
6 ..........................................................................................
9 ..........................................................................................
10 ........................................................................................
Total ....................................................................................
Grand total ..........................................................................
```

Consider the above grand total as a percentage relating to performance against the factor of *communication*. Those organizations which we believe measure up as effective virtual organizations tended to score in excess of 80 per cent.

In this chapter we have looked at the third factor in the model, communication. We see effective communication as the fuel for the journey towards becoming a virtual organization. Despite the fact that many organizations try very hard to improve the effectiveness of communication by implementing formal initiatives, it seems that there is a need to actually address more fundamental issues such as creating an open culture and climate where communication, or the 'fuel', can flow through the organization.

In the virtual organization there is evidence of strong communication at all levels within the organization, but also with external contacts who are viewed as valuable resources to draw on.

We said that one of the major inhibiting factors which organizations need to be aware of and manage is the need for unlearning. Often the block to effective communication, or, for that matter, change, exists because of entrenched habits, values and beliefs. In the next chapter we will pick up the subject of learning which was discussed originally in Chapter 3 and look in more detail at how organizations are using learning as the means of adapting and managing change.

References

Belbin, R.M., *Management teams—Why they succeed or fail*, Heinemann, 1981.

Handy, C., Trust and the Virtual Organization, *Harvard Business Review*, May/June, 1995.

Katzenbach, J.R. and Smith, D.K., *The Wisdom of Teams*, Harvard Business School Press, Boston, 1993.

Lorenz, A., BAe Plans Sweeping Changes To Boost Efficiency, *The Sunday Times*, 18 February, 1996.

Peters, T. and Waterman, R., *In Search Of Excellence*, Harper & Row, New York, 1982.

Tichy, N.M. and Sherman, S., Jack Welch's Lesson For Success, *Fortune*, January 25, 1993.

Tuckman, B.W., Development Sequences in Small Groups, *Psychological Bulletin*, 63, 1965.

Test driving the future

Things do not change; we change

HENRY DAVID THOREAU, *Walden*

In this chapter we turn our attention to the final of the four factors which comprise our model of successful organizational change and which is managed effectively in the virtual organization, *adaptation*. Specifically in this chapter we:

■ Explore the process of adaptation and look at the hierarchy of stages related to effective change management and learning
■ Explain the reason that it is becoming increasingly important to manage change effectively and look at how some organizations constantly adapt to meet the changing needs of their environment
■ Demonstrate the links between the process of change and learning and show how in the virtual organization learning, adaptation and change are occurring constantly and more often informally than formally
■ Explore the competencies related to both successful individual performance in the virtual organization, as well as the critical managerial behaviours
■ Look at how organizations formally and informally benchmark their performance against the best in their field and use this as a means of constantly adapting
■ Show how one specific organization, AlliedSignal, is managing a major culture change process in one of its European manufacturing plants

The case for adaptation

Change, adaptation and learning are constant characteristics of the virtual organization. In organizations which might be considered to be 'learning organizations', as discussed in Chapter 3, there is a recognition of the need to encourage continuous learning and it has been argued by some proponents of the learning organization concept that the ultimate goal is for the organization itself to actually learn. It may sound over ambitious to expect that the organization as an entity can really learn, however the concept is an imaginative one. Organizational learning might be said to take place when the organization is not so dependent on the skills and knowledge which its members possess that when individuals leave the organization it then becomes vulnerable or exposed. This suggests both a requirement to ensure that learning is continuously transferred among members of the organization and that learning as a behaviour becomes accepted and welcomed as part of the organizational culture.

Organizations which we would describe as virtual organizations appear to have taken the concept of learning beyond just the acquisition of knowledge and skills required to meet the immediate challenge; they have institutionalized the behaviours of learning to the extent that it is the expectation of everyone that they will need to continually learn and change in order to perform effectively. Learning does not simply focus on the knowledge and skills; there is a major emphasis on developing the right attitudes and behaviours and the ability to constantly adapt.

In these organizations learning or adaptation is seen as a hierarchical four-stage process.

Level 1—Knowledge (We know ...)

This is the level at which an organization actually acquires the knowledge necessary for success. To utilize knowledge, organizations need to acquire information that is relevant. This may be a formal process but, as previously described, it is more likely that such knowledge is obtained by having regular contact with customers, suppliers and competitors. In many ways getting the information is for most organizations the easy part, what separates traditional organizations from the virtual organization is how this data is processed and disseminated across the organization. Critical issues here are related to communication and making information available to all employees.

Gaining information and knowledge is the foundation block upon which adaptation is built; yet knowledge alone is insufficient in ensuring a successful result. This brings us to consider a higher level of organizational change which builds on this foundation.

Level 2—Skills (We can ...)

This is the level of adaptation that is concerned with the acquisition and development of core competencies within a business. As a prerequisite this requires knowledge, but is primarily concerned with application. Although skills may be obtained through training and development, it is evident in the virtual organization that traditional sources of skills such as courses and formal programmes are more likely to be developed by less formalized approaches. Included in this would be the development of learning processes, for example understanding what training is available and knowing how to access such resources.

In the case study below it is interesting to see how a major multinational organization is taking an innovative approach to both developing a learning culture and collaborating with suppliers. Here we see how the organization has stepped back from the routine of annual training programme planning and taken a refreshing look at the provision of training in order to create a positive learning environment.

British Petroleum (UK)

As part of their recognition of the importance of developing learning process and learning behaviours, BP (UK) have adopted an integrated development strategy entitled Learning For Success. A tactical outcome from this strategy is the provision of an 'annual training fair'.

This event is provided in the spirit of partnership between BP and their suppliers and is seen by both sides as providing synergy in their relationships. Interestingly, some suppliers will be working alongside other suppliers and they may actually be direct competitors of one another.

In the training fair it is interesting to note that some of the training provision might be viewed as not being directly business related. Clearly there is an underlying assumption that learning in its own right is good, and actually the subject content is less important. So some of the provision might be seen as more entertainment related, while some clearly carries a subject focused approach. Included in the last fair were activities as varied as lessons on juggling, short personal skills courses and career development counselling.

At the 'training fair' employees are invited to attend for brief 'taster' seminars where they are exposed to gaining an understanding of the structure and content of various programmes or training courses. Those employees that attend get the opportunity to check out the style of the material as well as to interact with the trainers. This 'chemistry' with the supplier is seen as being especially important in ensuring success of a particular programme and to an extent feedback from participants allows the providers to subsequently make informed decisions regarding which programmes and suppliers to bring on stream in the following year.

This event is highly visible and is supported by senior management. As a result, it also has a highly positive impact on the motivation of individuals and apart from entertainment value it is recognized that individuals actually take some specific learning from each event they attend. It is also significant that employees volunteer to attend the fair and they choose the events they wish to take part in; it is believed that this also helps in terms of motivation of attendees.

What is noticeable in the above case study is that the organization uses this approach to serve many different but important purposes.

Specifically, it achieves the following objectives:

- Raises the profile of learning as a subject
- Provides a limited level of knowledge and skills development
- Helps the organization to identify potential subjects and suppliers for learning events in the future
- Fosters relationships with new suppliers
- Keeps the organization up to date with external developments and topics
- Offers a fun and exciting environment for learning
- Gets employees used to the idea of having to learn new skills but in a non threatening way.

Clearly, the acquisition of both knowledge (I know) and skills (I can) are important stages of adaptation, yet knowledge and skills alone will not necessarily ensure success. There are many organizations that have invested in both knowledge and skills, in major change programmes, only to be surprised that nothing, or very little, seems to have changed.

Level 3—Motivation (We will ...)

Arguably this is the most critical level of the four levels of adaptation and indeed our experience suggests that this is where many organizations fail in the process of adaptation or change management. Often organizational change initiatives are started with a fanfare of trumpets and a flurry of activity and positive words of encouragement by senior management, but after a few months the loud and visible support has significantly diminished to such an extent that the impact of the initiative is seriously reduced.

In the virtual organization considerable effort is directed to ensure that motivation is maintained and that when seeking to bring about change people are personally motivated to change. This is primarily about ensuring that there are in place processes which will perpetuate the desire for change and success.

Level 4—Action (We do ...)

This is the final level of adaptation and the transition into this from the previous level often goes by without being noticed. This is the level at which the individuals internalize change and as a result such change becomes well accepted in the organization. Now the organization is no longer in a state of change—rather, perpetual change is the norm.

We refer to the term adaptation because we believe this suggests something beyond learning in the traditional sense. The virtual organization is able to adapt to its environment almost at will. This necessarily means being able to draw on a range of technical and behavioural skills in order to meet both the immediate and future demands of the business. It means that individuals are not intimidated when required to do things which they have never done before; they will rise to the challenge and if this means acquiring new skills or knowledge, then this is accepted as a normal part of such a challenge.

To achieve this, organizations will provide training in order to equip members with the technical skills required to do the current job and more importantly to prepare them for future roles. In the virtual organization individuals are aware of the need to continually update knowledge and skills and as such they tend to be prepared to invest a certain amount of their own time and energy into personal development. While some organizations, including many quoted by other authors as learning organizations, clearly work hard at trying to generate this self-development culture, in the virtual organization this occurs in a relatively effortless way. This is partly due to the fact that apart from making training and development readily available and accessible, in the virtual organization members tend to be psychologically receptive to learning in different ways other than simply through the use of formal training events.

In this chapter we look at the subject of adaptation from two perspectives. First, it is instructive to look at the way the organization establishes systems and processes which are conducive to adaptation. Included here for example are training and development programmes and processes for ensuring that skills are transferred and shared within the organization.

In the virtual organization, however, there is an equal emphasis placed on the importance of the behaviours required in order to create a culture of adaptation. Individuals need to be receptive to learning in many ways other than just through formal training provision. Furthermore, they need to display certain behaviours which arguably are not easily developed through formal training—behaviours such as initiative, tenacity and risk taking.

Establishing systems and processes

In the virtual organization technical and professional training is clearly seen as important, but it is viewed as the means to an end rather than as an end in itself. What we mean by this is that in the more traditional organization there is a tendency to feel that employees should possess certain qualifications and should have progressed through normally arduous training in order to be able to justify holding a particular position in the hierarchy. In one extreme case, tradition had it that in order to progress from the position of clerk to secretary there was a need for such staff to have a shorthand qualification even though there was no evidence that managers still used shorthand dictation. This was a classic example of the requirement in terms of supposed learning failing to keep pace with the actual business practice. We found examples of this at all levels of the organization including the requirement if one was to work in certain functions, for professional qualifications. When the content and relevance of training related to the attainment of such qualifications was examined more closely, it became apparent that the policy was influenced more by the need to restrict numbers at the higher levels of the organization or to be able to present the right image externally, than by a genuine desire to develop or improve competencies.

In a similar way, so were training and development systems seen to be based around a fundamental requirement to maintain the *status quo*. In such traditional organizations there would tend to be a suite of training courses offered which mirrored the organizational hierarchy; in many cases managers would attend such company courses after some time working at the appropriate level. In this sense the provision of training support might be viewed as 'pulling' people up to the right skill level after appointment rather than 'pushing' them.

In contrast, the approach taken in the virtual organization is to push people into taking on new responsibilities and roles and by providing whatever support might be required in terms of training and development. Such support would be seen as integral to the job rather than something which is offered as a 'bolt on'. Because of this, development would occur in many ways rather than relying on the formal training course as the main medium for learning. In the virtual organization there is a strong emphasis on learning from others and as such coaching and mentoring approaches are seen to take a high priority.

At this stage it is appropriate to look at one organization in particular, which clearly can be described as close to the virtual organization model and which demonstrates a high level of adaptability in terms of how it trains and develops its personnel.

Learning and adaptation at Compaq Computers

Compaq is one of the world's leading manufacturers of computers and is strategically repositioning its business away from the production of PCs in order to focus on integrated computer systems.

The company has a clearly defined vision statement that is widely distributed among its employees; but more than this it has clearly identified the core values of the organization as follows:

Our collective human potential is Compaq's most strategic advantage in satisfying our Customers. To this, Compaq is committed to the following principles to continually foster human innovation, creativity and productivity.

Compaq then goes on to describe some specific beliefs that are seen as core; these among others include the following:

- Fostering human dignity, treating fairly and with respect
- Building constructive trusting relationships in teams
- Fostering individual responsibility
- Open two-way communication
- Creating an environment that is enjoyable and fun.

Clearly Compaq is committed to the utmost utilization of its human resources and this tends to be manifested in some of their leading edge approaches to managing people. In particular they appear to be leaders in the sphere of performance management, as well as the integrated use of competencies.

Overall their human resource management is very much seen as contributing to the business in a positive way, whereas in many traditional companies this function is often seen as the custodian of people policies and procedures as well as having a policing function.

In their training function they have recognized the importance of coaching as a critical skill primarily to support their performance management programme and have developed a significant programme in partnership with two different consultants, both of whom might be viewed as competitors under different circumstances.

The programme itself takes the view that coaching is the balance between maintaining the relationship and achieving the task and that there are four clearly defined stages in the process. Within each of these stages they have identified the critical competencies and as a result, in training they focus on developing only the defined skills. Consequently, this approach is being used as they develop a complementary programme in the area of influencing and negotiation skills.

The approach in Compaq is typical of those organizations that are operating like virtual organizations, in particular they have a well known and understood vision that is supported by clear statements relating to their beliefs. These beliefs are consistent with the findings of our research as to what is culturally important in these change focused organizations. Equally important, Compaq often work in collaborative relationships with suppliers, customers and competitors; likewise, their approach to training and development is to build the learning process skills of the organization through the institutionalization of the coaching process. Finally, it is interesting to note that in Compaq the competencies that they are building in their people are the same sort of skills that we have identified as being important to the virtual organization. This is discussed in more depth later in the chapter.

New ways of thinking about learning

There seems to be much evidence to support the views of Lombardo (1989), who suggested that often being given jobs for which one is not qualified probably provides some of the best learning opportunities available. In the virtual organization this approach to development is often taken as opposed to holding people back until they had served what was perceived as sufficient time before progressing.

In the virtual organization it might not at first glance appear that training is taken as seriously as in the traditional organization. In the traditional organization there is more likely to be a dedicated training team who would probably be able to show a detailed course brochure and a host of training materials and might proudly boast about the number of staff training days provided each year.

In our own research (Whitlam, 1990), we surveyed over 1000 organizations as we sought to identify some of the key factors which influenced powerful learning. This has led us to question some of the common assumptions upon which traditional provision of training has been based. These are summarized below:

- Specific training programmes appeared to be valued greater by the providers than the recipients.
- Taking risks and making mistakes was perceived as a powerful route to personal and organizational learning.
- It was seen as critical to communicate effectively what resources for personal development were available and to understand the roles of different members of the organization.
- Formal training processes such as training courses, were perceived as significantly less useful than learning opportunities which were presented through informal processes such as through involvement on project teams.
- Sloman (1989) demonstrated the way in which on-job training is significantly undervalued and we found that in general the vast amount of individual learning that takes place in the organization does so in the context of informality.
- Internal training was seen as more beneficial than similar externally provided training due to relevance and the improved opportunity for internal communication.
- Where training systems were in evidence, training was found to be more effective when focused around individual needs rather than 'sheep-dipping'.
- For learning opportunities to be maximized there is a need to address the issue of 'unlearning' inappropriate behaviours and accepted wisdom which may actually inhibit the development process. This

finding is supported by the work of other researches such as Newstrom (1983) and Hedberg (1981).

The above tends to illustrate some of the thinking that exists in the virtual organization so much as it challenges our traditional way of looking at things. In addition the virtual organization would be less likely to have such obvious offerings in terms of formal systems and processes for training and development as the traditional organization. First, you would be less likely to find a permanent training team; it is more likely that most if not all employees would be seen as having core responsibilities for managing both their own learning and that of their team. Second, it would be difficult to realistically quantify the amount of training taking place because training and development is considered an integral part of the job rather than a discrete activity.

If one was to focus on actual learning, though, and to ask individuals to reflect on their own learning over the past year then the virtual organization would clearly come out on top. Only in this case the learning will have taken place through a combination of formal training, self-managed learning, role-modelling and on-job development.

It is as though in the virtual organization there is a transcendence of formal training as the medium for learning and an integration of learning with everyday activities. Such learning is often associated with real business activity. So business activities, projects, presentations and meetings will be critically reviewed in order to glean and reinforce key learning points. This might take place through formal review processes but is just as likely to be seen through informal everyday discussions taking place among members of the organization. Contrast this with the approach taken in some organizations where one sees what can best be described as a blame culture, where if something goes well it is often put down to a stroke of luck and where if something goes badly then there is a post-mortem and witch-hunt to find someone to blame.

Benchmarking as an adaptive process

Many large organizations in recent years have recognized the benefits to be gained from looking outside of their organization and learning from others. The practice of systematically looking at the methods of other organizations as a source of learning, that is benchmarking, was pioneered by the Xerox corporation in the 1970s, originally as a way of seeking ways of fighting the commercial threat from the Japanese. Now, of course, the threat to organizations in the West comes not only from Japan but from other Asian 'tigers', as well as smaller or more virtual organizations in the West. The need to benchmark one's activities and processes, whether formally or informally, is more necessary now than ever. As organizations continue to learn and innovate, state of the art knowledge is more likely to be held in the organization currently leading the way in a particular field than in the ivory towers of academia. Furthermore, as the body of knowledge is changing more rapidly than in the past, organizations are gaining competitive advantage from their ability to gather in ideas from outside the organization and translate their learning into useful business activity.

Many organizations take a systematic approach to benchmarking and approaches taken here can involve collaborating directly with other organizations which feel that there is some potential value to be gained from sharing information, or engaging an intermediary organization or consultancy which processes information on behalf of participating organizations. Of course, the advantage of direct collaboration is that there is an opportunity to enter into useful interactive discussions and even to build relationships. Potential difficulties are that it may be considered inappropriate to make such direct contact, particularly if dealing with competitors where there are fears about disclosing commercially sensitive information or information which will give away competitive advantage. Advocates of formal benchmarking would argue that if one is selective regarding what information is shared and if the focus is on specific processes or techniques then this issue of confidentiality need not be a major problem. It is also increasingly recognized that valuable insights can be gained from looking outside of your own business sector as a source of learning.

Using a third party to process benchmarking data can have advantages, particularly in being able to offer detailed quantitative data drawn from many organizations. Typically the organization which engages in a formal benchmarking process will undertake a series of steps as shown in Fig. 8.1.

This shows that the organization will define its performance indicators, that is the key measures of success which will be benchmarked. These may relate to a range of technical, managerial, human resource or skill related issues. Having established the means of measurement, then data is collected and compared against that gathered from external organizations. Having analysed the results of the exercise, then areas for particular attention are defined and plans are implemented for continuous improvement.

Saratoga International is one organization which provides an international benchmarking consultancy service. Organizations provide Saratoga with information on a regular basis and central co-ordinators collate the information and feed it back to participating organizations in various ways. Saratoga have collected performance data on around 800 organizations world-wide. Once areas for particular attention are identified, organizations then seek ideas by looking at best practices elsewhere

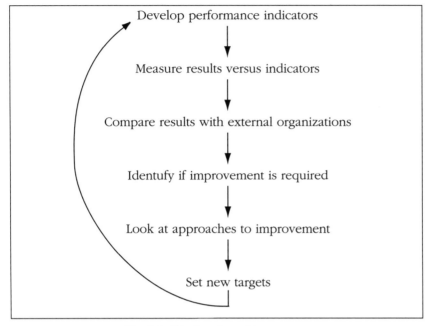

Fig. 8.1 The benchmarking process

and considering new ideas and breakthrough thinking which have taken place. Saratoga recommend there should be a clear understanding of the definitions for each data item (Saratoga has an international set of definitions for core metrics which are reviewed twice a year with clients). Data is submitted every six months and reports are produced which give data by industry, by number of employees and by revenue growth. Additionally, some organizations are provided with data which is integrated with the Harvard Business School scorecard approach and European Quality awards. The key is, of course, to turn the data into value-adding activity. This means looking at trends and identifying which activities are improving and which are declining against the activities of others. Organizations may then seek evidence regarding how other organizations regarded as the leading edge against particular indicators, have achieved such status. Also user conferences and special interest groups provide a forum for discussion between participating organizations.

While major corporations have used benchmarking in the formal sense as described above in order to look at their own processes, it is also noticeable how the virtual organization will constantly scan the external environment and identify learning opportunities which exist from looking at how other organizations operate. Interestingly, virtual organizations tend to be less concerned with the importance of drawing comparisons with organizations in the same business sector, whereas traditional organizations tend to be preoccupied with their own uniqueness and do not realize the opportunities which exist from looking outside of their own specific sector or industry. Virtual organizations are not inhibited by a fear of copying others; they recognize that others may also be operating at the leading edge and in the absence of a body of knowledge will recognize the need to pioneer the development of the body of knowledge in their own field.

Key behaviours of adaptation

In the virtual organization it can be seen that people display certain key behavioural traits which are a fundamental requirement for success. Interestingly, such behaviours tend to be difficult to train into people, rather they are thought to be personality based. This suggests there is a need to recruit people who already show evidence of possessing these attributes. Some organizations will also be quite open in declaring their expectations of employees. Hewlett Packard, for instance, in its statement of organizational values, 'The HP Way', says that:

> HP people should personally accept responsibility and be encouraged to upgrade their skills and capabilities through ongoing training and development. This is especially important in a technical business where the rate of progress is rapid and where people are expected to adapt and change.

Styles of learning

In terms of their ability to learn, members of the virtual organization will tend to be capable of learning in each of the four ways described by Honey and Mumford (1986): as 'Activists', 'Reflectors', 'Pragmatists' and 'Theorists'.

As 'Activists' they will learn from new experiences and will be prepared to take opportunities which are presented for learning. To an extent this calls for risk taking and a willingness to learn from experience and by exchanging ideas with other people within the organization or outside of it. In the virtual organization learning is seen to take place almost regardless of time and physical constraints and it is integrated into the jobs of organizational members.

As 'Reflectors' there is an ability to stand back from events and to assimilate information before acting and to review events critically afterwards. In the virtual organization, though, reflection tends to be realistic and is focused on the needs of the business rather than being a painstaking and laborious process. There is a willingness to look at real life projects and review in a positive way what has been learnt and how to continuously improve.

As 'Theorists' there is an ability for most people in the virtual organization to understand relationships between ideas, events and experiences. This calls for a certain conceptual ability throughout the organization, whereas in the traditional organization such abilities may be the preserve of senior management or specialists. In the virtual organization, however, there is often a need to cope with ambiguity and uncertainty and people tend not to become too obsessed with there always being a right or wrong answer.

Finally, in the virtual organization there is strength in terms of a 'Pragmatist' learning style. There is a willingness to try out new approaches and techniques without becoming unduly concerned about perfection. There is an ability to look to the examples of successful activity elsewhere and to learn how things could be improved within the organization. There is a willingness to take ideas and to try things out and the fact that the organization needs to be responsive and flexible means that individuals have to take a pragmatic approach.

PAUSE FOR THOUGHT

What is the predominant style of learning in your organization?

To what extent do people learn by doing things and taking risks?

What level of reflection is there before and after taking actions?

To what extent do people make connections between ideas, events and experience in order to seek learning opportunities?

How conducive is the working environment to trying out new ideas and approaches?

Now let us consider some of the specific critical competencies that are required for success by an individual operating in the virtual organization. It will be seen that many of these competencies are difficult to learn in a traditional way, for instance how do we teach tenacity? Consequently, this presents the organization with a need to provide the environment within which such behaviours can flourish and to support this with some innovative development practices.

Creativity

The ability to achieve a new or unique way of thinking about things and to be able to use such a thought process to suggest ways of developing new products or services.

Organizations of the future will need to develop the use of creativity in all their employees as well as in all aspects of their business. This will be more difficult in organizations where there is a high degree of rationality and logic, for instance in financial services; however, high technology (sunrise industries) businesses will probably find this easier to achieve. From an organizational perspective, there is a need to create a climate that develops and supports creativity; this will require the fostering of spontaneity and almost childlike behaviour. Mature, sophisticated and traditional businesses will find this difficult to achieve.

Innovation

The ability to see opportunities for developing new ideas or adapting existing ideas in order to gain some sort of advantage.

In many ways this is similar to the competence of creativity. However, innovation is focused on individuals who themselves may not necessarily be creative in terms of having lots of original ideas, but can often see 'chances' that others cannot see. The ability to be innovative will be linked to the person's beliefs about him or herself and so developing this behaviour may involve changing or managing personal beliefs.

Decisiveness

Being able and willing to take a timely decision and being conscious of the danger of prevarication.

Clearly this is a personality trait and one that is to be evidenced in the virtual organization where empowered individuals are enabled to act quickly and without hesitation. Judgement is critical and individuals can be provided with a number of techniques that would help in the process of decision making. However, more importantly the individual has to be given the confidence to take the decision.

Initiative

Actively influencing events rather than passively waiting for something to happen.

This is not really a trainable behaviour; more specifically, this is something which people tend to either possess or not. In the virtual organization there is a need for members to possess a high level of personal drive and initiative—this could mean generating new business, changing the shape of the business, forming new alliances or trying out new approaches.

Some traditional organizations, in contrast, suffer from a kind of paralysis brought about by an over emphasis on reflection and a tendency to want to weigh up from every angle the pros and cons for a particular course of action. Initiative, of course, calls for an element of risk taking and this in itself is not a behaviour which can be easily taught to people.

Risk taking

Ability to use judgement in taking a calculated risk, showing awareness of the probability and impact of risks materializing and an ability to engage in contingency planning.

Linked to decisiveness is the process of taking the risk. Although rooted in personality this behaviour can be supported by teaching techniques based on probability theory, but the behaviour will need to be supported by the corporate climate, particularly where failure is involved. One well known soft drink manufacturer that we know actually awards a prize each quarter for the 'best individual manager' who takes a chance without necessarily gaining any advantage—the object here being to send messages around the organization that taking a chance is alright even if they do not always come off.

Tenacity

Perseverance—keeping going when things get difficult or problems arise. Not giving up, yet being able to judge when an original goal may not be realistically obtained.

Another personality based competence which is really untrainable. Perseverence is seen as critical in managing all aspects of change, as, in general terms, most change looks like a failure somewhere in the middle of implementation. Arguably the critical part of the definition relates to knowing when to give up; many traditional organizations persevere too long, as the original goal is superseded.

What we have tried to do here is consider the personal competencies for success by an individual operating in the virtual organization; however, it should be noted that we believe that these competencies will complement the following sorts of managerial skills:

- ■ Vision
- ■ Urgency
- ■ Emotional muscle
- ■ Responsibility
- ■ Leadership
- ■ Influence
- ■ Empowerment.

It is interesting to note the absence of competencies like control or dele-gation in the above list; in the virtual organization these behaviours will be present but excessive use will almost certainly inhibit performance.

PAUSE FOR THOUGHT

To what extent are the personal competencies for success demonstrated in your organization?

How do you ensure that you recruit people with these behaviours?

How can you foster the development of a climate that supports these behaviours?

From a traditional to an adaptive culture

In this section we take a look at how one particular organization has approached the subject of bringing about major organizational and cul-tural change. Of particular interest here will be the fact that a number of organizational and environmental complexities exist.

The organization, AlliedSignal, is a leading international player in the automotive market and operates manufacturing plants world-wide. In the case study we look at how the requirement to bring about a major change in one of the European plants was managed.

Adaptation at AlliedSignal

Background

AlliedSignal Turbocharging Systems is part of the Automotive division ($4.5b) of the US AlliedSignal ($12b) corporation. The Turbocharging sector has fac-tories world-wide and the Skelmersdale factory in the north west of England is part of the European group. Skelmersdale has been structured around three product groupings: passenger, medium commercial and large commercial vehicles. There are around 720 employees on site.

The turbo/diesel   market has been expanding and in this sense Skelmersdale has not really felt the effect of the recession. There has been a low turnover of staff and a history of full capacity.   Volume output has increased considerably in recent years. The projections are that the business is set to continue to expand in terms of demand.

It has been recognized, though, by those responsible for the plant that there are issues which could, if not addressed, present a threat in the future. There have in the past been instances of failing to meet customer demand, arrears of production and lower productivity than other AlliedSignal factories. Despite this there has been an upward drift in terms of shopfloor remuneration.

The factory is, though, undergoing dramatic change relating to its culture, structure, working practices, shopfloor layout and management.

A number of initiatives are being driven through in a determined way and there is evidence of senior managers and those newly recruited into new roles being highly motivated and able to bring about the changes which are required. There is a commitment to being a centre of excellence and a 'lean cellular business'.

There is much evidence of the influence of the US parent through, for example, the Values Statement, The Code of Conduct and much of the terminology associated with organizational initiatives. Interestingly this is overlaid on what is a very traditional British manufacturing working environment and workforce and there are conscious efforts being made to integrate corporate thinking with the local business and social culture.

Attention is being given to more effective human resource management and with this in mind the plant manager, senior managers, human resource and organizational development specialists are closely involved in driving through the structural, organizational and cultural changes. This involves a major training and development effort.

Against the organizational model presented throughout this book, there are a number of issues which are being addressed in a concerted effort to manage the change process effectively and expediently.

Direction

Whereas the business has always appeared secure there is a recognition of the need to become increasingly competitive. In specific terms this means addressing quality and productivity and this message is continually emphasized to all employees throughout the plant.

The clarity of direction has been given clear focus due to the fact that the factory faces a crisis if it does not change and the bottom line is that this could result in closure; in the face of adversity the goal of the organization and its sense of purpose has become clear. The leaders of the organization have pulled no punches in making this clear through briefings. In order to focus all employees on what is required, very specific productivity targets are set and feedback regarding performance is immediate; there are cell level and plant level results published on a daily basis. Additionally, a number of key metrics have been defined relating to issues such as customer satisfaction, quality and internal measures of efficiency; feedback regarding these is provided through notice boards throughout the plant.

There is a strong sense of direction provided from the US parent in the form of a regularly reviewed business plan and the publication of the corporation's core values and beliefs. These emphasize the importance of:

- Customers
- Integrity
- People
- Teamwork
- Speed
- Innovation
- Performance.

Additionally, a code of conduct focuses on relationships with:

- The company
- Each other
- Customers
- Suppliers.

In the past the values of the company have been well publicized through notice-boards and booklets; however, there is a recognition that there is a need to do more in order to ensure that employees, in the words of the code of conduct—'live their values'. This has meant taking each of the values and defining them in terms which are applicable at a local level. Importantly, these values have also been integrated into selection and career development systems to ensure that the people who are recruited and developed in the business are able to relate to and work in accordance with these values.

Also, at a corporate level, there are a number of initiatives, training programmes and resources which are drawn on by the local plant.

Form

In the past the structure of the organization at the local level has in many ways complied with the traditional pattern for a manufacturing organization in the automotive sector. This has emphasized the importance of time-serving, and seniority had often been related to length of service. Different production processes were handled by discrete sections and there were many employees who were not really encouraged or motivated to be concerned with functions or parts of the manufacturing process other than their own.

Major structural changes have been introduced in order to both improve the manufacturing process and to encourage the development of a new philosophy and mind set on the part of employees. A cellular working structure has been established and has involved the selection of personnel for teams and the establishment of a team structure with team and group leaders. The title 'leader' has a particular significance, as the intention has been to encourage leadership and the use of initiative and the development of business awareness at all levels.

The group leaders and team leaders have been selected from within the organization and existing employees have been invited to apply for these positions. They have then been selected against their ability to demonstrate the key competencies required, which were related to the company's stated values. Significantly, it was not assumed that those previously holding supervisory positions would take up the new leadership roles.

With regard to manufacturing employees, a new structure was established which replaced the previous hierarchy and function-related titles with just three job titles (Manufacturer 1, 2 and 3). These levels were very tightly linked into the achievement of different levels of competence in the job as defined by nationally recognized standards.

At the same time as establishing this structure, a redundancy programme was implemented which encouraged voluntary redundancy and provided an opportunity for those who felt unable to adapt to the new way of working to leave with a favourable redundancy package. Those taking redundancy were offered outplacement to help them prepare for life outside of the organization.

Key personnel were recruited into positions which might be seen as change agent roles; included here were human resource, training and development, and organizational development staff. Some were brought in from outside the organization and some were pulled into such roles from line positions in the business. Additionally, there was a system in operation where certain employees, referred to as 'Black Belts', with a special role of facilitating change and spreading best practice, were trained up as facilitation experts with a wandering remit.

Additionally, a number of shopfloor employees were given special responsibilities for training and development and were provided with training to be able to operate as training facilitators.

In terms of organizational form, as we discussed it in Chapter 6, this organization clearly recognized the need to redefine the way it operated and therefore was structured. This has meant establishing some major departures from the traditional structure and apart from implementing the changes described above, employees are encouraged to see organizational change as the norm.

Communication

Communication is seen as a critical factor in determining the success of this culture change initiative and there is acceptance of the need to communicate regularly in all directions and using several different channels.

In the past there have been attempts to communicate down through the organization, but this had mainly involved literal transfer of information coming from the corporate headquarters or regarding production targets. There was previously a strong sense of 'them and us' between the shopfloor and management. As people from the shopfloor are increasingly involved in managing their own change process through collaborative working with managers and leaders, this is evidently breaking down and a sense of trust is emerging.

Communication takes the form of many written and face to face approaches including, for instance, regular plant manager updates, two-way communication meetings, daily cell shift meetings, audio tapes from the CEO and newsletters. What is significant in this organization is that the drive to improve communications is working—people read the notices, they read the newsletters and they raise topics for the agendas of meetings.

Generally, there is a sense that communications are opening up as a sense of trust is being restored. This is an environment which has traditionally been heavily unionized and in the past there has been a reliance on the trade union as a channel of communication between the shopfloor and the management. Gradually the significance of this channel of communication, which was prone to distortion, is being eroded as sense of common purpose is being established and as the distinction between shopfloor and management becomes more blurred.

Adaptation

The plant recognizes that it must adapt or die. Change is increasingly being seen as the norm and people at all levels are encouraged to challenge the previously accepted wisdom. There is also a sense of realism and acceptance that not all individuals will be prepared to make the transition required to cope in the organization of the future. So a combination of approaches can be seen to be operating; those who wish to leave are being given an incentive to do so, while those who are staying have to demonstrate a commitment to the change process and are given plenty of support and training to help them develop the appropriate skills and attitudes. There are a minority who do not wish to leave the organization   and who are unable to buy into the change process. Typically, these employees will engage in passive resistance; however, they are being directly challenged and confronted. It is felt that by combining an approach which builds the confidence of the 'early adopters' of the change process and challenges the obvious cynics, there is more likelihood of moving the critical mass of the organization in the right direction.

There is a major emphasis on learning and training and this focuses not simply on equipping people with the relevant technical skills, but just as importantly providing them with process skills and behavioural insights which will help them to operate successfully in the organization in the future, whatever the technical requirement.

Many training programmes built around the subject of change are designed to help employees better understand the process of change and to give them confidence in a fast changing environment. There has been a recognition of the need to ensure that learning achieved through off-job events is transferred back to the job environment and indeed there are a number work-based training initiatives underway.

There is naturally some evidence of resistance to change and of one of the-first psychological defence mechanisms—that of denial of the need to change. The company is confronting such resistance head on.

A number of external standards have been adopted and clearly some of these relate to industry or sector requirements. Some of these initiatives actually help in providing focus for managing change and for defining minimum standards which should be achieved. Included here are ISO9001, AlliedSignal corporate standards and the Investors in People Standard in the UK. Similarly, there are numerous initiatives underway which seek to learn from and imitate best practice elsewhere. There has been considerable learning from within the industry by looking at how competitors, suppliers and other AlliedSignal companies operate.

In an attempt to create a learning culture, employees are being given incentives to study with financial support offered for further and higher education and rewards being offered to individuals who achieve high standards.

So we can see a number of important principles being adopted in the above case study. The organization is clearly attempting to bring about a major culture change and it is interesting to note that this has not been triggered by a decline in the organization's fortunes and abilities; but rather by the increasing and changing demands of the market place and the need to meet the changing needs of the customer. For the organization to stand still without adapting it would, in relative terms compared to its competitors, fall behind. The threat actually exists on two levels; if the plant fails to meet productivity and quality targets then the corporation as a whole could lose business—even if this is not the case, then there is a real possibility of the corporation moving production to a different country or other more productive location which would have a devastating effect on the local community.

The key points to note in this case study are how:

■ The company recognized that to bring about dramatic change called for dramatic measures.
■ A combination of sensitivity and confrontation was deployed.
■ There was a need to translate corporate values into a meaningful and workable language for use in the local nation and plant.
■ People in both central and line roles were given responsibility for driving the change process; also there was movement of personnel between the line and human resource functions.
■ Clear measures and targets were defined in order to create a picture of success.
■ The structure was redefined and many people had multiple responsibilities and interests other than their immediate job role.
■ Leadership was encouraged at all levels.

- Communication channels were numerous and constantly used; there was no such thing as over communication.
- Learning was seen as a continuing and critical process which took place both on the job and off.

Kotter (1995) has suggested that a number of key factors need to be addressed when managing the change process and he points out that many change efforts fail because one or more of these issues are not tackled effectively. As we review these factors, we will also refer back to the case study organization to demonstrate how it is tackling these factors. The key issues which need to be addressed are as follows.

Create a sense of urgency

Successful organizations in managing change are able to create a sense of urgency among members of the organization. They find some impetus or catalyst which ensures people realize the implications of not changing and they broadcast widely the message about the need to change. AlliedSignal took the measure of taking the whole workforce off site, significantly to a local school, where a major presentation was given emphasizing the need to change and giving the broad picture regarding potential threats to the business. As if this was not enough they were then invited to raise questions and concerns and these were answered both there and then and subsequently in writing with the summary of questions and answers being sent to every employee's house. In line with the observations of Kotter, this organization also drew on external experts and internal surveys to highlight the need for change.

Establish a guiding coalition

Successful transformation means there must be a powerful enough body of people who work together to publicize the need for change and to actually drive it through. These change agents are drawn from various parts of the organization, regardless of the hierarchy. It has to be accepted that not all of the senior team will necessarily commit to change and the guiding coalition will include managers from outside of the top team. This was certainly the case in AlliedSignal; the guiding coalition comprised central change agents from staff functions, senior managers, including of course the plant manager, and representatives from the shopfloor. Importantly, the shopfloor representatives were not in any sense there in a token capacity—they had a real role in driving through change and influencing others throughout the plant. And, as Kotter suggests, it is in fact possible to take time-served 60-year-old employees with traditional organization mind sets and not only encourage them to accept the need for change but to help in driving it through. In the case study organization such people were indeed co-opted onto the guiding coalition group.

Create a vision

As we discussed in Chapter 5, when the organization is faced with uncertainty and the need to change a critical factor is the need for a vision. This needs to be expressed in such a way that it is easily understood and so proves to be a motivational force. For AlliedSignal, in the case study, the vision was of becoming one of the most productive plants world-wide. All change processes seem like a mess when you are in the middle of them and it was noticeable how during times of difficulty the more visionary leaders in the case study organization would simply reiterate their vision. Kotter points out that without the vision there is a danger that the various initiatives which are being taken simply seem like a confusing jumble. This was a real danger in AlliedSignal, as there were many initiatives at various stages of implementation including the introduction of, for instance, Total Quality Management, *kaizen* and high performance work teams.

Communicate

Kotter suggests the need for multiple communication and, as discussed in the case study, this is what occurred. All existing channels of communication were used and still further channels were created in order to ensure the messages regarding the changes in culture, systems, processes and structure were not simply broadcast, but received and understood.

Remove obstacles

In the case of AlliedSignal, there were many potential obstacles which might have and in fact did threaten to prevent the organization from achieving successful change. Such obstacles came in the form of, for instance, people and systems and structural barriers. These were identified and tackled in a direct way. People who were unable or unwilling to co-operate in the change process were expected to leave. This may sound ruthless, but considerable support was offered to those who wanted to make the transition to the new way of working but simply needed help and training. Structurally, the organization chart was rewritten. This meant certain jobs which worked against the new philosophy were stripped out and new roles were created.

Plan for and create short term wins

Kotter suggests that there is a need for organizations to plan for and create short term wins when managing the change process. This may sound manipulative, but there is no doubt that in bringing about change there is a need to mobilize the critical mass of opinion so that eventually, rather than simply the guiding coalition believing in the need for change, the majority see that in the new style organization there is evidence of success. Bringing about major change in organizations does not happen overnight; furthermore, when one is in the middle of the change process it is very easy to only see confusion, difficulties and the barriers. In fact in the case of AlliedSignal it was interesting how part way through the change process it took the objective views of the external advisers to demonstrate the progress which was being made.

Having suggested the importance of creating short terms wins, Kotter warns against declaring victory too soon and suggests there is a need to anchor changes which are made into the company culture. AlliedSignal did this by ensuring that development and assessment centres and hence recruitment and promotion decisions and succession planning were built around the ability of people in the future to work within the new culture.

Assessment of adaptation

Finally we provide you with an opportunity to consider your own effectiveness against the critical factor of *adaptation*.

The statements below are designed to assist you in identifying ways in which you can focus on your organization's approach to adaptation. Essentially, this is seen as a prerequisite for helping you move towards becoming a virtual organization. These questions should not be seen as a test; there are no right or wrong answers. However, their effectiveness relies on the frankness of your responses.

Listed below are ten focused statements relating to our research findings about the virtual organization. You may use this brief questionnaire to assess your own department or organization. This is a forced choice questionnaire requiring you to respond against each statement.

Please read each statement carefully and respond by answering either Yes (agreeing) or No (disagreeing) to each statement. There is no time limit; it will probably only take two minutes to complete.

1. Process review to assess how we are doing is a frequent and regular part of how we work in teams.   Yes/No

2. We have highly structured and formalized systems for providing training and development to employees.   Yes/No

3. The word learning is a common part of our vocabulary and is frequently used in the business.   Yes/No

4. We are frequently encouraged to challenge existing policies and procedures.   Yes/No

5. People progress or are promoted in our organization only when they are ready for it.   Yes/No

6. We value loyalty and conformity.   Yes/No

7. We have few specific objectives but a clear understanding of the overall goal.   Yes/No

8. As individuals we are encouraged to learn anything as any learning is seen as good.   Yes/No

9. Our planning skills are very strong, we like to predict and manage things well ahead of time.   Yes/No

10. In our business we tend to rely on training courses to meet development needs of employees.   Yes/No

Scoring

If you answered Yes to any of the following statements give yourself 10 points for each Yes.

1 ....

3 ....

4 ....

7 ....

8 ....

Total ....

If you answered No to any of the following statements give yourself 10 points for each No.

2 ....

5 ....

6 ....

9 ....

10 ....

Total ....

Grand total ....

Consider the above grand total as a percentage relating to performance against the factor of adaptation. Those organizations which we believe measure up as effective virtual organizations tended to score in excess of 80 per cent.

In this chapter, then, we have taken the fourth and final factor in the organizational model and described some of the approaches taken by organizations attempting to bring about major change initiatives. We have also suggested that those organizations which measure up effectively as virtual organizations tend to view change and therefore learning as a continuous process. In effect, they are prepared to test out new approaches without necessarily knowing the consequences. They do, though, approach new activity with an open mind and they are prepared to take risks. In terms of the analogy of the journey towards becoming a virtual organization, we would liken adaptation to the idea of test driving—the organization will try out new approaches and use this as a way of finding out what is likely to work and what approaches should be adjusted, changed, adapted or even abandoned.

As far as the individual qualities needed to cope in this environment, it would seem that there are a number of personality related competencies or skills which are needed. It is not necessarily easy to develop all of the abilities from scratch; some behaviours need to brought into the organization through effective selection and then fostered from within.

So in the last four chapters we have looked at the key issues which need to be addressed by organizations in managing the move towards virtual organization status. We have given examples from a range of organizations which might be seen as being at different stages on the journey. Additionally it should be acknowledged that each organization is moving forward at a different pace and arguably some of the more traditional organizations we have discussed are not actually moving forward at all. For these organizations the danger is that as the number of companies adopting the virtual organization philosophy increases so the traditional organizations will become even more isolated. Their difficulty will stem not just from their own inability or unwillingness to adapt, but also from the fact that they are more likely to have to face up to the reality of working with or dealing with virtual organizations.

In the final chapter we will provide the reader with a summary of the key messages from the book.

References

Hedberg, B., *How Organizations Learn and Unlearn.* Oxford University Press, 1981.

Honey, P. and Mumford, A., *Using Your Learning Styles,* Peter Honey, Maidenhead, 1986.

Kotter, J.P., Leading Change: Why Transformation Efforts Fail, *Harvard Business Review,* March/April, 1995.

Lombardo, M., The Road to the Top is Paved with Good Assignments, *Executive Development,* 2 (1), 1989.

Nystrom, P.C., Management of Unlearning—Exploding the Clean Slate Fallacy, *Training & Development Journal,* August, 1983.

Sloman, M., On Job Training: A Costly Poor Relation, *Personnel Management,* February, 1989.

Whitlam P., Assessing Organizational Learning Effectiveness, M.Phil Thesis, International Management Centres, 1990.

Reviewing the journey

In this final chapter we:

■ Review the key messages from the book, highlighting relevant aspects of each chapter
■ Consider some recent independent organization based research which draws similar conclusions to our own regarding the future shape of organizations
■ Provide a unique vision of what it might look like to work in the organization of the future through a future-focused case study

Review of the book

Throughout the book we have suggested that the process of moving towards becoming a virtual organization can be likened to a journey. In a sense it might be considered more of a journey than a destination or an end in itself. In our work with even the most advanced organizations against our criteria of direction, form, communication and adaptation, it is unrealistic to expect that such organizations will have achieved all there is to achieve in becoming successful virtual organizations. The fact that adaptation is in itself a key criterion suggests that there is a process of continuous change which such organizations will accept they need to commit to; they recognize the need to constantly adapt and change in order to fit in with their environment and to cope with the accelerating change curve.

Here we provide a review of the key aspects of the journey which have been discussed throughout the book. This should serve as a useful revision chapter for those who have read all of the preceding chapters, or it will no doubt help fill in some of the gaps where the reader has taken a more selective approach.

Throughout the book we have liberally shared a number of examples of real organizational practice in order to ensure that the subject of organizational change and the virtual organization is seen as a live and dynamic matter, with a real range of experiences across the corporate spectrum. In this chapter we will adapt the case study approach by presenting a fictional case study based on our view of how organizations might well operate in the future. While this is an unconventional approach it is designed to help the reader visualize the changing shape of organizations and to catch a glimpse of the environment he or she may be working in in the virtual organization of the future.

In the introductory chapter we first introduced the model and the use of the term *'The virtual organization'*. It is important to recognize that the word 'virtual' is bandied around quite liberally and often with different interpretations and meanings. In the context of the book, the virtual organization is taken to mean any organization which successfully manages the four key factors which form the basis of our research based model, namely, direction, form, communication and adaptation. Some people in considering their own definitions of the virtual organization have tended to stress the importance of issues which we would categorize under the heading of form—they might see virtual organizations as one's which typically have no real physical base or presence and which are extremely flexible in terms of how they do business and which exploit the use of technology. We would agree that these are all key factors which distinguish virtual organizations from more traditional organizations, however we also consider that other key factors which are discussed in the book are of equal importance.

We introduced the Change Assessment Orientation Survey (Ch.A.O.S.), which is designed to help organizations to assess their position against the model of the four key factors and in this respect we have provided some generic sector based benchmarks to compare against.

In Chapter 2 we took a global standpoint and looked at some of the major trends and challenges which organizations are facing on a macro level. This is considered a key first step in looking to bring about effective organizational change. A key concept was discussed, that of the accelerating change curve. If one is operating in a climate of accelerating change, and this might encompass organizational and extra-organizational change, then it is clearly less easy to find a recognized source of knowledge in order to decide how to do things—if no-one has previously encountered the latest problem, then there are no guidelines regarding issues such as how to structure, organize, think or manage.

The accelerating change curve and the reducing body of knowledge mean that more and more organizations will need to look to a new set of predominant skills and behaviours if they are to remain competitive and if they intend to play a significant role in the corporate environment of the future. Whereas traditional organizations have been able to rely on classic approaches to strategy and long range planning, the virtual organization will excel in new areas. Employee involvement will encompass the challenge of leading and co-ordinating diverse and dispersed human resources. People will be expected to genuinely contribute to the development and growth of the organization and to question and test systems and processes which inhibit innovation.

For some of the more traditional organizations there is evidence of denial that such forces will affect them; such denial is dangerous and we looked at how in some cases the organization is being driven to change by the force of not just the competition but its customers and suppliers.

In Chapter 3 we explored some of the literature and views expressed by those who might be described as the proponents of the 'learning organization'. It seems that many of the writers and researchers in this area have tended to focus on formal learning systems and our research suggests that, increasingly, organizations will be driven to focus on the development of appropriate behaviours and attitudes, many of which are actually difficult to teach or train.

Some of the learning organization proponents believe that organizations should seek to continually evolve and develop by encouraging learning as a way of life. We would agree with the view that organizations in the future will certainly need to prioritize learning and adaptive behaviours and in the best examples these will become institutionalized.

We suggest that in the virtual organization learning is something which almost goes without saying; in other words learning actually transcends systems and formal processes, it happens at all levels and at all times and is welcomed by all as a catalyst for individual and organizational progress.

We presented a model of organizational behaviour which was drawn from our initial research into the process of change and the achievement of potential which suggests that organizations develop strong values and beliefs which can serve as either extremely liberating or inhibiting forces in their development. Just as individuals develop a self-concept which is influenced by the forces of external ëexpertsí, so do organizations. For organizations to develop there is often a need to question established views and perspectives regarding its capabilities and limitations. For many this means engaging in a process of unlearning in order to move outside of their comfort zone.

Here the process of vision building can be particularly effective in helping members of the organization to unite and mobilize in order to move towards a common picture of the future.

In Chapter 4 we moved on to discuss the nature of our own research in some depth, in particular showing how we developed the model which defines the four factors which the virtual organization addresses effectively.

We believe that whereas in the past we have been able to look to the large corporations as models for others to follow, this is not necessarily so when looking at the virtual organization model. Indeed, it seems that many smaller organizations, often less well known, are actually leading the way when measured against our model.

We showed how our model evolved from our research which used a combination of case studies, structured interviews and questionnaires. The four key factors which were ultimately incorporated into the model were:

■ Direction
■ Form
■ Communication
■ Adaptation

and we contrasted the approaches taken to these factors by traditional organizations and those which might be considered as virtual organizations.

The Change Assessment Orientation Survey (Ch.A.O.S.) was developed as a practical tool which can be used within organizations by either individuals or groups in order to assess the preparedness of organizations for change and, in particular, for movement to becoming a virtual organization. The reader is introduced to this instrument and encouraged to consider his or her own organizations status by completing the survey or introducing it on a broader basis. We show how the Ch.A.O.S. was used by a number of different organization's with rather different objectives and, for that matter, results.

In Chapter 5 we explored in some depth the first of the four key factors in the model, *direction*. Here we looked at a range of issues associated with leadership and strategy in organizations. There have been a number of different perspectives on strategy presented over the years and we suggest that as it is becoming less easy to predict the future and we are all having to operate in a climate of accelerating change, the relevance of traditional approaches to strategic planning has to be questioned. In the virtual organization it is more likely that issues of a strategic nature, that is to do with the direction and purpose of the organization, will be discussed with members at all levels, including those with a more operational remit. It is recognized that strategy is dynamic and rapidly changing and all members of the organization have a role to play in determining how it develops.

We suggested the need for the organization to strike a good balance between the use of hard measures, such as financial performance and output measurement, and the use of systems which attempt to measure behaviours. If one has a clear picture of the behaviours which are required in the organization, then it is possible to recruit, train and develop people against such a profile. We believe there is generally a move away from strict job descriptions and towards a more flexible approach whereby the organization focuses on the critical behaviours required for success; this is seen as more appropriate because the actual roles and responsibilities, or tasks, of individuals change in a very dynamic way.

In some organizations job titles are fast becoming a thing of the past and in the virtual organization titles which suggest hierarchy and reinforce status are less apparent. Leadership at all levels of the organization is coming to the fore, as the classic skills of management, such as planning, organising and controlling become less important. Organizations which are able to create an environment where effective leadership is seen at all levels tend to have clearly defined the key behaviours or characteristics of leadership which they wish to foster—and more than this, they even define the behaviours of followers within the organization. In part, leadership is about defining a clear vision or picture of where the organization or function or team is heading and we looked at approaches to defining a vision of success in order to mobilize and motivate others.

In Chapter 6 we explored in some detail the concept of organizational *Form.* This word was carefully chosen as it is meant to encompass more than just the issue of organizational design and structure. Whereas in the past it may have been appropriate to start by defining organizational structure and building the business around this, in the virtual organization we suggest that the predominant factor defining issues such as structure and more, are driven by the business and by how it is best considered that the organization can serve the needs of its customers or clients.

Virtual organizations tend to be capable of adjusting their form, including their organizational structure, how and where they physically work and how they manage people, both within the organization and outside of it, in order to respond to a changing external environment.

This throws into question many of the long held beliefs about the nature of the job and the individual's career. Virtual organizations will tend to be flexible with regard to how they use the services of people and are able to contend with the challenge of managing portfolio knowledge workers, as well as people who may have loyalties to organizations other than their own. Such developments are likely to change the nature of the role of the human resource specialist significantly; and there is clearly a move away from the policing and welfare role towards a genuine need for people to be able to contribute to the development of the organization and to cope with ambiguity and change.

We looked at some of the truly innovative approaches already being adopted in terms of organizational form and suggest that these point to the likely future shape of organizations. Included here were examples of virtual business parks, hot-desking, teleworking and telecottages.

Many of the trends suggested by our exposition of organizational form are demanding an enlightened approach to communication, both within the organization and with respect to communicating with contacts outside of it, and in Chapter 7 we explored the third factor, *Communication,* in more depth. In the virtual organization communication may often appear to be messy and informal, however it is likely to be more effective than in traditional organizations which may establish deliberate and contrived strategies and processes to improve communication. While the virtual organization may have any number of formal communications systems, it will also create a climate whereby people feel free to communicate with others at all levels and in all functions of the business in an open and candid way; they are not stifled by rules, regulations and protocol. In this way many of the larger corporations are now looking to smaller organizations in order to identify ways in which they can break down the boundaries which evolve over time.

Similarly, in the virtual organization a fine balance is struck between building trust and taking a realistic and commercial approach to building contacts and relationships with people both inside the organization and outside of it. While there is likely to be a nucleus of entrepreneurial personnel who may not personally perform as the best team players, there is a predominance of team-working. People may simultaneously act as members of several teams, some of which may be geographically dispersed; this calls for individual competencies such as being able to cope with ambiguity and the ability to take ownership of one's own personal organization as well as strong team working skills.

In Chapter 7 we looked at how organizations are making use of technology as a means of improving communication. Whereas in the past organizations may have faced the challenge of operating with too little information, increasingly the problem is that there is too much data and information to work with. The virtual organization will be capable of scanning the environment for information and sucking it into the organization and then making good use of it. Technology will be embraced as a means of improving communication both internally and with external contacts such as alliance organizations, customers and suppliers.

In Chapter 8 the subject of organizational change or adaptation was discussed and we looked at how in the virtual organization change and learning are closely related. It is recognized that the organization is a continually evolving entity and that due to the requirement for organizational adaptation so there is a need for individuals to constantly learn new skills and behaviours.

Learning or personal adaptation in the virtual organization is something which takes place through both formal interventions and through the open mindedness of members of the organization regarding their own personal development. People are developed for the future rather than simply equipped with the skills required for their current role.

At an organizational level it is interesting to note how in more forward thinking organizations there is a willingness to look outside of one's own organization and even sector in order to seek to learn from others who might be considered as best in their field; this contrasts with many traditional organizations which tend to suffer from what we describe as a 'terminal uniqueness', that is, a belief that they are so different from others that there is nothing to be learned from looking outside of their own narrow domain.

We looked at some of the key factors which organizations successfully managing the process of adaptation tend to address. Included here were, for instance, the ability to create a sense of urgency and the ability to form a guiding coalition of positive people who would create the climate for change.

Research supporting our findings

In our work with the major international market research company, ACNielsen, which is part of the Dun and Bradstreet organization, we recently came across some interesting research which has served to support some of our own findings and predictions regarding the nature of the virtual organization. This is briefly summarized here because it provides for useful comparisons to be drawn between our own research and that of another independent researcher.

Stephen Shearon (Shearon, 1991), Director of Human Resources at ACNielsen chose to draw on Handy's model of four organizational cultures (Handy, 1976), in order to provide a framework for considering the characteristics of leadership and a range of human resource issues in both ACNielsen and other organizations.

Handy, some time ago, proposed a model of four organizational cultures or ideologies, and these have provided us with a very useful basis for looking at real organizations and discussing how they both structure themselves and how people are expected to operate.

He proposed that the 'power culture' organization tended to put faith in individuals, focused on control around the centre and operated in a very political way. Shearon found that where this culture existed, communication tended to be focused downwards, management style was exploitative and authoritative, training was mainly for replacement, people were assigned to one job, there was a lack of real trust and co-operation and status differentials were actively promoted.

In the 'role culture', which stresses the importance of jobs and roles, he found that communication tended to be written and downwards in direction, management style might be described as benevolent, training focused on skills development and flexibility was limited.

In the 'task culture', where the organization was focused primarily on the achievement of tasks or activities for the good of the business, it was found that communication tended to be downwards and lateral with limited feedback. Management style was consultative and there was more flexibility and co-operation across boundaries.

When Handy first wrote of the 'person culture', he suggested that this was probably more of a concept than a reality. In the person culture he suggested that the organization would tend to exist to satisfy the needs of a number of different individuals who might actually be driven by a loyalty to their own profession or expertise. Here all would contribute to the business equally and influence would be shared. It is here that we have probably seen most movement since Handy first wrote on this subject and Shearon's work has suggested that there is real evidence of the person culture where the following characteristics are present.

- Communication is free flowing in all directions
- Selection and recruitment are excellent
- Management style is participative
- Payment systems are related to individual and company performance
- Training is for continuous development
- Job flexibility means that people are multi-skilled
- Members are committed to a shared vision of the company's objectives
- Objective setting is clear and understood by all
- There is a continual improvement mentality
- All employees are appraised
- Status differentials are reduced.

It is not difficult to see here the correlation between our exposition of the virtual organization, with respect to direction, form, communication and adaptation, and that of Handy's early concept and Shearon's more recent studies.

Finally, by way of a footnote to the book and in order to maybe provide more food for thought for the reader, we end below with a glimpse into the future and the virtual organization as we see it evolving. Here we have taken the approach of presenting a future-focused case study. We challenge you to consider what part you might be playing in such an environment in the future.

CASE
STUDY
9.1

The virtual organization in the year 2020

Luke Jameson was woken up by his electronic personal assistant at 6 a.m. and his schedule for the day was presented to him on his wrist-based personal organization system. He felt rather tired—he had been working late in the office the previous evening. One of the difficulties he had been trying to come to terms with over recent months was the pressure of working from a home-based office, both continuing his principal career as a business consultant specializing in product design and starting a new business as an antiques dealer.

The first two hours of the working day were spent in a meeting with his eldest son who was in the process of completing his secondary education, but was also training his father in the use of the latest technology. This was considered a useful session for Luke, who would be able to apply his newly acquired knowledge in his businesses, and as for his son it was good to be able to gain some work experience before moving into part-time employment.

After dropping his son off at school, Luke returned home for a virtual conference with a client when he had been advising for the last two years. This was an interesting meeting in that the attendees were spread across the globe at the time of the meeting, yet it was still possible to work in real time on the design of a new product and due to the fact that there were direct links into the production company in South East Asia the design was going directly into production. Luke felt confident that this product would be shipped within days—his only concern was ensuring that as he had played a key role in the development of this product, he needed to protect his own rights to intellectual property which he felt he could market elsewhere.

In an immediate effort to follow this concern up, he consulted his virtual lawyer, a software system which simulated a visit to the legal practice which took care of commercial law issues for his businesses. An internationally legally binding agreement was produced and this was briefly reviewed by his actual lawyer before being e-mailed to relevant parties. This gave Luke some reassurance: while he felt there was a good level of trust with his clients he knew from previous experience you could never be too careful, particularly as the actual contacts within the client business were apt to change with the next corporate clear-out.

In the afternoon, Luke decided to drop into his local teleworking centre. This was partly to satisfy his need for some sort of real social interaction and partly because he was picking up some useful contacts who could help him in his new business venture. He always met new people at the centre and this afternoon there were one or two newcomers as well as the regulars, a few of whom were long term unemployed and some who worked regularly at the centre in providing office services to local businesses. Luke spent two hours on the Internet gathering data on antiques and eventually bidding for some new purchases in a computer-based auction; this was all part of his strategy of building up some stock for the antiques business before he started, though he realized there was little need to open an actual shop as such because most of his dealing would take place electronically.

On the way back home, Luke dropped in on his elderly parents who were employed by him to help with some of the routine administrative tasks. He was pleased to see that they were on top of their part of the business and he left them with the next work package which would keep them occupied for the next two weeks prior to their vacation.

In the evening, Luke divided his time between eating with his wife and children and exercising in his personal gymnasium while listening to relaxation tapes. The only distraction was the on-line link he had to the world stock market which gave 24-hour live updates on developments relevant to his business interests—there were some concerns here regarding the threat to the electronics industry coming from the increasingly powerful environmental lobby.

He slept well that night, having been told by his electronic personal assistant that he had achieved 78 per cent effectiveness throughout the day against his own targets.

References

Handy, C., *Understanding Organizations*. Penguin, Middlesex, 1976.

Shearon, S.A., 'Gaining Commitment Through the Management of Culture', M.Sc. Thesis, Leeds Business School, 1991.

The modified change assessment orientation survey (Ch.A.O.S.)

Introduction

The modified Ch.A.O.S. instrument is designed to assist you in identifying ways in which it can adapt, evolve and manage change more effectively in the future. Essentially, this is seen as a prerequisite for any organization which is seeking to move towards becoming a virtual organization.

It is not a test; there are no right or wrong answers. However, its effectiveness relies on the frankness of your responses.

Instructions

Listed below are 40 statements relating to what may happen within your department/organization.

Please read each statement carefully and using the columns provided indicate your response by circling the letter in the appropriate column; the stronger your agreement, the nearer the left-hand column.

There is no time limit; it will probably take 10–15 minutes to complete.

SA = Strongly agree
A   = Agree
D   = Disagree
SD = Strongly disagree

It is important to note that this instrument is a modified version of the full instrument, consequently it should not be assumed to have the same level of reliability and validity.

If you are interested in using the more comprehensive version of this instrument, or if you would like us to compare your results against other organizations please contact us at the following address:

The Asset Partnership
21 Cliff Drive
CROMER
Norfolk NR27 0AW
United Kingdom

Tel: +44 1263 515150

Fax: +44 1263 515150

CHANGE ASSESSMENT ORIENTATION SURVEY

		SA	A	D	SD
1	Employees have specific individual performance objectives	D	C	B	A
2	We work mostly in our team, rarely do we mix with other groups or teams	A	B	C	D
3	As a business we are good at listening to each other	D	C	B	A
4	We are encouraged to be open and honest in all our communications	d	c	b	a
5	Our performance is regularly monitored	D	C	B	A
6	We are encouraged to change jobs in the business	d	c	b	a
7	We are encouraged to do new things, irrespective of what they are	D	C	B	A
8	We seldom take risks	A	B	C	D
9	We constantly seek ways of improving the products/services we provide	d	c	b	a
10	We tend to solve problems by a step by step approach	D	C	B	A
11	When we learn a new skill, we are actively encouraged to practise	D	C	B	A
12	We seldom challenge others, including management, in order to find ways of improving things	A	B	C	D
13	Feedback on our performance is quick in coming	D	C	B	A
14	Teamwork is not crucial in our business	a	b	c	d
15	Delegation is actively encouraged	D	C	B	A
16	We are encouraged to be innovative and creative	D	C	B	A
17	Training is given a high priority in our organization	D	C	B	A
18	We could make better use of technology to provide quality information	A	B	C	D
19	Insufficient time is made available for learning things	A	B	C	D
20	Fun and enjoyment are encouraged while at work	D	C	B	A

21	When feedback is received, it is provided in a manner that is helpful for the future	D	C	B	A
22	The way we are organized does enable us to get the best out of people	d	c	b	a
23	Within our business employees are encouraged to manage their own learning	D	C	B	A
24	Generally communication in our business is a one-way process	A	B	C	D
25	We keep in contact and review what other businesses are doing	D	C	B	A
26	We have procedures that are fairly inflexible with many rules and policies	A	B	C	D
27	We are encouraged to seek help when needed	D	C	B	A
28	Trying new things or experimenting is often undertaken in our business	D	C	B	A
29	We involve individuals in setting their own targets and objectives	D	C	B	A
30	We operate a casual approach to appraising performance of individuals	a	b	c	d
31	We value maturity, gained through long service and experience in a particular job	a	b	c	d
32	In our business communications are generally slow in coming	A	B	C	D
33	We regard people by their individual or team contribution to business success	d	c	b	a
34	Flexibility is seldom found as a feature of our structure	A	B	C	D
35	We actively ask for feedback as to how we are doing	D	C	B	A
36	Access to information is limited in our business	A	B	C	D
37	Consultation between management and employees is a regular part of how our business operates	d	c	b	a
38	We pride ourselves on our standards of quality	D	C	B	A
39	We are often asked to do jobs or tasks for which we may have little experience	D	C	B	A
40	Within our business we have a high self esteem and believe we are valued by our customers	D	C	B	A

Scoring

Direction		Form		Adaptation		Communication	
1		2		3		4	
5		6		7		8	
9		10		11		12	
13		14		15		16	
17		18		19		20	
21		22		23		24	
25		26		27		28	
29		30		31		32	
33		34		35		36	
37		38		39		40	
Sub total		Sub total		Sub total		Sub total	

Instructions

Letters are translated as follows:

A = 1   B = 2   C = 3   D = 4

Upper and lower case letters are scored in the same way.

Transfer the translated scores from the survey into the appropriate columns, then add up each column.

Summary overview of industry benchmarks against Ch.A.O.S. Instrument

Plot the scores from Appendix I onto the scale below to identify whether you have given low, moderate or high score against the scores obtained by others who have completed the Ch.A.O.S. Instrument. If the actual number you scored is not shown then assess its position on the relevant scale.

Direction	Form	Adaptation	Communication	
40	40	40	40	
38	35	38	37	High score
36	30	36	34	
31	25	31	30	Moderate
26	20	27	27	score
21	15	22	24	
16	10	18	20	
8	5	9	10	Low score
0	0	0	0	

Next add up the total for the four factors, Direction, Form, Adaptation and Communication in order to identify your total score compared to benchmarks by organizational sector in Appendix II

	Score	Your score	Industry/Sector averages
H I G H	160 150 140 130 120		Small Businesses (general), Communication and Insurance
M E D	110 105 100 90		Electronics, Consulting, F.M.C.G., Computers, Manufacturing (light), Retail and Multi-Nationals
I U M	80 70 65 60		Brewing, Hotels, Petroleum, Transport, Maunfacturing (heavy), Printing/Publishing, Education and Building Societies
L O W	55 50 40		Public Sector (general), Building/Construction and Hospitals

The research path

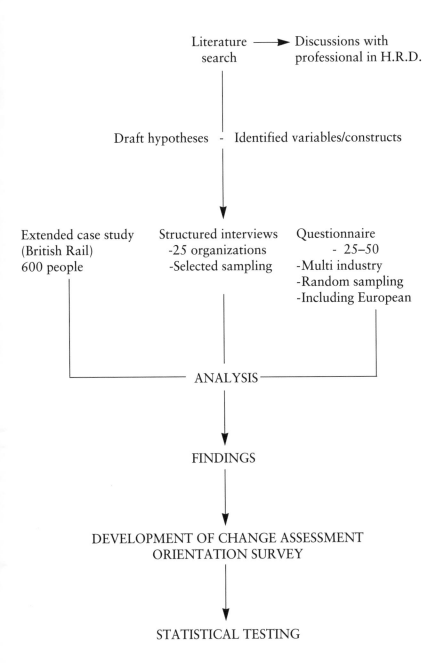

Literature ⟶ Discussions with
search   professional in H.R.D.

Draft hypotheses - Identified variables/constructs

Extended case study   Structured interviews   Questionnaire
(British Rail)   -25 organizations   - 25–50
600 people   -Selected sampling   -Multi industry
                                                 -Random sampling
                                                 -Including European

ANALYSIS

FINDINGS

DEVELOPMENT OF CHANGE ASSESSMENT
ORIENTATION SURVEY

STATISTICAL TESTING

Analysis of respondents to primary research

Age profile

	Structured interviews			Questionnaires		Case study
	%	No.	%	No.	%	No.
Under 20	(5)	2		(4)	15	(2)	5
21–30	(80)	32		(17)	63	(9)	21
31–40	(10)	4		(42)	156	(38)| 86
41–50	(5)	2		(27)	101	(40)| 90
51–60	—			(7)	26	(9)	21
+ 60	—			(1)	4	(2)	5
Unknown	—			(2)	7	—	
Total	40			372		228	

Gender profile

	Structured interviews		Questionnaires		Case study	
	%	No.	%	No.	%	No.
Male	(55)	22	(76)	283	(89)	203
Female	(45)	18	(20)	74	(11)	25
Not stated	—		(4)	15	—	
Total	40		372		228	

Job profiles

	Structured interviews		Questionnaires		Case study	
	%	No.	%	No.	%	No.
Administration		—	(6)	22	(15)	34
Education	(90)	36	(7)	26	(8)	18
Engineering		—	(7)	26	(9)	21
Finance		—	(16)	60	(15)	34
H.R.M.	(10)	4	(8)	30	(15)	34
M.I.S.		—	(2)	7	(2)	5
Marketing		—	(4)	15	(4)	11
Purchasing		—	(1)	4		—
Production		—	(3)	11		—
Sales		—	(23)	85	(3)	7
Other known		—	(19)	71	(28)	64
Unknown		—	(4)	15		—
Total		**40**		**372**		**228**

Industry profile

	Structured interviews		Questionnaires		Case study	
	%	No.	%	No.	%	No.
F.M.C.G.	(5)	2	(10)	38		—
Electronics	(10)	4	(6)	23		—
Manufacturing	(5)	2	(2)	8		—
Financial	(10)	4	(30)	114		—
Hospitality	(5)	2	(4)	16		—
Multi-services	(10)	4	(2)	8		—
Transport	(15)	6	(33)	125	(100)	228
Authorities	(3)	1	(4)	16		—
Government	(5)	2	(3)	12		—
Small businesses	(32)	13	(3)	12		—
Total		**40**		**372**		**228**

Summary of data gathered from research

The following pages show a summation of all the data. The key to the sources are shown as follows:

1 = Other case studies, meetings with other researchers and literature review
2 = Structured interviews
3 = Questionnaires
4 = Extended case study

FEATURES	1	2	3	4
STRATEGY				
Allocation of resources				
• Finance	*	*	*	*
• People		*		
• Time		*	*	*
Degree of customer orientation	*	*	*	*
Visibility of senior management		*	*	*
Mechanism for involving others in the process of business planning			*	*
SYSTEMS—Structure				
Less hierarchical structures		*	*	
Greater flexibility in organizational design	*			*
Role clarification, definition of competence		*	*	
SYSTEMS—Communications				
Volume and appropriateness of data		*	*	*
External sensors	*	*		
Speed of communication		*	*	*
Effectiveness in managing meetings		*	*	*
Understanding of broader business performance		*	*	*

FEATURES	1	2	3	4
SYSTEMS—Learning processes				
Recognition of need/identification		*	*	
Importance of self-motivation	*	*	*	*
Knowledge of resources available		*	*	
Need for self-insight/awareness		*	*	*
Influence of trainer/coach/mentor or other supporters		*	*	*
Quality of learning materials			*	*
Availability of time		*	*	*
Affiliation needs		*	*	
Managing mistakes positively	*	*	*	*
Taking risks	*	*	*	*
SYSTEMS—Learning systems				
Being given a role for which they have little experience, and where learning is critical for success or survival	*	*	*	*
Career counselling and individual development		*	*	*
Working in project teams		*	*	*
Having increased delegation		*	*	*
Access to self-study/open learning resources		*	*	*
Improved performance review		*	*	*
Extended use of action learning			*	*
Sponsorship (vocational training)			*	
Counselling		*	*	*
Coaching		*	*	*
Mentoring		*	*	*
Extended availability of training		*	*	
• Problem solving		*	*	*
• Interpersonal skills, including assertiveness		*	*	*
• Team building		*	*	*

FEATURES	1	2	3	4
SYSTEMS—Learning behaviours				
Observing others (right and wrong)	*	*	*	*
Practice	*	*	*	*
Visualizing	*	*		*
Listening	*	*	*	*
Questioning	*	*	*	*
Initiating				
Problem analysis	*	*	*	*
SYSTEMS —Process of management				
Need for an effective process of objective setting and monitoring		*	*	*
Improve team effectiveness/interdependency of teams	*	*	*	*
Processes for problem solving	*	*	*	*
CULTURE—Values and beliefs				
Importance of enjoyment/fun	*	*	*	*
Need for openness and honesty	*	*	*	*
Challenging	*	*	*	*
Need for high self-esteem		*	*	*
Value of learning for its own sake	*	*	*	*
Trusting/responsibility	*	*	*	*
Innovation	*	*	*	*
Empowerment	*	*	*	*

Index

accelerating change curve 25–30, 210
Adair, J. 105
adaptation 8–9, 18–19, 68, 80–1, 86, 209, 214–15
  assessment of 204–6
  case for 181–2
    action (We do...) 184–5
    case study 182–4
    knowledge (We know...) 182
    motivation (We will...) 184
    skills (We can...) 182–4
  establishing systems/processes 185–6, 187
    benchmarking 189–92
    case study 186–7
    new ways of thinking/learning 188–9
  from traditional to adaptive culture 196, 201–2
    case study 196–201
    communicate 203
    create a sense of urgency 202
    create a vision 203
    establish a guiding coalition 202–3
    plan for/create short term wins 204
    remove obstacles 203
  key behaviours 192
    creativity 194
    decisiveness 194
    initiative 194–5
    innovation 194
    risk taking 195
    styles of learning 192–3
    tenacity 195
AlliedSignal 23
  adaptation 196–7, 200–4
  communication 199–200
  direction 197–8
  form 198–9
Andersen Consulting 173–6
Apple Computers 144
Argyris, C. 51
'Askit basket' 155, 156
aspiration statements 107
Avon Internet Business Park (AIBP) 140–1

Baisley, L. 145

Barham, K. *et al* 52
Barnatt, C. 143, 144
Bartle Bogle Hegarty 143
behaviours 48, 51, 99, 131, 185, 211
  adaptive 192–5
  managerial 56
Belbin, R.M. 171
benchmarking 43
  as adaptive process 189–92
Black and Decker 41
Bridges, W. 124, 127, 131
British Aerospace 159–60
British Telecom 141, 144
Burgoyne, J. 50
Burns, T. and Stalker, G.M. 25
Bushe, G.R. 89
business parks 140–2
  case study 140–1
business process re-engineering 35, 102
Buxton Mineral Water Company 63–4

change 49
  in the business environment 1–2, 11–12
  as effective 67–9
  realisation of 57–64
Change Assessment Orientation Survey (Ch.A.O.S.) 9–11, 13, 69, 210, 212, 221–33
  as change management tool 87–8
  as diagnostic instrument 88–90
  and learning 90–1
  modified 219
  specifically using 91
'clear desk policy' 143
clover leaf model 25, 132
Coca-Cola
  improving responsiveness through outsourcing 100–1
  vision for developing people at 114–16
collaboration 56, 98
comfort zone 211
  expansion
    desensitisation 62–3
    flooding 62
    vision 63

communication 7–8, 16–18, 55, 68, 77, 79–80, 85–6, 148, 151–3, 199–200, 203, 209, 214
  assessment 178–9
  characteristics 152
  external 172–4
    case study 174–8
  forcing improvements 156–60
    case study 155–6
  internal 153–5
    case study 153–4
  openness 159
  speed 159
  synergy through teamwork 167, 169–72
    case study 168–9
  top-down 158–9
  trust and integrity 160–2, 166–7
    case study 163–6
communications industry 24, 27
Compaq Computers, learning and adaptation at 186–7
competencies 131, 185
computing industry 26–7, 106, 131–2, 186–7
conferences 161
continuous improvement 35
cottage industries 139
Craig, C. 145
Cranfield School of Management 124
Culpin, R. 30
cultural differences 24
culture 75, 77
Current Experiences and Perspectives for Teleworking (EC) 145
customers 12, 27
  communication with 172–4
    case study 174–8
  focus on 41–2
cyberspaces 139

decision-making 17, 36–7
desensitisation 63
Digital Equipment (DEC) 142
direction 6–7, 14–15, 68, 78–9, 82, 83, 94, 197–8, 212–13
  assessment of 116–18
  leadership/followership 101–10
  strategy 94–101
  vision 111–13
    case studies 113–16
Dolan, S. 52
double loop learning 51
Dun and Bradstreet 215

Eccles, T. 36
education and training 32, 48, 53–4, 186
  assistance in 54
  assumptions 188–9
  at Sheffield Forgemasters Ltd 75–7
  continuous 132
  in the Post Office 71–5
emergent strategy 95–6
employment 11–12, 23
  boundary workers 56
  categories of 32
  changes in 124
  continual employee involvement 33–8
    case study 34–5
  contract by contract 138
  death of the job 126–35
  educational assistance 54
  encouragement of entrepreneurial skills 38–40
  importance of concern for people 30–3
  and job description 99–100, 212–13
  managing culture change 163–7
  part-time 129–30
  patterns of 137–8
  traditional 25
empowerment 17, 33, 35
entrepreneurial skills, encouragement of 38–40
environment 22, 144
Ernst & Young 143
European Community 124
European Quality awards 191
European Union 144
Evans, D. 160

finance industry 27–8, 84
  case study 174–8
flooding 63
followership 109–10
Ford 24
  Employee Development and Assistance Programme 54
form 7, 15–16, 54–5, 68, 79, 84–5, 118, 198–9, 213
  assessment of 146–8
  changing organisational landscape 123–5
    case study 125–6
  death of the job 126–9
    HR specialist 129–33
    professional 'portfolio worker' 133–4
    'white collar labourer' 134–5
  defined 121–3
  innovations in 136, 139–40
    case studies 140–6
    virtual partnership 137–8

garden city movement 139–40
Gardner, H. 107
Garratt, R. 52–3
General Electric Company (GEC) 98, 159
globalisation 23, 27, 160
goals 43, 58
Grand Metropolitan Brewing, using
    Ch.A.O.S. in 90–1
Greengard, S. 144
Guest, D. and Mackenzie Davey, K. 25

Haas, R. 107
Hale, R. and Whitlam, P.J. 44, 109
Handy, C. 25, 84, 124, 130, 133, 161,
    215, 216
Harvard Business School 191
Hedberg, B. 189
Hewlett Packard (HP) 131, 140, 141, 171,
    192
Hitachi 36
Hofman, F. and Senge, P.M. 49
Honey, P. and Mumford, A. 192
hot-desking 142
hotel industry, using Ch.A.O.S. in 88–90
'hotelling' system 143
human resource specialist 122, 129–33

IBM 26, 142, 143
individual 130
    beliefs 49
    learning 50, 53
    and the organisation 28–9, 32–3
information 56
innovation 40–1, 194
    multimedia 175
inputs/outputs 99
Institute of Manpower Studies 32
Institute of Personnel and Development
    (formerly IPM) 98
integrity see trust and integrity
Intel Corporation 131
intent 96–100
Internet 24
intrapreneurship 96
Investors in People 43

Japanese model 35–6
jobs see employment
Jobs, S. 106

kaizen 35, 36
Katzenbach, J.R. and Smith, D.K. 171
Kinsman, F. 142

Kotter, J.P. 202, 204

leadership 43, 104–10, 213
    compared with management 104
    effective 118
    flexible 109
    innovative 107
    intimidation by 168
    ordinary 107
    perceptions of 49
    qualities/characteristics 105–9
    team, group, project 104
    traits 105
    visionary 104–8
learning
    styles of
        Activists 192
        Pragmatists 193
        Reflectors 192–3
        Theorists 193
learning organisation 12–13, 29, 67–9
    aspiration or reality 47–9
    critique of literature on 49–52
    practical steps 52–6
    qualities of 65
    realising change 57–64
Leeds University 141
Levi Strauss 107
Lombardo, M. 188
Lorenz, A. 160

3M 40, 41, 156
management
    behaviours 56
    compared with leadership 104
    competencies 103–4
    McGregor's Type X manager 33–4, 102
    role of 102–3
Management By Objectives (MBO) 98
Management Charter Initiative (MCI) 103
measurement, hard and soft 42–3, 98, 99,
    118, 212
Microsoft 131
MIT, Center ror Organizational Learning
    49
Morgan, G. 56
motor industry 24, 26, 54, 84
Motorola 32–3, 38, 107, 157, 171

Naisbitt, J. 22–3, 53
National Power 41
Nationwide Building Society 84, 173
    creation of interactive banking at 174

benefits 177
challenge 174–5
future 177–8
innovation 175–6
project management 176–7
solution 175
New York Life 145
Newstrom, P.C. 189
A.C. Nielsen 215
'nomad' meetings 143

Open University 161
organisations
and accelerating change 25–30
adaptive 50
behaviour 59
boundaryless 159
changing landscape of 123–5
case study 125–6
comfort zone 62–3
contrasting traditional and virtual 81–6
do-nut 132
eggs 132
and external change 21–5
habit driven 50
and the individual 28–9, 32–3
innovations in form 136–46
internal dialogues 59–60
power of vision 63–4
realising change in 57–65
redefining concept of 122
self-concept 60–1, 64, 211
significant trends 30–45
continual employee involvement 33–8
emphasis on measurement 42–3
encouraging entrepreneurial skills 38–40
focus on customer orientation 41–2
focus on innovation 40–1
importance of demonstrating concern for people 30–3
influence not authority 43–5
stable 50
subtle 50
values and beliefs 49, 58–9, 106

outsourcing 100–1

Panucci, D. 144
partnerships 24
virtual 137–8
Pedler, M. et al 50
Perrier (UK), group mission statement 113–14

person culture 216
Peters, T. and Waterman, R.H. 34, 41, 153
Pinchot, G. 96
planning 95
policy making 55
Post Office, redefining learning at 71–5
Pritchett 27
'professional portfolio worker' 122, 133–4

Railtrack, using Ch.A.O.S. in 87–8
Rank Xerox 143, 144
remuneration 15
'cafeteria benefits' 32
research
aims 70–1
analysis 70
decision making 70–1
planning and implementation 77–8
case studies 71–7, 87–91
contrasting traditional and virtual organisation 81–6
summary 69–70
support for findings 215–16
variables
adaptation 80–1
communication 79–80
direction 78–9
form 79
Revans, R. 47
Rifkin, J. 23
'right first time' 41
Rogers, R. 146
role culture 215

Saratoga International 190–1
Saztec 145–6
Schor, J.B. 124
science parks 140, 141–2
Scottish Hydro-Electric plc 159, 162
managing culture change at 163–6
devolution of power and authority 165–6
management competence 163–4
staff motivation 164–5
succession planning 166
self-help approach 53–4
Semco, redefining the organisation 125–6
Semler, R. 125
service sector 123–4
Shearon, S. 215, 216
Sheffield Forgemasters Ltd, organisational learning at 75–7
Shetland Isles Telecroft 145
Sloman, M. 188

SMART (space, morale and remote
   technology) 142
Snell, N. 130
societal change 21–5
strategy 55, 75, 77, 212
   approaches 94–101
      case study 100–1
      emergent 95–6
      intent 96–7
      intrapreneurship 96
      planning 95
      virtual and traditional 97–100
suggestion schemes 157–8
Swift, J. 106
Syrett, M. and Lammiman, J. 124
systems 75, 77
systems transforming innovations (S.T.I.)
   89

task culture 215
Taylorism 102
teamwork 18, 213, 214
   briefings 158
   dysfunctional 168–9
      blame culture 168–9
      escapist behaviour 169
      failure to challenge 168
      functionally focused 169
      intimidated by their leader 168
      introspective 168
   leader 104
   successful 171–2
   synergy through 167, 169–72
      case study 168–9
technology 23, 26–7, 55, 124, 175, 214
telecommuting centres 144
telecottages 145–6
   case study 145

teleworking 144
'Theory X' type managers 33–4, 102
Thompson, J.D. 29
Tichy, N.M. and Sherman, S. 159
Total Quality Management (TQM) 35, 40,
   155
Toyota 23, 24
training see education and training
Truman, H. 109
trust and integrity 17, 160–2, 173, 214
Tuckman, B.W. 170

uncertainty 29, 49
unlearning 22, 211

virtual
   learning space 54
   offices/workspaces 139
   partnership 137–8
virtual organisation 55, 67–9, 210
   concept of 3–6, 13–14
   contrasted with traditional organisation
      81–6
   year 2000 case study 216–18
vision 43, 63–4, 96, 203, 213
   building 138, 211
   case studies 113–16
   developing 110–13

Weinstock, A. 98
Welch, J. 159
'white collar labourer' 122, 134–5
Whitlam, P.J. 23, 30, 48, 51, 132, 188
Wilson, S. 142

Xerox 189